Beyond Tribal Loyalties

Beyond Tribal Loyalties

Personal Stories of Jewish Peace Activists

Edited by

Avigail Abarbanel

**2018
Second Edition
Amazon KDP**

Beyond Tribal Loyalties: Personal Stories of Jewish Peace Activists
Edited by Avigail Abarbanel

First published 2012 Cambridge Scholars Publishing
Second edition 2018 Amazon
(Ver. 26th June 2018)

Copyright © Avigail Abarbanel & Contributors

Cover image: An olive tree in Ni'lin, Occupied West Bank.
© Valérian Mazataud/Focus Zero. Montreal Canada.

All rights for this book reserved. No part of this book may be reproduced, stored in a retrieval system, or transmitted, in any form or by any means, electronic, mechanical, photocopying, recording or otherwise, without the prior permission of the copyright owner.

*This book is dedicated
to my late grandmother Rivka who
has sown seeds in the soil and in me,
to my grandmother's Palestinian friends
& to activists everywhere who are working
for what should be a given:
justice, safety, dignity, compassion
& equal opportunity for everyone
to develop our human potential.*

Table of Contents

Foreword 9

Introduction to the 2012 Edition 11

Introduction to the 2018 Edition 25

Australia

Am I an Activist? - *Sivan Barak* 37

The Road to Hell is Paved with Tribal Loyalties - *Ray Bergmann* 47

Once You See You Cannot Unsee - *Nicole Erlich* 59

I am Now Again the Zionist I Once Was (But the Zionist Caravan Has Moved On) - *David Langsam* 67

A Secular Jew From the End of the Earth - *Vivienne Porzsolt* 77

A Troublemaker in Exile - *Margot Salom* 85

The Wicked Son: Hemlock and *Cherem* - *Peter Slezak* 93

Canada

The Courage of My Convictions - *Lesley Levy* 113

The Hole Truth - *Ronit Yarosky* 121

Israel

Comprehending Oppression, or How I Came to Understand Occupation and Resist It - *Jeff Halper* 131

Conversion - *Dorothy Naor* 141

Eucalyptus Tree - *Maya Wind* 149

United Kingdom

Leaving Israel - *Avigail Abarbanel* **159**

Journey Out of Zionism - *Susan Nathan* **173**

Out of the Frame: The Journey Out of Zionism - *Ilan Pappé* **179**

The Birth of the Israeli State Was my Birthday: Re-living the Past Through a Child's Eye - *Ruth Tenne* **187**

United States

**Shattering the Israel Barrier
(A Tikkun Olam Mosaic) -** *Rae Abileah* **199**

1996 - *Jesse Bacon* **209**

Confronting the Sacred Cow - *Anna Baltzer* **217**

A Startling Awareness - *Rich Forer* **227**

An Accidental Activist - *Hazel Kahan* **237**

Hybrid States - *Yaniv Reich* **245**

The Cult of Atheist Zionism Posing as Judaism - *Rich Siegel* **255**

How I Became a Self-Loving Anti-Occupation Jew -
  Wendy Elisheva Somerson *265*

My Journey Home - *Ariel Vegosen* **273**

A Lighthouse in Gaza – *Ariel Vegosen* **281**

Afterword - *Avigail Abarbanel* **283**

Foreword

As I write this, the United Nations is about to vote on the recognition of a Palestinian state on pre-1967 borders and institutional membership. Regardless of whether one supports the UN initiative or not—and supporters and detractors can be found among Palestinians, Israelis, Arabs, Americans, Europeans, Jews and others, each for their own reasons—the reality of the event itself is of enormous political and symbolic importance. For it restores the Palestinian issue to a central position internationally—demanding attention and redress—and it does so without violence.

The need to keep the Palestinian issue focal to the Jewish discourse on the Israeli-Palestinian conflict is a theme that runs through this very important collection of works by Jewish academics, writers and activists who have broken from the mainstream of the Jewish community in their own countries including Israel. Their journeys are individual and profound, some involving considerable struggle while others less so; yet they are all animated by the same set of ethical imperatives that speak to the humanity of the other, an essential humanity, they argue, which must be incorporated within our own moral boundaries and understanding of Jewish history. The imperative is proximity over distance, embrace over exclusion—to maintain a living connection with the people we are oppressing, to enter their predicaments and do what we can to end their subordination and pain; to see Palestinians as we see ourselves—human beings seeking an ordinary life for their children in a home of their own. Only by fighting for their freedom, the authors believe, can we truly secure our own. At its core—to borrow from Professor Marc Ellis—this book calls for reflection not celebration.

Many important and disquieting questions, once silenced, are voiced: Who are we as a people and what should we stand for? Why do so many—indeed the majority among us—so easily and willingly tolerate the suffering inflicted in our name? What are Jews now capable of resisting? What is our narrative of victory and defeat? What are the boundaries of our rebirth after the Holocaust? Where do we belong?

The tension between Zionism and Judaism inevitably emerges, as it must, around the following challenge: Can Jewish power and sovereignty, and Jewish ethics coexist in the face of our continued oppression of the Palestinian people? Can empowerment and compassion ever be reconciled? Each author in this collection finds his or her own answers and they are not all the same. But they show, poignantly and without equivocation, that our salvation as a people lies in a return to, and renewal of, our ethical tradition.

More than anything, the essays that follow show—and this is crucial—that our identity as a people can move beyond a life made of barriers and as such, we must resolve, as the writers here do, never to leave the world as it is.

Sara Roy
Center for Middle Eastern Studies
Harvard University
September 2011

Introduction to the 2012 Edition

This book owes its existence to my friend Kenneth Ring, the editor of Letters from Palestine. In early 2010, not long after my husband Ian and I moved from Canberra, Australia to the Scottish Highlands, Ken contacted me and suggested that I write a book about my journey to becoming an activist for Palestinian rights. He felt that there was something special about my transition from growing up in Israel and serving in the military there, to becoming an activist, and that it was a story worth telling.

Ken is a persistent fellow, so I decided to give it a try and started to write down my story. But soon I began to feel uncomfortable. It just didn't seem right to me to have a book entirely about myself. I knew that I was not that special, and that there were other Jews who have been through a similar journey.

One afternoon on the bus home from Inverness, while I was reading Ken's book, I suddenly had an idea. What if instead of writing a book only about myself, I edit a collection of personal stories of Jewish activists? Letters from Palestine is an anthology of personal stories of Palestinians. The contributors in Letters from Palestine—several generations of Palestinians who have lived in the shadow of the Nakba[1] and of Israeli Occupation—were prepared to share their thoughts, feelings and experiences with the world, and Ken provided the platform. It occurred to me that the same model could also be applied to stories of Jewish activists.

Although I started my activism in what felt like isolation, I discovered over the years that there was a growing community of Jews who had similar thoughts and feelings to my own about Israel and Palestine. They too have been through the challenging personal journey to come out of Zionism. Jesse Bacon, one of the contributors, said to me that this book was creating a community. Editing the book certainly made me feel like a member of a community of like-minded (but not

---

[1] *Nakba* is Arabic for "catastrophe". It refers to the deliberate and systematic ethnic cleansing of the Palestinian people. The *Nakba* included massacres like the ones in Deir Yassin and Tantura, as well forced expulsions, destruction and appropriation of Palestinian cities, towns, villages and property, by the Israeli forces during and after the war of 1948. The state of Israel is either denying the *Nakba* or justifying it on the grounds that it was OK to do what was necessary for the 'survival of the Jewish people'. To the best of my knowledge the Nakba is not mentioned in any Israeli school textbook.

identical-minded!) people. Having my story included with the stories of others felt a lot more authentic than telling it in isolation.

The idea felt right but I also had reservations about this book. My reservations are reflected in Anna Baltzer's regrets about the way she initially approached her activist work. In her piece she says,

> *"I was reinforcing the idea that Jewish voices and opinions are more important than the voices and needs of the oppressed themselves, the Palestinian people, the experts and leaders on their plight and struggle."*

In my years of public speaking about Israel-Palestine in Australia, I consciously used the Western bias in favour of Jewish voices. I knew that as a Jew, and especially one who was born in Israel, I was more likely to be listened to than a Palestinian telling exactly the same story. In this book, once again Jewish voices were going to be given a stage, and I was concerned that I was colluding with this bias rather than challenging it. After all, haven't Jewish voices been heard enough? Isn't it now time for more books like *Letters from Palestine*, *A Doctor in Galilee* by Hatim Kanaaneh or *Nakba: Palestine, 1948, and the Claims of Memory (Cultures of History)* edited by Ahmad H. Sa'di and Lila Abu-Lughod? Perhaps we don't need another book of Jewish stories, even if they are supportive of the Palestinians.

But I think that perhaps this book does have a place. The Jewish voice in this book is fundamentally different from the mainstream Zionist and Jewish voice. This is the voice of individuals who were able to transcend something powerful about their upbringing: the requirement to turn Zionist ideology into an inseparable part of their identity, and ensure that they always see themselves, the world and Israel in particular, through the perspective of this ideology[2].

Another reason that I believe this book has a place is because each author, in his or her way, validates the Palestinian narrative. They testify to what the Palestinians themselves have been saying all along. By so doing, their stories might just help the Palestinian voice to be heard better. There is a chance that some people who wouldn't otherwise listen to Palestinians, might be more open to learn about Palestinian history and present reality from Jewish stories.

---

[2] To readers who are less versed in the history of the Israeli-Palestinian conflict, I recommend Ilan Pappé's book, *The Ethnic Cleansing of Palestine*.

Another reservation I had is once again echoed in one of Anna Baltzer's regrets,

> "...as a Jew, I was giving permission to non-Jews—especially Christians otherwise hesitant to speak out due to the Church's history of antisemitism and complicity during the Nazi Holocaust—to criticise Israeli atrocities, when what needed to be said was that non-Jews do not need permission from Jews to do what they know is right..."

Baltzer is absolutely right of course. Why should non-Jews need permission to speak up for the rights of a persecuted people just because they happen to be victims of the Jewish state? But unfortunately, the reality is that they still do.

My husband Ian, who is not Jewish, wrote a letter to the *Canberra Times* a few years ago, protesting against something that Israel did, that was in the news at the time. A swift response followed from a Jewish reader who among other things wrote, "...and we know what you are..." A German friend told me the other day that while sitting with a friend at a café during a recent visit to Germany, she voiced her criticism of Israel. As soon as she raised the topic, her friend began to appear nervous, looking anxiously over her shoulder, clearly worried that someone might overhear the conversation.

In the first example Ian suffered direct backlash for voicing his views publicly. But the second example was closer to self-censorship. People worry about what might happen if they voice criticism of Israel or are in the company of someone who does. They choose to gag themselves or their friends voluntarily, fearing to be seen as, or accused of being, antisemitic. It is clearly not permissible to voice criticism of Israel in public in Germany and possibly elsewhere in the West. Israel and its supporters have been successful in equating criticism of Israel with antisemitism. It doesn't have to make sense logically to be effective. It just has to press the right emotional buttons.

Given that this is how things are, I think a book like this is needed. Although non-Jews shouldn't need permission from Jews, under the circumstances I do hope that this book will empower and encourage more non-Jewish people to speak up with confidence and without fear.

In 2002 in post 9/11 Australia, Muslim women identifiable by their traditional dress were being spat on, called names and physically threatened and assaulted in the streets of Sydney and Melbourne. In response I initiated National Headscarf Day3. On 29 November that year, I asked women of all backgrounds to wear a headscarf as a gesture of solidarity with the women who were being attacked. It was meant to send a message to the attackers that their behaviour would not be tolerated, and that Muslim women had support in the general community in Australia. National Headscarf Day drew a great deal of media attention and almost every interviewer wanted to know why I was doing this. Implied in the question was the assumption that the last thing a Jewish person would want to do is to support Muslims.

I thought that I didn't need a reason to support Muslim women, or anyone else for that matter. When people were singled out and attacked by prejudiced and ignorant mobs because of who they were or what they wore, I felt that I had a duty to do something about it. It shouldn't matter who I am or what my background is.

In this book I wanted to explore not so much the question of why Jewish activists support the Palestinians. I think I know the answer to that. I wanted to know what is different or special about these activists that they are prepared to do this, when the vast majority of Jews do not. What might be the factors that help them to do what they are doing? Is there something about the way they were brought up, or the values they were taught; are they more caring than others, less fearful perhaps? I am curious to know what enables these people to stand up against powerful opposition and express views that are so unpopular in the mainstream Jewish community around the world and in Israel, and that often invite abuse, threats, violence, rejection and labels like "self-hating Jew", "Nazi", "Israel-hater" and even "antisemite".

In a conversation with Hazel Kahan, another contributor to this book, I once lamented that there are plenty of Jewish human rights lawyers and activists who would fight for the rights of anyone except the Palestinian people. Somehow their moral indignation and need to help others come to an abrupt halt and the "shutters go down" when the suffering of the Palestinians is mentioned. Hazel told me that this

---

[3] You can read about National Headscarf Day in Dr Shakira Hussein's chapter, "Looking in or looking out? Stories on the multiple meanings of veiling" in *Beyond the Hijab Debates: New Conversations on Gender, Race and Religion*.

selective attitude to justice and human rights is well recognised, and that there is even a term for it: PEP, Progressive Except on Palestine.

The purpose of this book is to try to understand why the contributors are not PEPs. I am curious to know how they were able to break out of a powerful prison of belief, tradition and identity; a belief system that taught all of us that Palestinians are our mortal enemy and that any sympathy towards them amounts to a complete betrayal of our people, not to mention an existential threat to the state of Israel.

Over the years I have been told that I was "courageous" for standing up for Palestinian rights. I have often wondered about this. Why exactly does it need to take courage to stand up for Palestinian rights? Should people need courage to protect the rights of abused children, to stand up against human trafficking, domestic abuse or racism? But I am certain that it took courage for William Wilberforce to stand up against the slave trade, and for the suffragettes to demand that women be given the right to vote.

It takes courage to object to, or protest against something that is still an accepted, well-established mainstream ideology or practice. I hope that those who fight for the rights of children or against human trafficking are not told that they are silly or bad and that abuse of children or human trafficking are perfectly fine. But when Wilberforce fought against the slave trade, he was certainly told that the slave trade was not only accepted, but that it was a good practice that was essential for the British economy; and that in any case dark-skinned people weren't human beings like white people and did not deserve the same rights. I am sure that there were people who just didn't understand what he was on about, just as there were people (including many women) who didn't understand why women needed the right to vote. Back then, most people believed that women were less intelligent than men, and that it was unnatural for women to participate in politics.

Zionism is the name of the Jewish nationalist ideology and programme that dreamed up and executed the idea of a Jewish state in Palestine. Despite the fact that the creation of a Jewish state came at the expense of another people, the Palestinians, Zionism is still seen as legitimate. Israel enjoys relatively widespread Western support despite the fact that it is a colonial and apartheid ethnocracy; despite the fact that in the service of colonialism and apartheid it commits human rights violations, war crimes, oppression and theft of land, water and other resources. Against the backdrop of general support for Israel, and the refusal of the world's power brokers to intervene to stop or change the situation, the only people left to protest (except the Palestinians themselves) are individuals and groups who are not part of the world's power elite. These people are being told that they are stupid and bad because they don't understand that the oppression and dispossession of the Palestinians is necessary for Israeli "security"; that the Palestinians are bad people who are "not like us", and that they are not really victims but rather "terrorists" who endanger the entire Western world. When this is the general mindset it very much requires courage to stand up for the rights of Palestinians.

But there is another important reason why Jewish people need courage to object to Zionism and to Israel's behaviour. This reason has to do with the nature of Zionism itself, and the way it is being taught. Despite being a secular ideology, Zionism has a quasi-religious quality to it, and it seems to elicit strong emotions and zeal in people, in the same way that religion often does. Zionist ideology has also found a way to tie itself to people's identity. One does not believe in Zionist ideology, one is a Zionist.

But Zionism doesn't just have a religious quality to it. In many Jewish communities it has taken the place of religion or has at least become blurred with it. This is reflected in quite a few of the stories in this book. I remember how surprised I was the first time I saw David Ben Gurion's [4] portrait on the big sign outside the synagogue in Canberra, where I lived for eleven years. I am not religious, but if for some reason I wanted to attend a service at that synagogue, I would effectively be endorsing Israel and Zionism regardless of my values, just by sitting inside that building. With the exception of some anti-Zionist ultra-Orthodox Jewish groups, Zionism and Jewishness are offered as a package to Jews, inside and outside Israel. In most cases if you are a member of a Jewish community or a synagogue, it is understood and expected that you would also be a Zionist and support Israel no matter what.

This blurring of boundaries didn't happen by accident. From its very beginning Israel understood that it needed the support of Jewish

---

[4] David Ben Gurion was a prominent Zionist leader, Israel's first Prime Minister and is a Zionist symbol. He was one of the people responsible for the ethnic cleansing of the Palestinians in 1948.

communities around the world. It needed their donations, and it needed to make sure that they would represent Israel's interests in their countries.

Diaspora Jews are also important to Israel because of demographic reasons. Creating a Jewish ethnocracy was the whole point of Zionism. Israel as it is, is not the creation of a fanatical few or an unintended mistake. The Zionist movement never set out to create just another Western style liberal democracy for everyone. Jews wanted a state where they could live only, or mostly with Jews, where they can run the country themselves and make their own laws without worrying about others hating them, discriminating against them, legislating against them, expelling them, forcing them to convert or persecuting them. Given that the Palestinian citizens of Israel are a large minority of over 20%, Israeli Jews are afraid that one day they would outnumber the Jews and take over the country. To them this would mean the end of the dream of a Jewish state, and consequently the end of safety for Jews. Israel therefore feels the need to ensure that there is an ample supply of Jews who could be convinced to come and live in Israel in case the Jewish birth rate in Israel isn't enough to keep Jews a majority.

The Zionist programme to create a Jewish state in Palestine was morally wrong not because the idea of a Jewish state is particularly wrong but because the land of Palestine was already populated. It took ethnic cleansing, the 1948 Nakba (that is still ongoing) in order to appropriate it. Sadly, to a Jew, the argument for an ethnocracy, an exclusively Jewish state on the historic land of Palestine, can sound logical and certainly necessary, even in the face of this terrible injustice. In the eyes of many Jews the long record of Jewish persecution culminating in the Holocaust, seems to justify the desire to have an exclusively Jewish state, no matter the cost. Many Jews feel that they do not trust the world and are afraid that what happened before will happen again. To them Zionism offers the solution to these anxieties— the state of Israel, the Jewish safe haven—the place they can run to when they are persecuted and that will accept them with open arms, no questions asked. Many Jews feel that they simply cannot afford not to have Israel, even if it's far from perfect, because an Israel that isn't exclusively Jewish cannot guarantee to be a safe haven for Jews. It will be just another country that can reject Jewish refugees just like so many countries rejected Jewish refugees before and during the Second World

War. The exclusively Jewish state is intended as a guarantee against such circumstances. No matter the cost.

I and many other Jews are now questioning this equation. We have opened our eyes to the price the Palestinians have been paying for the existence of the Jewish state, and we do not accept it. Fundamentally we do not believe that it is OK to hurt another people in order to save our own. But many people (Jews and non-Jews) still do, or otherwise deny or ignore the fact that the existence of Israel comes at a terrible cost.

Israel has been using its Hasbara programme to achieve its goals. The literal meaning of the Hebrew word hasbara is simply "explaining": explaining Israel's position, its history and its needs for the purpose of gaining support for Israel. But hasbara is a euphemism for propaganda that entices and excites, uplifts and inspires. It preys on deep feelings of fear (of antisemitism), on loyalty, and on the need to belong. It also makes immigrating to Israel seem like a noble goal that should be the life purpose of every Jew in the West.

The Hasbara programme teaches Israeli mythology to Western Jews from early childhood in a variety of contexts: Jewish schools, synagogues, Sunday schools and youth movements. It sponsors and runs various programmes for young Jewish people to visit or study in Israel in the hope that they would develop a sense of connection to Israel and would one day come to settle there, or at least continue to support Israel financially and politically. The mythology that the Hasbara teaches is based on the official and dishonest version of the history of Israel and the Israeli-Palestinian conflict. Margot Salom refers to this as the Leon Uris version of history as depicted in the novel Exodus. Zionist mythology can be powerful enough to move even non-Jews to tears. But in Jews it is designed to create a particularly personal sense of identification with Israel, and a strong desire to support it and be a part of it.

Jewish culture, which is already based on a sense of victimhood, relates easily to a view of Israel as an innocent victim state, surrounded by enemies who wish to destroy it and push its Jewish inhabitants into the sea. The Palestinians, if they are even mentioned, are presented as antisemites who just hate the Jews and don't want them to have a state of their own. Nowhere in this official mythology is the ethnic cleansing of the Palestinians mentioned. In fact, Israel is presented as a just and peace-loving, enlightened Western-style democracy whose noble and innocent military force follows the principle of "purity of arms", doesn't harm civilians, and only fights unavoidable wars of self-defence.

A key point in this mythology is that the Palestinians left voluntarily in 1948. I was taught at school in Israel that the "Arabs"—I wasn't exposed to the word "Palestinians" until my mid-twenties—were "just peasants" who didn't mind leaving, because it didn't really matter to them where they lived. In his piece, Ilan Pappé calls the historians responsible for this version of history, "fraudulent". But fraudulent or not, this version of history has been effective in ensuring widespread Jewish support for Israel.

The stories in this book show that some Jews begin to question their loyalty to Israel when they learn the truth. So, it appears that Israel's fear of losing support if people knew the truth is in fact justified, and that lying or "massaging the truth" has been a successful, if immoral, tactic.

Israeli Hasbara succceded in making a powerful link between Jewishness and support of Israel. This link has become almost a fact of life and has long been taken for granted in most Jewish communities in the West. So, when Jews begin to stand up against the Occupation, against Israeli apartheid and for the rights of the Palestinians, they are in fact decoupling this automatic link. They are saying that it is possible to be Jewish and not support Israel.

Because of the nature of Zionism, Jewish people who question must wrestle with the very essence of who they are. They have to examine their sense of belonging and what it means for them to be Jewish, not to mention face heavy guilt that by "supporting Israel's enemies", they believe they are undermining the Jewish state and helping to destroy it. For the reasons I explained earlier, in the minds of many Jews the idea of the destruction of Israel (or if Israel stops being exclusively Jewish) is synonymous with the annihilation of the Jewish people, their very own destruction. Most Jews can't or won't confront or challenge this belief. They think it's nothing short of collective suicide.

The more blurred the boundary between our beliefs and our identity, and the more strongly our beliefs are linked with our existential fears, the harder it is to question or let go of them. To question and reevaluate our sense of who we are, is one of the hardest things any human being can do, and few choose to take this path.

The contributors in this book belong to the minority that does. Some had to abandon their idea of Jewishness altogether. They no longer feel a need for tribal identification. Others found a new understanding of what it means for them to be Jewish—one that rejects the view of the Jew as the eternal and only victim, and that refuses to live in fear. Some have found, and even founded, new Jewish communities and groups of like-minded people, where it is safe and permissible to be critical of Israel, while retaining a sense of Jewish identity. These people are "coming out" of a collective cultural closet. They have chosen to join the rest of the human race as equals, not as people whose identity is founded on fear and anticipation of the next Holocaust. They are unusual.

Some of the contributors responded to my invitation to participate in this book, and others volunteered to have their stories included when they heard about this project. Sometimes it took a little convincing on my part because none of the contributors think that there is anything special about them and what they are doing. They feel that they are just doing what they know is right and are responding to their own need to live with integrity and according to their values.

This book was not meant as a political debate or a collection of political essays or statements. There is no shortage of those. It was intended as an exposé of challenging personal journeys. It's another angle on the Israeli-Palestinian conflict, one we don't often encounter.

The contributors don't share a political position on Palestine and Israel. In fact, there is quite a diversity of opinions and of ideas about the way forward. Some of the contributors belong to activist groups, while others are private people who do their work alone.

Most of the stories were written in response to a brief that I initially sent around. I asked the contributors to say something about their background and their relationship to Zionism. I wanted to know whether they had experienced an evolution or change in their views and if so, what caused it. I asked whether there were special events, incidents, books or figures that had influenced or inspired them to move in the direction they have chosen. I asked each contributor to share something about his or her inner journey. I was curious to know what it was like emotionally when views were beginning to change and evolve. I also asked if there were any important turning points on their journey, and asked authors to comment on what they think made them choose to become active in this area, when so many choose the opposite. Another question I asked was whether the authors suffered in any way for their views and their activism, and whether they paid a price for them.

As you will see, the contributors responded each in his or her own unique way. To me the stories seem to complement each other, and together paint an interesting and valuable picture of the Israeli-Palestinian conflict and of activism in this area.

I was careful that my editing did not compromise each writer's style. I wanted to honour each writer's authentic voice as much as possible. I was especially careful with Ruth Tenne's story because Ruth wrote it from a child's perspective and it was important to her that this perspective was preserved.

Because the book is published in the United Kingdom, and for the sake of consistency, I changed the spelling into British English. This means that even American or Canadian contributors may "sound" British, although they wrote their stories in their respective English dialects.

Over the past few years I have noticed that when people use the word "Israeli" they refer to the Jewish citizens of Israel. The reality is that the Palestinian citizens of Israel who make up more than 20% of the population are also Israelis, but the word "Israeli" does not include them. This is an interesting example of how language can reinforce the idea that Israel is a country only of Jews, and only for Jews. Therefore, for the sake of accuracy and to avoid colluding with this, I have replaced, in many places, the word "Israeli" with the phrases "Jewish Israeli" or "Israeli Jew".

In some places I added footnotes, where I felt that it was necessary to explain or clarify something. I was particularly aware that some readers may not be familiar with certain Jewish terms, concepts or organisations. To distinguish between my footnotes and those offered by the authors, I added my initials (AA) at the end of my footnotes.

I wasn't sure about the order in which the stories should appear. In the end I decided to group them according to country of residence, and then in alphabetical order of the author's surname. It's not necessarily the best order, and certainly not the only one possible. But I have tried to reflect the fact that I view all of us as equal.

The number of stories included under each country is not representative of the number of Jewish activists in that country. It is simply a reflection of the number of stories that I was able to invite to this book.

Except in Ruth Tenne's case, I did not include a biography with the stories. I think the writers do a good job of describing their background and their activism. Ruth's story however, focussed more on her childhood experience of witnessing the establishment of the state of Israel and the 1948 war, and I felt that there was a need for a short biography to describe her more recent activist work.

I feel privileged and humbled to have had the opportunity to edit this book, and I am deeply grateful to all the contributors who made the effort to write their stories. I know that for many, if not all, writing for this book was not easy, as they had to delve into deeply emotional issues and share personal details. I am grateful also to my husband Ian for his ongoing support, and for his help in typesetting and designing this book.

The process of editing was an emotional experience, and I found myself crying on a few occasions along the way. Many of the experiences, emotions and realisations that the contributors describe, resonated with my own, and many of my own memories surfaced as I was reading the stories.

I hope that reading these wise, brave and often moving stories will encourage you, the reader, to think about your place in the world, your loyalty and attachment to your particular group or belief system and your values. I hope that they will encourage you to seek truth and question everything, even long-held and cherished beliefs. As the contributors have all learned, we cannot assume that everything we are taught is always the truth, even if it is comfortable or attractive, and even if we want very much to believe it. It is our individual responsibility to make sure that we are well informed and exposed to as many sources of information as possible.

There are injustices everywhere that affect individuals and groups. Somewhere along the way I learned that every crime, violation or act of injustice requires three participants: a victim, a perpetrator and a bystander. As long as bystanders exist, so will crime and injustice. The role of perpetrators is obvious, but it is bystanders who guarantee that trauma, humiliation and suffering will continue to reverberate for generations and prevent millions of human beings from fulfilling their potential.

This book is a tribute to those who will not keep quiet, who make trouble, who refuse to be bystanders, and who intervene to let perpetrators know that what they are doing is wrong, and to support and protect their victims. These courageous souls are an example of what humanity can and should be. The more people join them and refuse to remain bystanders, the harder it will be for perpetrators to commit their crimes.

If you are already involved in some form of activism, you are a part of a noble tradition, and I am sure you will find kindred spirits in this book. If you are not, I hope these stories will encourage you to see that it is possible to stand up for the rights of others, even against strong opposition. It isn't easy, but it's fulfilling and it's right. It is certainly life, and world-changing.

I welcome thoughts and comments from readers. You can write to me at: avigail@fullyhuman.co.uk.

Avigail Abarbanel
Inverness-Shire
March 2012

Introduction to the 2018 Edition

It's hard to believe but *Beyond Tribal Loyalties* has been out now for six years. The publication of a second edition offers me an opportunity to write a new, more up-to-date introduction.

I wish I could say that things are better in Palestine compared with how they were back in 2012 when the paperback edition was first published. Unfortunately, things are not only not better, they are far worse for the Palestinian people.

The recent brutal Israeli attack on unarmed and peaceful Palestinian protesters in Gaza, the targeted shootings of twenty-nine medics, killing two, while they were treating wounded on the ground, the use of snipers to shoot down protesters including children, as if on a hunting spree, are the latest examples of how settler-colonialism handles even peaceful resistance.

100% of Gaza's children and probably most of the adults there suffer from Post-Traumatic Stress. Almost two million people are trapped in the largest open-air prison on the planet living in hellish conditions without any hope of release, under an illegal Israeli siege. Although Israel 'withdrew' from Gaza it still controls directly and indirectly what every individual there does, how much and what they eat, their access to education and work, their ability to travel, their access to medical care and whether or not they have building materials, clean water, sanitation or electricity.

Daily injustices continue, incarceration without trial, incarceration and abuse of Palestinian children, including but not limited to keeping children in adult prisons and preventing their families from seeing them. There are recurring cruel and senseless crimes against Palestinians that can only be described as psychopathic. They are committed both by colonisers (aka settlers) who go unpunished and by Israeli forces. These stories rarely make it to mainstream news.

The infiltration of Palestinian society by Israeli secret agents is common practice.[5] The job of those agents is to sabotage community relationships and break down Palestinian society from within, all in the service of weakening resistance and ultimately eliminating a people.

---

[5] I strongly recommend the film 'Omar'. It depicts accurately how Israel operates in the Occupied and Colonised West Bank.

The 'shoot first ask questions later' policy, and Israeli racism demonstrate how little Palestinian lives matter to Israel.

Israel continues to enact laws and implement policies that marginalise the Palestinians a little bit at a time, thus making it easier one day to remove them completely one way or another. Ilan Pappé calls what Israel does to the Palestinians an 'incremental genocide'. If we take a step back from the intentionally complex picture Israel tries to paint for us, we can all see that this is indeed what it is.

Israeli settler-colonialism in Palestine is progressing largely unchallenged by those who have the power to stop it. If it were not for the persistent work of grassroots groups, the Palestinians would have been all but forgotten by now. Although the situation on the ground in ever shrinking Palestine is worse than it was six years ago, the biggest success of grassroots protest is in not allowing the topic of Palestine to disappear from public awareness.

The Boycott Divestment and Sanctions (BDS) movement, alternative news outlets like *Mondoweiss*, *The Electronic Intifada*, *Middle East Monitor (MEMO)* and others, independent journalists and activists like Jonathan Cook and dedicated historians like Ilan Pappé are all ensuring that the Palestinian cause remains on the world's agenda. Anti-Zionists and BDS supporters from within Israel are making an invaluable contribution. Despite the fact that they are a small minority, they lend their voice from within to Palestinian resistance and to the larger context of opposition to Israeli settler-colonialism.

Occasionally articles are published in mainstream newspapers that are sympathetic to the Palestinians. But even the most sympathetic writers are still caught up in what I call the Israeli 'language trap'.[6] They still use words like 'conflict', 'peace', 'war' and 'negotiations', implying false symmetry between Israel and the Palestinians.

Many writers in mainstream media outlets still insist on 'balance' in their reporting and make a big point of representing 'both sides of the story'. While in principle neutrality and balance can be seen as expressions of thoughtfulness, reason and calmness, they are only appropriate where there is equality of power. If exercised in situations where there is an inherent imbalance of power, neutrality or balance become active enablers of an abusive system. It is appropriate and

---

[6] See my article on *Mondoweiss*, 'The Palestine Israel Language Trap' at: http://mondoweiss.net/2016/08/palestine-israel-language/ (last accessed 8th June 2018)

necessary to remain unbiased when dealing with two sides with equal power, whether they are a couple attending relationship therapy at my practice, or two organisations or countries who have a dispute.

Where there is an imbalance of power, maintaining a 'neutral' or 'balanced' position is by definition harmful to the less powerful side[7]. In the field of psychotherapy, we do not engage in relationship therapy if there is an imbalance of power manifesting for example in violence or coercive control by one side[8] against the other. Our first priority is always to dismantle the power structure and protect the victim.

A 'balanced' position enables toxic and abusive power structures to continue. This not only causes more harm to victims, it also gives permission to perpetrators to continue the abuse. This is precisely what a 'balanced' position on Palestine is doing.

There is no 'other side to the story' in settler-colonialism just like there is no 'other side' to the story in slavery, racism, discrimination, or child abuse. A long time ago we stopped debating with those who oppose women's equality or women's right to vote. It would be preposterous and possibly even criminal in some countries to suggest that child molesters have a valid point of view, that slavery is useful to our economy, or that Hitler's genocidal racial ideology had merit. But settler-colonialism in Palestine is still exempt.

I am yet to see one mainstream newspaper that is prepared to call a spade a spade and name Israeli *setter-colonialism* for what it is. Settler-colonialism is a crime against humanity and it needs to be recognised and named as such. When we deal with a crime the focus must be on the crime not on identities. Jewish Israelis, the perpetrators of settler-colonialism, do not deserve special treatment or consideration for any reason. Neither do the Palestinian people, the victims of Israeli settler-colonialism, deserve to be seen as lesser victims. A crime is a crime.

As in all historical cases of settler-colonialism, it is the settler-colonisers who usually have the advantage. They have more advanced weaponry and they mobilise all of their resources to achieve their goal. They also control the narrative, what is talked about, how much is talked about and what is permissible or not permissible to say.

---

[7] As Desmond Tutu said: "If you are neutral in situations of injustice, you have chosen the side of the oppressor. If an elephant has its foot on the tail of a mouse and you say that you are neutral, the mouse will not appreciate your neutrality."

[8] Violence and coercive control in personal relationships are criminal offences in the UK.

Settler-colonisers have always done everything in their power to obscure the reality of settler-colonialism and its inherent crimes, and to dehumanise and demonise their victims. Israeli settler-colonialism is not original and is no different. According the late Australian scholar Patrick Wolfe, settle-colonisers engage in a 'policy of elimination'[9] of the native populations they aim to replace. The Palestinians have always known they are the victims of settler-colonialism. The know they are being slowly eliminated and replaced. They have been crying out for help for decades, but no one in positions of power is listening.

Elimination is not just physical. For any settler-colonial movement to succeed it has to ensure that there is no resistance. After all, successful resistance could mean failure for the settler-coloniser. Resistance is not just armed resistance. As long as a colonised people hold on to their identity, their culture, their memory and their dignity they are a threat to the colonisers. It has therefore always been part of colonial and settler-colonial movements to do everything possible to damage the very spirit and humanity of their victims. Colonisers and settler-colonisers have always portrayed their victims as 'primitives', 'inferior', 'terrorists', 'bad' humans or even non-humans, who do not deserve sympathy from anyone and who do not have a right to exist. This is helpful if you want to get the support of others for the crime you are committing and enable your own people to obey orders without questioning.

One of the most successful tools used by Israel and its supporters to silence opposition and weaken support for the Palestinians is to equate criticism of Israel with antisemitism. This has been quite an effective way of silencing criticism and disempowering protesters. During my seventeen years of activism I have witnessed this cynical Israeli tactic become increasingly more effective. We all saw its impact on the British Labour Party in recent times.

With varying degrees of success Israel has been attempting to use its political influence and the legal systems in different countries to criminalise criticism of Israel and the BDS under existing racial vilification laws. Antisemitism as a form of racial vilification is already criminalised in a number of countries. If you can legally equate criticism of Israel with antisemitism, then criticising the state of Israel and supporting the BDS automatically become crimes. Israel would like to

---

[9] Patrick Wolfe (2006) Settler colonialism and the elimination of the native, *Journal of Genocide Research*, 8:4, 387-409. Published online: 21 Dec 2006 (The full article is available online).

argue that if you disagree with the right of Israel to exist *as an exclusively Jewish state at the expense of the indigenous people*, you are effectively calling for the destruction of all Jewish people everywhere. Israel is trying to shift the focus from legitimate objection to settler-colonialism to illegitimate racism against Jews.

This is one of the many mechanisms Israel uses to try to smooth its path to completing its settler-colonial project in Palestine and the elimination of the Palestinian people. It is unprecedented that criticism of a state's policies should be seen as racism. This has to be opposed not only because it is false. It has to be opposed because it constitutes interference in the democratic process in other countries and the right, duty and freedom of citizens in any country to protest against human rights violations and crimes against humanity committed *by anyone*.

Equating criticism of Israel with antisemitism doesn't just harm the Palestinian cause, it also trivialises the meaning of real antisemitism, which is a form of racism directed specifically against Jews. But Israel does not care much about whether or not the word 'antisemitism' is losing its meaning. From Israeli perspective, the end justifies the means.

In the eyes of Jewish Israelis, Jews are the ultimate victims and the most important victims that have ever existed in human history. Jewish culture is based on an identity of persecution and a belief that Jews are never safe among non-Jews. Mainstream Jewish culture shares a belief that Jews can only be safe with other Jews and that it is the duty of all Jews to do whatever is necessary to preserve the Jewish people[10]. Growing up in Israel I learned that the only thing standing between me and annihilation is the state of Israel. It therefore followed that if I wanted to survive I would have to dedicate my life to protecting the Jewish state, no matter the cost. I was raised to believe that the survival

---

[10] The definition of what constitutes Jewishness is a complex topic that deserves separate discussion. It's important to realise though that Israel has adopted a racial, blood definition of Jewishness. The idea of Jewishness as a race was adopted by Hitler and the Nazis and it fitted well within their race (pseudo) science. In Israel any person is considered Jewish if their mother is Jewish regardless of whether they follow Jewish religion or identify themselves as Jewish in any way. How the mother is identified as Jewish is because her mother was Jewish and so it goes on. Records of Jewish religious populations that traditionally avoided marrying out became the basis for identifying Jewish people and that has become confused with a Jewish 'race'. This racial definition allows Israel to 'speak' for people who do not have any affiliation to the Jewish state, and who do not agree with Zionism. Israel wants to be a 'national home' for all those Israel considers to be Jewish regardless of where they live or how they see themselves.

of our own people is more important than anything, including universal human values and a greater sense of purpose.

Despite the blatant imbalance of power between the Israeli state and the Palestinian people most Israeli Jews still believe that they are just fighting for their own survival against a dangerous annihilator. This victimhood complex has always been embedded in Jewish culture. I grew up with it and it kind of makes sense when you are on the inside and are brought up only on the narrow and blinkered version of history Israel teaches.

Those in Israel who would be sympathetic to the suffering of the Palestinians can easily be overpowered and silenced because they too know and believe this narrative of eternal Jewish victimhood. Jewish victimhood is the central pillar of Jewish identity Israel-style, and it is an unspoken social taboo to question it[11].

Israel's unique take on demonising the indigenous people it is seeking to replace fits well within traditional Israeli Jewish narrative. Israel has succeeded in portraying the Palestinians not as victims of a settler-colonial state who are fighting for their survival, but as enemies of the *Jewish people*. In Jewish Israeli eyes the Palestinian people are just the latest in a long list of groups who have been hell-bent on annihilating the Jewish people for their own reasons[12]. Until people grasp this, they cannot properly understand what is going on in Palestine and what Israel is doing there.

Only when you come out of the fog of insular Jewish Israeli brainwashing and gain a broader perspective, you begin to see how flawed and out of touch with reality this way of thinking is. I have long been equating Jewish Israeli culture to a cult, precisely because of its insular view of the world and the requirement that individuals submit their unique identity and replace it with group identity. Although questioning or criticising Jewish Israeli mindset and policies are not

---

[11] I am not talking here about Holocaust denial. The Holocaust was a horrific attempt to annihilate all of Europe's Jews in the Twentieth Century using the machinery of a modern state. The Nazi regime murdered, displaced and scarred millions of Jews. The devastating impact of the Holocaust reverberated for generations. I'm talking about the perception that Jews are *always* victims. Israeli Jews believe that the Holocaust isn't over, and that without the state of Israel it is only a matter of time before someone carries out another attempt to annihilate the Jewish people. Sadly, the lessons Israel learns from Jewish persecution and the ones it teaches its citizens are inward looking. They are not generalised to include all human beings. Israeli Jews believe in 'never again *for us*', not necessarily in 'never again for anyone'.

[12] See Peter Slezak's story for an example of this in the Jewish Passover liturgy.

formally punishable in Israel – at least not for Jews – there is a great deal of informal and effective pressure on people to conform and self-censor.[13]

As a psychotherapist I have worked with many cult survivors over the years. I can see many similarities between the Zionist belief system and a cult. One of the most obvious similarities lies in the process of leaving or trying to leave Zionism. Leaving cults is always psychologically complex and incredibly difficult and leaving Zionism is no different. The stories in this book are largely about the process of leaving the Zionist cult, what it is like to do this and the challenges and opposition you face when you try to leave.

Since the original publication of this book many have joined the ranks of 'cult leavers', and it has been suggested that I consider putting together a second volume of stories. Having met so many new courageous people over the past six years who have been on this journey, I am tempted.

❦

The machinery of Zionist Israeli settler-colonialism is intended ultimately to replace the entire Palestinian population with Jews on all the land of historic Palestine. Israel is on track to complete its plan with considerable military, political and financial backing from countries like the US, UK, Germany and others. Many countries support Israel in spirit, or at least do not offer any significant opposition to Israeli settler-colonialism except for the occasional and toothless 'condemnation' of events that are usually perceived in isolation. The grassroots campaign continues to bite and annoy Israel, but we are still a long way away from official support for the BDS from our governments.

This universal support for Israel is a de-facto endorsement of settler-colonialism and is therefore collusion with a crime against humanity. This should be extraordinary in a 'post-colonial' world. Sanctions against Israel should be a no-brainer for societies that routinely talk about democracy, freedom, equality and human rights.

---

[13] See my Mondoweiss article, 'Why I left the cult' at
http://mondoweiss.net/2016/10/why-i-left-the-cult/ See also Gideon Levy's testimony at:
http://mondoweiss.net/2018/03/gideon-question-crushed/

Post-colonial lessons and reflections are indeed common in progressive scholarly circles. But we still live in a world largely run by colonial and imperialistic interests, complete with the belief that there are worthy and less worthy humans.

Present day political and economic imperialism are often also accompanied by military might as evident in the foreign policies of countries like the US and the UK, and the propaganda they use to justify their actions. For example, the US presented its invasion of Iraq ostensibly as a way to deal with the risks of weapons of mass destruction. But in truth, the US-led invasion, which caused the destruction of a country, the deaths of around half a million people and well over four thousand US soldiers[14] was a cynical means to increase the influence and control of US energy interests in the region.

While this goes on, who is going to stand up to Israel? To take Israel to task, current imperialist countries would have to acknowledge and abandon their imperialistic ambitions and policies. Israel has never had it so easy and so good and that is because the rest of the world, or at least the significant world powers in our time are not behaving any better. The fact that official sanctions or any real attempt to stop Israel's relentless march to complete its settler-colonial project seem so impossible, exposes a global problem of hypocrisy and double standards. It also highlights the discrepancy between the laws we have inside our societies and the rules we live by internationally.

The closest internal equivalent of settler-colonialism would probably be a house invasion. In Western societies there is no question whose side the law is on and who it protects. Our laws would not tolerate it if one person invaded the home of another and attempted to replace the inhabitants with their own family, no matter what reasons or justifications they would cite. In Palestine we not only tolerate it, our own governments actively enable this house invasion and everything that goes with it.

ᛝ

---

[14] There number of deaths caused by the invasion of Iraq is still debated, which in itself should worry us. How can we not know how many died or were otherwise harmed unless we don't really care...? (See: https://www.huffingtonpost.com/2013/10/15/iraq-death-toll_n_4102855.html?guccounter=1)

When I started to work on the first edition of this book, the idea that Jewish people could stand up to Israel, challenge its policies and support the Palestinians was still seen as something of a novelty. This is no longer the case. More Jews than ever before question the expectation that they have an automatic obligation to support Israel 'right or wrong', and the idea that their very identity is linked with Israel's fate. However, despite the slow increase in pro-Palestinian activism in Jewish circles, there is still significant Jewish support for Israel around the world.

I am often asked by Israeli Jews and supporters of Israel to justify myself for my activism. But it is not I or people like me who need to justify ourselves. I believe that it is Jews and non-Jews who support settler-colonialism in Palestine that have the duty to explain why they support it. You can't be a nice person in one area of your life, profess to believe in social justice, peace and fairness on one hand, and at the same time support the idea that one group of people has more right to exist or survive than another. Those who support Israel are the ones who owe the Palestinians an explanation and an apology.

Those Jews who begin to see the reality of Israel for what it is, still have to wrestle with issues of identity, fear of antisemitism and tribal affiliation. I have always hoped that this book will offer support and inspiration to those who are just starting on this difficult journey.

If any good comes out of the existence of Israel is that it its increasingly visible unfolding settler-colonial agenda will inevitably lead to a crisis in Jewish identity. I have no doubt that there are already the beginnings of a re-evaluation and a re-thinking of what being Jewish means. Seeing your own people as a perpetrator and not as history's biggest victim is a major shift, likely to lead to a psychological crisis. Learning not to live in fear of antisemitism, that mythical, almost supernatural monster that is such a central part of Jewish identity, requires recovery from the elements of trauma embedded in Jewishness.

It's a big journey that will take time; time that the Palestinians do not have! What we all have to focus on as a matter of urgency is changing the power imbalance and stop enabling Israeli settler-colonialism. Jews who are still on the journey can deal with their identity crisis and psychological problems later.

I have left all the stories in this book as they are. They are valuable as they are and have in themselves become part of history. Sadly, we lost Margot Salom in 2016. But her powerful voice carries on through her story and her other writings. Her courage and passion and the legacy of her activism for justice live on.

What has changed in me in the past six years, apart from just growing older, is that I see myself more than ever before as a member of the human species, rather than a member of any particular group. We all need to move beyond tribal loyalties. Our existence and survival as a species depends now more than ever on cooperation, not on isolationism or competitive tribal, ghetto mentality. Even more so, if we want more for ourselves then just survival, if we want to develop and see what is possible for us, if we want to fulfil our potential, we cannot continue with our short-sighted and narrow-minded tribalism. It simply gets in the way and keeps us in a permanent state of war that is self-inflicted and completely unnecessary and preventable. The narratives and testimonies in this book are examples of the personal process of moving from a narrow definition of identity to a broader and more compassionate one, that embraces the entirety of our species.

I do not have good news. Our politicians and elected leaders do not have the courage, vision or compassion to do the right thing and fix a suffering world, despite the fact that most of our suffering is human-made and avoidable. It is therefore up to each one of us to continue to cooperate, provide leadership, courage, a non-adversarial model of activism, cooperation, openness, compassion. We must insist on being heard. We can't wait for our political 'mummies' and 'daddies' to know what's best for us. They do not necessarily represent the best of us and they have no idea what they are doing.

We don't have to like everyone, we just have to realise we are all members of the same species and that it is up to us to transform this world if we want to thrive rather than just survive and increase our numbers.

Defeating Israeli settler-colonialism will not only be liberating for the Palestinians, it will also symbolise our refusal to accept the law of the jungle that currently drives our world.

Avigail Abarbanel
Scottish Highlands, June 2018

Australia

Am I an Activist?

Sivan Barak

My name is Sivan Barak. I'm a sister, a mother, a daughter, a friend and in my humble opinion I may well be an activist. But the question that is far more interesting to me is why I became one, and this is still not clear to me.

My education, both formal and informal, has not been mainstream. Learning to question everything has probably been the best lesson I ever learned, but it has also caused me and my family much turmoil.

Questioning is an incessant quality that has affected every aspect of my life. There have been many questions, big and small, but one particular question recurs in a multitude of scenarios, and it is a complex one to ask. So, I always place it within a story.

Let me ask you, the reader, my question and I ask that you share it also with your friends and family.

Imagine two close friends driving along a beach road on a lovely spring afternoon, listening to music, seemingly without a care in the world. Suddenly a car swerves towards them, an accident occurs, the cars are destroyed yet the two friends are untouched.

After the terrible sounds of glass shattering, smell of oil and burning rubber, the adrenaline rush subsides, the body stops shaking. Then there is silence.

In these moments a shift could occur for the two involved in the incident, a deep shift in their perspective on life.

Why is it that one friend may emerge from this traumatic event with a renewed attitude to life, seeing it as a precious gift to be cherished and relished? Perhaps even re-evaluating her attitude toward what is most important, deciding to live life fearlessly from now on, take risks, "stop putting it off" as she comes to a realisation that life might end tomorrow?

Meanwhile the second friend could see it in a completely opposing light. She could cling to the fear and drama experienced at that moment of impact, seeing the near-death experience in a fatalistic way, and from that day on live in perpetual victimhood.

What lies within our minds or hearts that leads us down these two opposing paths?

Crossroads or turning points, and the choices we make, have always fascinated me. Is it the way we are wired, our genetics, or our upbringing and family values?

On the surface my destiny as an activist was set before I had any political or social awareness. But the road taken, and the path down the Yellow Brick Road, never led me to the Emerald City, and I am still not sure where home is.

To understand who Sivan Barak is and why I am in this book, I need to tell my story. It began in the United States in 1964, it spans across three continents and ends in Australia in 2011. To pinpoint the precise crossroad that morphed me into an activist I will trace my life junctions from both ends chronologically, applying a magnifying glass to significant moments that made me the woman I am today. To be honest, until I was asked to write this chapter I never gave this a thought. So, in the process of writing this, I'm hoping to locate the "car crash" that affected my inner moral compass so deeply that I became the person I am today.

My story will move between past and present dates, working slowly towards that one definitive moment, that is probably somewhere in the middle.

Flashback to Scene 1

Cedars of Sinai Hospital in Beverly Hills in Los Angeles, 2 February 1964. I entered the world, the first-born of a Jewish mother and Buddhist father. Sunny California is filled with organic food, hippies, soul music, peace activists, patriots, anti-Vietnam demonstrations, macramé bags and tie-dye clothes.

My mother was born in Palestine in 1943 to Jewish Polish parents who immigrated to Palestine in the early 1930s. My father was American-born, the son of a Russian Jewish immigrant father, and a thirteenth generation American born ex-Mormon mother. Confused yet?

With this kind of a start I was seemingly on an inevitable path to activism, or at least to soul-searching. At birth I was bestowed with three citizenships, American, Israeli and Australian. Thus, began my wandering years in the quest for a sense of identity and belonging to a place, a people, a tribe.

Flash forward Scene 10

Café on Glenhuntly Road in the midst of the Jewish Ghetto, Melbourne, February 2011. I'm a mother of two teenagers: one grumpy fourteen-year-old son, and one effervescent nineteen-year-old daughter. I work full-time as a designer in a wholesale jewellery business, and study for a Masters in Social Work.

In my spare time I volunteer in advocacy groups such as WIB (Women in Black), calling for the end to the occupation in Israel-Palestine, AJDS (Australian Jewish Democratic Society) sounding a progressive voice among the Jews and a Jewish voice among progressives, and ASPIRE (Australian Supporters for the Palestinian Iraqi Refugees Emergency), advocating for the human rights of Palestinian refugees from Iraq. I learn belly dancing, participate in interfaith dialogue, study Arabic and keep up with current affairs in the world.

To all intents and purposes, it seems that in my forty-seven years I have indeed remained on the Saffron Highway of activism that seems to have been my destiny from birth. But this ain't necessarily so!

Flashback scene 2

Kibbutz Nahal Oz in the Negev, Southern Israel, 1970. My mother, younger brother and I immigrated to Israel and settled in a kibbutz neighbouring Gaza. The kibbutz was a socialist project in which I lived wonderful carefree days barefoot, free to roam, surrounded by nature and freedom. Hebrew became my language, Israel my Homeland, and picking her wild flowers in springtime was a favourite pastime.

My mother remarried a young Israeli kibbutznik who worked in the fields and befriended several of the farmers from Gaza who worked across the fence. We often hosted the Gazans and their families in our home and would drive down to share a magnificent meal at their home in Gaza. In my young mind I knew only of peaceful coexistence between "us" Jews and "them" the Arabs, but then I was told very little of the narrative of the Palestinians. There seemed to be many blanks and fuzzy anecdotes around our histories.

Following three peaceful years, came the Yom Kippur war in 1973. My new father was a paratrooper with a beautiful red beret and olive uniform, and he soon left for the Suez Canal to fight the terrible enemy. I was told we were fighting the Arabs and that they wanted to kill us all. During those months the kibbutz was suddenly empty of men. It was run by the women who worked in the fields, milked the cows, fed the chickens and baked cakes for care packages sent to their brave fighting husbands, brothers, sons, fathers and friends.

For me these days were exciting. School was out, and we spent many nights in the bomb shelters, eating chocolate and watching television. In those days the kibbutz was truly a socialist project so television was not allowed in the members' rooms, only in communal spaces like the shelters and club room. This was for the sake of equality for all. When my dad returned for a rare visit, he told us heroic tales of battles won, about a bicycle he found in one of the villages, which he wanted to bring back for us, the awful food they ate and how little they slept.

Flash-forward scene 9

Welcome hall, arrival lounge, Melbourne Tullamarine International Airport, December 2009. I'm clasping a video camera, finger poised on the Record button, waiting with nervous anticipation for the arrival of the most precious human cargo, sixty-eight Palestinian Iraqi refugees coming to Australia for resettlement.

We have never met in person but for the past year and a half I have been a part of an organisation called ASPIRE, made up of a random group of people in Melbourne who applied on behalf of these refugees to seek asylum in Australia.

We heard about the plight of the Palestinian refugees who fled persecution in Iraq and had been staying in Syria near the Iraqi border since 2005. Being stateless, these people found no country that would take them in. For sixteen months we worked furiously through mountains of documents needing translation from Arabic to English, applications to be filled in, passport photos, identification documents and hundreds of telephone calls to the refugee camp. Finally, the big day arrived.

The families were about to arrive and I wanted to document the moment on my camera because it was too great to believe. Suddenly they begin to appear, slowly pushing huge trolleys laden with overflowing suitcases, plastic bags and clothing, tired bewildered eyes of people who have seen too much and have never experienced a welcome of any kind.

I document a strange "greeting dance" between the men arriving and the men welcoming. My camera captures it so beautifully. "*Ahalan, ahalan*", then two or four kisses on either cheek; an intimate gesture between men who have never met but who are bound together.

The women too start to kiss each other shyly on both cheeks whilst saying a quiet "*Ahalan*". I watch the local Western women guiding the new arrivals towards the door to a new land, that for the first time in three generations they can call home. I managed to capture all this on the video camera for ours and their children to see.

Back again scene 3

Flying over Melbourne, about to land, 1975. Immigrating to Australia. After the war my parents decided to leave the kibbutz and move to Australia. I desperately wanted to stay and even found foster parents to look after me in the kibbutz. But my family weren't so keen to relinquish me. So grudgingly I left, vowing to return the moment I became an adult.

We settled in Kew, a white, upper middle-class neighbourhood. I entered a wonderful private open school and found new friends. Naturally we were drawn towards our Lebanese neighbours who owned the local milk bar (grocery store). Together we shared food, laughter and a common longing for the warm and friendly Middle East.

My teenage years were the time I began to mature and develop a sense of identity. I joined *Hashomer Ha'tzair*, a socialist Zionist youth movement, and learned about the Jewish diaspora's need for Israel. I was taught our narrative as a Jewish People, which was centred on our need for survival as a result of pogroms and the Holocaust.

Planting the seeds of the ideals of *aliyah*[15] was easy with me. I had already made a promise to myself when I was eleven that I would return. This flame stayed alive until I graduated from high school and got on a plane to join the army in Israel.

Back to the future scene 8

State Library Swanston Street, Melbourne, December 2008. Hosting an angry demonstration. About a week into Operation Cast Lead in Gaza, I've decided to join the masses. All alone I marched uncomfortably down the main street of our peaceful city beside very angry demonstrators shouting slogans of fury against the killing of innocent lives in the besieged Gaza.

Half an hour earlier another demonstration went down this same path, with many of my friends marching in support of the Israeli government. Now as I march I keep looking around to see if anyone recognises me. I'm genuinely concerned that I would be labelled an "Israel-hater" or "an enemy from within". Despite my fears I march, as my heart tells me to do the right thing. Let my friends gaze in horror. "Palestine will be free, from the river to the sea!" The chanting made me cringe, but I marched on.

Scene 4

Ben Gurion Airport, Israel, May1983. Strapped to a bright orange backpack with all my belongings. At eighteen I was a full-fledged Lefty Zionist who believed my country needed me to continue "flowering the barren land" that was founded by our forefathers in the 1948 "War of Independence".

I was familiar with the history of 1967, the Occupation, with Palestinian identity, but it was mostly equated with terror and fear. Certainly, this was without any question a Jewish homeland and my home.

---

[15]*Aliyah* is a Hebrew term for immigrating to Israel that literally means "ascending". By contrast, the term for leaving Israel is *yeridah*, meaning "descending". Both terms are imbued with a moral value. It comes from the idea that the only place for Jews is the state of Israel and that all Jews must want to live there. The words *yeridah* and *yordim*, those who leave, have traditionally been used in a pejorative way. (AA)

In 1984 I voluntarily enlisted into the Israeli army and served for two years and ten months. I remember one day during basic training I was at target practice. My target had an Arab looking face drawn on it, cartoon style. My stomach turned. I told my officer that I refused to shoot at this target and asked for a replacement. He rolled his eyes but did as I asked.

During six months duty in the West bank, I started to see the reality on the ground and questions arose in me. I noted a two-tiered society of "us" and "them". We rule and they are second class citizens with no voice or rights. I still felt we had a purpose to protect and defend the innocent from terror and hatred and stayed on the path.

Scene 7

Lobby of Armagh House with three Palestinian men, late 2008. Preparing a radio interview for the *Palestine Remembered* show. I wait for my colleague who is late, so I apologetically introduce myself, hand outstretched, "Hello, I'm Sivan, sorry we are running late." We chat a little and I reveal with confidence my origins. One of the men asks me with an obvious hint of distaste "Are you a Zionist?" I feel my heart sink and defences go up. I answer "Are you a terrorist?" We both look at each other in shock and realise for a second the sweeping generalisation and ignorance between us. I then suggest, "Can we start again?"

Not long after this exchange we became close friends. Several months later he said to me, "If all Israelis were like you, there would be peace and we would be sitting together in a Tel Aviv café sipping a latte." Today he is back in Gaza, teaching at the University and about to get married.

Back to scene 5

Office of Hadassah International in Caulfield. June 2008. Fundraising for a project in Jerusalem that treats children of all religions who suffer from trauma.

The phone rings and on the other line is an Israeli woman who invites me to participate in a workshop titled, "What do you think of me?" This joint Palestinian-Israeli project placed three Jewish Israelis and three Palestinians who currently live in Australia in a common space and filmed them interacting through a series of exercises such as creative writing, performance and drama.

I agreed wholeheartedly to participate and in July attended the first workshop day in a series of six meetings. The first meeting was to be a solo interview in which I was invited to share information about my identity, views of the conflict and of the "other".

Scene 6

Trades Hall, first day of "What do you think of me?" July 2008. Team building exercise in the big cold room. Six strangers standing awkwardly around sipping instant coffee and waiting for cameras to be set up so the workshop can begin. I'm feeling nervous and excited about this adventure. I love new experiences and this looks promisingly different to anything I have ever done before.

We introduce ourselves to the group whilst turning towards the facilitators for directions. We are asked to sit in a circle and the general idea of the workshop is conveyed to us. I eye the others, especially the Palestinians, with curiosity and some dread. "Turn to the person beside you, acquaint yourselves in five minutes, then in turn, introduce your partner to the group." I faced a strange man, who told me his story, where he, his father and his grandfather are from, how they lived in exile for sixty-three years as refugees. I sensed undertones of anger towards me when he was telling his story, but he was polite enough and non-confrontational. I introduce myself too, quickly, and then we did the rounds. The stories were interesting with many similarities across the national groups.

In the next exercise we asked were to stand up, a pair at a time in the middle of the large room and face each other while the rest looked on. My partner and I were first to stand up, facing each other approximately two metres apart, hands by our sides, no facial expression. We were asked to stare into each other's eyes and wait in silence. I could hear the film capturing the moment. I wriggled around uncomfortably giggling in nervousness. Our eyes locked. We looked at each other, not yet seeing each other. I could feel my heart beating fast, resisting staring deeply into the eyes of a stranger, an enemy, who probably hates me and blames me for generations of his family's suffering. But then I saw him, behind the conflict, the violence and the pain, beyond all that. For the first time in my life I saw the man opposite me. A human being like me, an equal, and the shift happened. It was a simple shift, it was over in a second but with no going back.

My crossroad was as simple as that. From the day I stared into the eyes of a Palestinian man and saw the human being, I started to see and fight against the injustices my people had instigated against his people. A cloud lifted in me and in those who watched us. It was palpable.

The path has at times been terrifying and ground shattering, but I will remain on it until peace and justice are set in place in the land I love, that is my home and his.

The Road to Hell is Paved with Tribal Loyalties

Ray Bergmann

"How wonderful it is that nobody need wait a single moment before starting to improve the world."
— *Anne Frank*

I peer back into my early life, with its intensely Jewish identification and background, to see how it came about that I became an activist for Palestinian human rights and for a just and negotiated settlement of the Israeli-Palestinian conflict. There are strong tribal loyalties that prevent most Jews from entertaining any doubts about the Zionist version of the conflict in Israel-Palestine. But I did react differently to the Israeli occupation of Palestine compared with the Jewish friends of my childhood who remain staunch Zionist supporters to this day.

I was born in January 1949 into a Jewish family in Brisbane, a relaxed and peaceful provincial city on the East coast of Australia, and the capital of the "sunshine state" of Queensland. It was a secure environment in an advanced Western country with a well-developed social security system; a good basis surely for the development of a well-balanced and cheerful child who was indeed well-spoiled by doting parents Leo and Betty Bergmann.

My elder sister was born two years previously. She was named Estelle, after our dad's mother who perished at Auschwitz together with Dad's father.

I was given the same Hebrew name as Dad's father, Israel. My Germanic-English name was registered as Raymond—the "Ray" part coming from the middle syllable in Is-ra-el.

I was born only months after the declaration of independence of the State of Israel, so my naming ceremony was also a celebration and recognition of this remarkable historical event. My father's sister Nora, who had been on a children's transport ship to England just before the Nazi Holocaust, arrived by boat in Brisbane on the very day I was born.

My mother's mother migrated to Australia from Palestine before my mother was born. Since my maternal grandfather was never spoken of, Nana was the only grandparent I ever knew.

I was a curious child, always asking questions. But neither my parents nor Nana ever gave much information about their own childhoods and background, which were not to be spoken about. Jewish community leaders that they respected, told them that it would harm children psychologically to know too much about traumatic events in recent family history, and they believed them. The only thing I remember Nana saying about Palestine was that, "It was no place to raise children." She came to Australia by boat from Jaffa with two children, Mum's sister and brother. My mother was born in Brisbane after they arrived.

It was in the early 1960s, when I was eleven, that this advice to spare children their families' traumas must have been changed. One night well past our bedtime, my sister and I were summoned to the lounge room to watch graphic scenes on our black and white television set, of what had happened to Dad's parents and millions of other Jews, singled out along with gypsies for genocide on the basis of their ethnicity. It was around that time, when I first learned the details of the Nazi Holocaust, that Nana passed away.

I began to develop religious habits more Orthodox than my parents. I regularly donned the *tefillin*. These are the small black leather boxes containing scrolls of parchment inscribed with verses from the Torah, with black leather straps that I would wind around my left arm and hand before saying morning prayers. I would often walk several hours alone to get to the Margaret Street synagogue on Saturday mornings in observance of the strict Orthodox Jewish prohibition on riding in a vehicle on the Sabbath. I was a member of the boys' choir that was active in the synagogue services.

My parents had always kept a kosher home, and attended synagogue on holy days and, like Nana, especially loved and celebrated all the Jewish festivals. But along with the rest of my extended family, they were not as strict in their observance of Jewish rituals as some members of the Jewish community who they respected as observing "the proper way". So, they enjoyed *naches*[16] from my stricter observance of the rituals and encouraged it.

The Brisbane River divided the city in two and there was a cultural difference between the north and south sides of the river. The Jewish subculture was also divided accordingly. The North side community was centred on the Margaret Street synagogue, which was founded by British Jews three generations earlier. The South side community lived closer to the Deshon Street synagogue, which was founded after the Russo-Japanese War of 1905 by Russian Jews from Harbin, a major junction on the Chinese Eastern Railway.

Nana lived just around the corner from the Deshon Street synagogue. Her many friends, who also lived within walking distance of the synagogue, were immigrants from varied far-flung parts of the world. Nana was a peddler who went door-to-door selling haberdashery and bed linen. Most households had a sewing machine in those days. My grandmother would take orders for rolls of material, dress patterns etc., pick up the orders at Malouf haberdashery in nearby Woolloogabba and deliver them the following day. The bed linen she sold was on consignment from local Jewish traders, many of whom were her friends.

Nana's parents were Russian Jews who emigrated to France in 1890 escaping antisemitic pogroms. They stayed in France until a wave of antisemitism rocked France during the scandalous Dreyfus affair[17]. So, they moved to Palestine, then a province of the Turkish Empire.

Although my parents and most of my relatives lived on the South side, they were members of the North side, Margaret Street synagogue. Dad's sister had married a third generation Australian Jew whose grandfather, according to a plaque on the synagogue wall, was the first president of the Margaret Street shul (synagogue).

Mum's sister Nellie had three daughters. The eldest, Judy, married the son of one of the Russian Jewish immigrants from Harbin and they attended the Deshon Street shul with Nana. The middle daughter

---

[16] Yiddish for satisfaction. (AA)
[17] Alfred Dreyfus was a young Jewish French artillery officer who was tried and convicted of treason in 1894 based on false evidence. He was sentenced to life in prison but was eventually acquitted in 1906. (AA)

married a Romanian Jew, and the youngest married a third-generation Australian Jew. They all attended the Margaret Street shul with their husbands and children.

My Aunty Dora was Mum's best friend from childhood. The information I have about Nana's life came from my cousin Judy, who was eighteen when I was born, and from Aunty Dora, to whom my mother confided some of her secrets. Aunty Dora, like Judy, attended the Deshon Street shul.

The Zionist Organisation of Queensland, its local branch of WIZO (Women's International Zionist Organisation) and its youth group Bei'tar, were centred at the Margaret Street Hall at the back of the shul. Our Sunday School was there, and after Sunday School I attended Bei'tar.

I recall objecting to the military nature of Bei'tar when I was eleven. I didn't like wearing the uniform, singing war-like songs or playing games like "Arabs and Jews". I protested first to the Bei'tar leaders and then complained to community leaders that in these songs and games they were teaching us to hate people we didn't know anything about. I was told by everyone, including my parents, that this was the only youth organisation we had, and that I should just ignore any aspects of the ideology I didn't like. They assured me that they did the same.

The stories I have from Aunty Dora and cousin Judy about Nana's life don't tally. But I know from Mum's birth and marriage certificates that Nana's country of origin was Palestine, although she was born in 1890 in Marseilles, France as Eva Camen (previously Kaminsky). I also know from Mum's birth certificate that the date of Mum's birth in Brisbane was 6 June 1920, that Mum's father Jacob Mendel (previously Mendelovitz) was born in 1882 in Bacău, Romania, and that Jacob and Eva were married on 16 December 1907 in Palestine. Mum's birth certificate lists "Previous Issue" of Jacob and Eva Mendel as "Leslie aged eleven" and "Nellie aged eight".

Mum and Aunty Dora told me that Eva, my Nana, left Palestine in 1919 and Mum was born soon after Nana arrived in Brisbane. Judy told me that Jacob and Eva left Palestine together to come to Australia in 1912 and lived at the corner of Brook Street and Annerley Road in South Brisbane, where Jacob had a tinsmith shop. Judy says that her mother Nellie was only ten months old when Nana's parents left Palestine. They first went back to Marseilles in France and then boarded a ship to Australia. None of my relatives can tell me where Nana's parents are buried.

World War I was between these two versions of the story, as well as the end of Turkish rule over Palestine and the commencement of the British Mandate. It is a little hard to figure out how my relatives could disagree over whether my mother's family came to Australia before or after these momentous events in world history, and why no-one knows whether Nana's parents are buried in Palestine, France or Australia. But there you have it!

Aunty Dora told me that my grandfather Jacob Mendel was a violent man who used to beat Nana up even when she was pregnant. They lived in Jaffa. One night when Jacob was out terrorising the neighbourhood with his mates, Nana left Palestine on a boat with her two children by her side and my mother in her belly. She said that Jacob followed them to Australia, but Nana would only allow him entry as far as the front veranda to visit their children.

My sister and I didn't learn that Mum and Nellie had a brother until we were teenagers. One day when Dad and Mum were getting ready to go out, I asked where they were going. Dad told me in a hushed tone that Mum had a brother called Leslie in Eventide Nursing Home, and that he was shell-shocked in his military service during the Second World War. One time I went to visit him by myself and introduced myself as Betty's son. He just turned around and walked away.

Aunty Dora told me that Betty told her that Mum and Leslie were arguing one day because Mum had taken over his bed on the front veranda, while he was away doing his basic military training. Their father appeared suddenly at the front gate and a fight broke out between them. Jacob threw Leslie over the veranda railing, and Leslie hit his head on the concrete below. He was never the same. Apparently, Mum always returned home upset after visiting Leslie at Eventide, as he relived their argument on the veranda over and over again. His memory was stuck at that event. Thus, I learned of our family secrets!

Mum and Dad were staunch Zionists. Dad regularly went around to other Jewish families collecting contributions for the Jewish National Fund from the Blue Boxes that were in every Jewish home. The JNF used these funds to create Jewish settlements in Israel and projects for "turning the desert green". Mum proudly showed me a group photo showing Nana in one of the first WIZO events that were held at the

Margaret Street synagogue in the 1920s. Aunty Dora pointed out in that photo that while Nana was standing at one end of the group, the man standing at the opposite end of the group was my grandfather.

Dora said that Eva and Jacob had opposing ideas on Zionism but everyone in the Jewish community attended WIZO functions. Just as I attended Bei'tar because it was the only Jewish youth group available in Brisbane, WIZO was the only Jewish women's group in Brisbane.

Dora said that Nana was a *Bundist*, a Jewish socialist who was opposed to Political Zionism and its focus on the creation of a Jewish state. She held the more traditional "love of Zion" position of the earlier Jewish settlers in Palestine before the concept was revised into a political ideology. Aunty Dora told me that Mum wanted to go out with boys from the Bei'tar youth group when she was a teenager, but Nana forbade her going out with any "revisionist"[18] like Mum's father!

My parents sent me to a state school for both primary and secondary education, and my best friends today are from my high school days. I hardly ever meet the best friends I had as a child, all of whom were Jewish and most of whom were in the synagogue choir.

When I was seventeen and in my final year of high school, my parents were beginning to despair of the views I was expressing on Zionism and on the Jewish community and its leadership. I claimed that the Jewish community was complicit in crimes that, while not of the same magnitude as the Nazi crimes against the Jews, were nonetheless of a quality that felt to me disturbingly similar. These crimes resulted in the apparently permanent displacement of most of the non-Jewish population of the Holy Land, and the persecution and denial of basic rights of those who remained.

My parents blamed what appeared to them to be my radical opinions, on the influence of my non-Jewish friends. They asked me not to see my non-Jewish friends any more but just to keep my friends within the Jewish community. I was astounded that they would demand such a thing in my last year of high school and flatly refused. I said that if they wanted me to be sheltered from the world beyond the Jewish ghetto, they should not have sent me to public schools[19] where I would be fraternising with non-Jews. Now that I had been exposed to a culture

---

[18] Revisionist Zionist ideology was developed originally by Ze'ev Jabotinsky. It was centred on the idea of creating a Jewish state in Palestine. (AA)

[19] In Australia a public school is a government-run school. Jewish schools are private. (AA)

beyond that of the Jewish ghetto, it was impossible to scrub the essentials of European enlightenment out of my character.

To some extent it is true that the influence of my non-Jewish friends helped to wean me away from what I had already considered at the age of seventeen to be an obsession with Jewishness. But these guys were not "radicals", and I did not learn what my parents regarded as "radicalism" from them. What I did learn from them was nevertheless important to the development of my character. I was a very opinionated person but my best friend had the habit of countering my generalised opinions with the question: "How do you know that?" In truth I had to admit, "I didn't know, I just heard it or read it somewhere." Only rarely could I defend my arguments with properly researched and properly presented facts.

One of my friends asked me how come they could not attend any parties or events of the Jewish community youth, when I was able to go to any of the youth events at the church he attended. How come the possibility of a Jewish girl falling in love and marrying him was a threat to the existence of the entire Jewish community, but if a Jewish male were to marry his sister it would be no problem for his parents, provided there was no pressure on her to change her religion? I realised then that Judaism was more about tribalism than a universal religion.

I was no longer following the rituals of Judaism and had become more interested in the philosophies of yoga, Vedanta and Hinduism. I had to ask myself in what way I was Jewish and came to the conclusion that it was more of an obsessive clinging to my tribal identity than anything to do with my essential identity as a human being.

I came to agree with Albert Einstein, who in his 1954 letter to philosopher Eric Gutkind said:

> "For me the Jewish religion, like all others, is an incarnation of the most childish superstitions. And the Jewish people to whom I gladly belong and with whose mentality I have a deep affinity have no different quality for me than all other people. As far as my experience goes, they are no better than other human groups, although they are protected from the worst cancers by a lack of power. Otherwise I cannot see anything 'chosen' about them."

But Israeli Zionists are not "protected from the worst cancers by a lack of power"! When I read on the internet today about people awakening to the appalling facts on the ground caused by continuing Zionist colonisation of Israel-Palestine, I am reminded of a critical awakening I had fifty years ago at the age of twelve. Only a year after my grandmother had passed away, I attended a Bei'tar youth camp in Sydney during the school holiday, and I noticed gross inconsistencies in the Bei'tar literature and songs. The analysis of supposed historical facts varied in its detail to such an extent from booklet to booklet, that I began to understand that it was biased propaganda. I complained that they were teaching us an obviously skewed history to justify an enormous war crime, the exclusion of Palestinians from their homeland since 1948. They were justifying a Jewish exclusivity that seemed little different from antisemitism but with the victim and oppressor reversed!

I was eighteen years old when the Egyptian naval blockade of the Straits of Tiran dominated the headlines of all the newspapers and was the focus of discussion amongst my friends at synagogue. When the 1967 war broke out I was one of six volunteers who heeded the call of the Zionist Organisation of Queensland to dedicate one year of labour to the Jewish Agency in Israel to bring in farm harvests while soldiers were at the front. I was surprised that none of the six volunteers were dedicated Zionists. My Zionist friends explained they were dedicated to Israel in the long-term. They wanted to finish their university studies first, so as not to be a burden when they finally migrated to Israel.

After arriving in Israel, we were sent to an army camp. I was naturally drawn to a small group of sceptical volunteers who were not pleased to be sent to an army camp instead of the harvesting as we had expected. The "Six Day" war was already over by this time, and we were presented with triumphant stories of the speedy victory, of the conquest of Jerusalem and the Biblical Judea, to which we were taken in army jeeps.

Coming over a rise on the road, we were suddenly confronted with miles of mud hovels of the overcrowded Jericho refugee camp below us. The American volunteer beside me gasped: "This must be a scene from MGM!" But we were to be more shocked a few days later when returning from this tour of the Occupied Territories, because from the same road we had travelled only days earlier the Jericho refugee camp looked to be empty! Where had they all gone? We saw that evening on the TV a mass of people scrambling across the broken Allenby bridge over the Jordan River to Jordan. Why were they fleeing now? Only a day before they had been passively waiting to see what would happen. What had happened to make them flee so suddenly?

We were back at work the next day digging trenches on Mount Scopus, when the small group of sceptics began comparing notes. Some of the group had been filling in trenches we had dug a few days previously and we had filled in trenches that they had dug previously. We were wasting our time here! I protested to the Jewish Agency that we were supposed to be bringing in harvest and insisted I be sent to a kibbutz with an *ulpan*, (a school for Hebrew language), where at least I could spend the year I had committed, to work in a productive way.

I was happy to work and study at Kibbutz Sarid in the Jezreel Valley. Across the road from the bus stop, the ruins of the Palestinian village that had been there until 1948 were still visible, covered with prickly pear bushes. Hitching a ride back from nearby Afula, I was given a ride by an Arab driving a donkey cart. Despite our lack of a common language, he was smiling and friendly. Surely there was no intrinsic enmity between Arabs and Jews—what enmity existed was political ideology and historical events. Surely a future co-existence could also be created by political ideology and historical events.

I went to Jerusalem one weekend with Swedish friends from Kibbutz Sarid and we stayed with a friend of theirs. The Mandelbaum Gate separating Arab East Jerusalem from Jewish West Jerusalem had been pulled down and the streets of West Jerusalem were full of cars with Palestinians going to take a look. We joined a mass of Israelis crossing over to East Jerusalem to take a look. Everyone seemed to be getting along fine. There were no incidents that day with Palestinians and Israelis thronging together at market places and historical sites. The government received a shock at how well Jews were interacting with Arabs. Just a few days later barbed wire went up separating the two populations again.

After I returned from Israel I was asked by the President of the Zionist Organisation of Queensland whether I would be available to speak about my experience in Israel at fund-raising events. He was shocked to hear that my views on Zionism had not changed even after a year of volunteering with the Jewish Agency in Israel. At that time, I still held the view that in the politics of the Middle East, Israel was more sinned against than sinning. But that view was to change during the following year as I read *The Arabs in Israel, 1948-1966* by Sabri Jurays, a 1968 publication by the Beirut Institute for Palestine Studies.

Sabri Jurays' book had a profound effect on me. It introduced me to well-documented evidence about the ethnic cleansing of Palestine, explaining how the Absentee Property Law was used to take land from Palestinian ownership and turn it over to the Jewish National Fund for resettlement by Jews. It gave me the Palestinian perspective for the first time.

The years following my return from Israel did not turn out at all as I expected. My university studies were interrupted by debilitating Pulmonary Sarcoidosis, and my mental balance was rocked by the shock of physical frailty. Finally, I recognised that hoping for healing of the body notwithstanding, my priority was to heal my emotional turmoil. I came to understand that peace of mind was what I needed. From then on, I began to focus my mind on regaining peace of mind whenever I became aware of severe mental disequilibrium or physical lassitude. As one of my yoga tapes has it: "Calm the breath to balance the mind, balance the mind to heal the body." I have since come to realise that healing the world must also begin with such a process.

It wasn't until many years later that I completed my university degree, majoring in Japanese and German Studies. During my studies I spent two years in Germany between 1974 and 1976 and two years in Japan between 1988 and 1989. I think the experience of living in Japan had a strong influence in shaping the inner identity I have today. My Jewishness is a matter of cultural inheritance and it is secondary to the effects of the many other influences that have shaped my personality.

Certainly, my antipathy to injustice is now much stronger than any tribal loyalty inherited from my ethnic background. This is remarkable when one considers that a foreigner in Japan always remains a foreigner, regardless of how well he functions within Japanese society. Returning from Japan to Australia gave me a much stronger Australian identity than I had prior to living in Japan, and Jewishness became a less dominant part of my identity, which by now was more universal in outlook.

When it came to the issue of the Israel-Palestine conflict, I felt there is no greater responsibility for a person of Jewish heritage than to demand that no crimes be committed in my name. Sabri Jurays' book informed me of the involvement of Ariel Sharon in the Qibya massacre in 1953. This knowledge eventually led to my seeking out Palestinian Solidarity groups, when Ariel Sharon became Israel's Prime Minister in 2001. It was because I knew of his involvement in massacres of Palestinians that I felt I had an obligation to start speaking out.

I discovered Margot Salom and Basim Faraj on the internet, where they were organising the Women in Black, "We refuse to be enemies" demonstration outside the Brisbane City Hall. These were the first people I met in Brisbane who were organising for Palestinian Solidarity, and Khalil Hamdan also met us through this demonstration. Khalil was a Christian Palestinian who was a Sabeel Ecumenical Liberation Theology member. He had fled Jaffa with his family in 1948 and grew up in a refugee camp near Nablus. It was through Khalil that we got introduced to Hashem Kleibo, president of the Queensland Palestinian Association.

Basim's cousin had co-founded an organisation in Canada called Palestinian and Jewish Unity and so Basim, Margot and I established a Queensland Palestinian and Jewish Unity group which counted Hashem Kleibo and Khalil Hamdan among its first members. We subsequently joined with the Fair Go for Palestine group to form the Queensland Palestinian Solidarity Campaign.

As president of the Queensland Palestinian Solidarity Campaign (QPSC) I took part in street demonstrations on the anniversaries of significant events in Palestinian and Israeli history, participated in forums and lectures on the Middle East conflict, and to this day I am the moderator of the QPSC Yahoo group that keeps supporters of Palestinian human rights in touch with Palestinian solidarity events and news articles that provide an understanding of the conflict.

QPSC sponsored events when the Ambassador of Palestine visited Queensland and facilitated meetings with local politicians for the Ambassador and other prominent speakers on the conflict. QPSC also joined together with Palestinian Solidarity groups around the country to forge a national voice moderated by Australians for Palestine.

The Gaza War during the winter of 2008–2009, brought a new generation into leadership of Palestinian Solidarity activism. In addition to demonstrations and forums, the Justice for Palestine group coordinates local actions related to the Boycotts, Divestment and Sanctions (BDS) campaign. This campaign will continue to target sponsors and supporters of the Israeli occupation until Israel begins to comply with international law and Palestinian rights.

These days, the main focus of my activism is as moderator of the QPSC. I have retired lately from activist leadership to focus on my work as a security guard at university campuses in order to save sufficient funds for my retirement from work, which is just a few years away.

I am pleased to see that today there is a stronger Palestinian Solidarity movement not only in Brisbane but around the world.

I remain a staunch anti-Zionist. I believe that because Zionism is responsible for terrorising and oppressing the Palestinians, it has significantly undermined the Jewish moral tradition. This tradition, which was enhanced by the European enlightenment, was substituted with a tribal code based on loyalty and revenge.

My favourite motto is the one professed both by Jesus and by Rabbi Hillel: "*Ve'ahavta le'rayacha kamocha*" (Hebrew for "Love your neighbour as yourself"). This is the basis of *tikkun olam* (repairing the world) in Judaism, and compassion for others is the universal basis of all religions and of humanism.

May Palestinians and Israeli Jews learn to share the Holy Land in peace.

"Never doubt that a small group of thoughtful, committed citizens can change the world. Indeed, it is the only thing that ever has" — Margaret Mead

Once You See You Cannot Unsee

Nicole Erlich

"The trouble is that once you see it, you can't unsee it. And once you've seen it, keeping quiet, saying nothing, becomes as political an act as speaking out. There's no innocence. Either way, you're accountable."
— *Arundhati Roy*

I was born as a first generation Australian in Melbourne in the mid-70s. As was the case with the vast majority of Jews of my generation growing up in Melbourne, our families had fled from Europe after World War II. They were hoping to be safe in a country that was as far away as possible from the atrocities they had experienced.

My father's family moved to Melbourne in the early 1950s from Poland. My paternal grandparents had spent time in concentration camps there and lost many of their family members.

My maternal grandparents managed to escape their native Czechoslovakia in 1938 on an immigrant ship to Palestine. My uncle, their first child, was born during that sea voyage. Upon their arrival in Palestine, British soldiers ordered their boat to turn around. As the story goes, my grandmother, screaming baby in arms, approached the soldiers and told them that she would rather die than be forced to go back. They were permitted to stay.

A little more than ten years later, my maternal grandparents decided to leave Israel and follow my grandmother's remaining siblings to

Melbourne. Their brood now expanded to four, and my mother was a little less than a year old.

Despite growing up in a non-observant household my two younger brothers and I were sent to a Zionist Modern Orthodox Jewish school, which was focussed on instilling a love of Israel and the Torah.

During the fifteen years I spent at that school, I was steeped in the pioneering myths surrounding Israel's birth. Not once did I hear the words "Palestinian" or "Occupation". The importance of Israel to the survival of the Jews, and the constant threat of their "innately antisemitic" Arab neighbours were stalwart themes. Given that the vast majority of students had family members who had suffered or died in the Holocaust, these themes resonated deeply and powerfully.

As far as I can recall, I never had strong feelings of religiosity, nor any desire to move to Israel. This is despite the fact that my school and wider community focussed on the virtues of religion and on encouragement to view Israel as our true homeland (including being taught to sing songs like "Blue and white, these are my colours").

I was taught that it was imperative that Jews stayed together and kept at a distance from non-Jews and had little quality contact with non-Jewish people during my school years. Despite that, I became increasingly frustrated with the underlying assumption that no matter how empathetic and well-intentioned, there was always the potential for dormant antisemitism to be stirred up within each non-Jew at the slightest provocation.

One peculiar corollary of this view was that being around too many non-Jews was in itself seen as being "anti-Jewish". I remember when I was applying for university, I selected an out-of-the-way university campus that had a particular combination of courses that was unavailable elsewhere. A family member then remarked that I wanted to go there instead of a more local campus "only because I didn't want to be around Jews".

At university I started making non-Jewish friends for the first time, solidifying my belief that I could, despite warnings to the contrary, have close friendships with people who did not share my ethnicity or background. These social realisations were cemented by my introduction to popular science, and particularly human evolution.

I found learning about "Mitochondrial Eve"—the "mother" of all humans from whom we can all be traced back 200,000 years to East

Africa—a much more satisfying and inspiring explanation of our origins than the myths surrounding her Biblical counterpart. Understanding the evolutionary history and interconnectedness of humanity (and all other biological organisms), made any focus on substantial ethnic and race differences seem extremely outdated and trivial. It also made the idea of an omnipotent being—particularly one that favoured any subgroup of people—entirely redundant.

At the same time that my worldview evolved along scientific and atheistic lines, both my younger brothers became increasingly religious. Books such as *Not by Chance* and *Permission to Believe* started appearing in my room, presumably in an attempt to curtail my "misguided beliefs". Their shift pushed me to form a coherent worldview faster. It no doubt made my parents wonder where they'd gone wrong with us all. Nevertheless, they were more accepting of my brothers' comparatively extreme views as my brothers were, after all, staying within the fold.

Over the next few years I continued to assimilate more into the wider community, moving first to study overseas and then to settle in Brisbane. Although it is difficult to remember the exact nature of the fleeting thoughts I did have about Israel, I believe I continued to reject Israel as being the Jewish homeland because of the Biblical nature of the mandate. But I had no reason to reject the notion that it functioned as a moral, egalitarian, largely secular democracy. This latter perception was constantly reinforced to me by the mainstream media. Everything I read in my local newspaper coincided with the narrative I had learned at school. It never crossed my mind that a mainstream Australian publication—with no conceivable reason to pander to a bias of an ethnic minority—would portray Israel in this light unless it were true.

The first stirrings of awareness occurred in early 2006, when I attended my brother's Orthodox wedding in Jerusalem. Although attempting to act graciously in what was a very foreign environment, I was unable to hold back when I started hearing what felt like an endless stream of anti-Arab comments from various people around me.

I was informed that the people who served us at restaurants and cleaned our rooms were nice on the surface but could turn into heartless murderers at any moment. Naïvely, until the people around me made these comments, I couldn't even tell that the targets of their derision were Arabs, rather than Mizrachi Jews (Jews of Middle Eastern descent).

I remember briefly wondering why it appeared that Arabs ("Palestinian" being a word with which I was still unfamiliar) did appear to have so many of the menial jobs. It wasn't as if they were new immigrants who needed to first learn the language and settle in before finding their feet.

Although this experience still didn't open my eyes to either the Occupation or the extent of the travesties committed against the Palestinians on either side of the Green Line, it paved the way for my awakening later that year.

At that time, I attended my other brother's wedding in Melbourne. Whilst there, I wandered into a bookshop to get some space. There I picked up the book *The Other Side of Israel* by Susan Nathan. The author, a British-born Jew and initially a passionate Zionist, made the highly unusual decision to move to the Israeli Arab village of Tamra to experience and document the lives of the indigenous population.

Nathan vividly described her experiences with the brutal and systematic discrimination faced daily by the people who lived there, as well as her own psychological transformation. Given my existing ambivalence towards Israel, and already expecting to hear similar criticisms to those of how Western countries treat the more disenfranchised members of their own societies, I was caught completely off guard about how it would affect me.

The book listed every atrocity of which I am now intensely aware, but that back then I could never have imagined. Nathan discussed the systematic discrimination of Palestinians in every sphere of life, including education, health and employment, the constant threat of house demolitions and the complete denial of Palestinian history and culture.

Suddenly, for the first time since my early days at school, being Jewish had again taken centre stage in my identity. I dearly wish it had been for any other reason. Instead, I was finding out that a group of people of whose existence I was barely aware, was undergoing state-sanctioned suffering and displacement to make way for—well, people like me. And for no other reason except that they had the "audacity" to have been born there.

I vacillated between intense feelings of shame and rage. I also had extremely strong feelings of betrayal. I realised that I had spent five days a week for fifteen years in an environment where I had been constantly lied to about a country that was discussed several times a day. I felt particularly manipulated remembering how I was encouraged to contribute to seemingly innocuous activities like donating money to plant trees. Now I realise that the organisation responsible for this used the planting of trees as another way of displacing Palestinians in body and in memory. I was also rather horrified to learn that the intra-school sports house to which I used to belong was named after a "flagship" illegal settlement in the West Bank.

I think two factors contributed to my rapid acceptance and reaction to the situation that Nathan depicted. First was the power of it coming from someone similar to myself (if far more committed), who underwent a dramatic psychological shift from being a very passionate Zionist and strongly attached to the mythology of Israel, to a firm rejection of unapologetic racism and colonialism. Following her transformation and thoughts throughout the book helped facilitate my own. Second, my feelings were all the more consolidated by this recent trip, where the small glimpses I saw of the indigenous population, and the questions these glimpses generated, were amply (if very depressingly) answered. These intense feelings seem all the more striking to me now because I felt them even before I knew much at all about the Occupation!

I spent the next few years undergoing an overwhelming learning process, reading everything I could find, and spending hours each evening scouring through alternative blogs and news sites. I felt like I was learning the history and politics of the region from scratch. I could also barely have a conversation with friends without the topic of conversation turning to the Middle East. I'm sure I alarmed many of them with my sudden obsession and fury over a country that was far away, and of which I had barely spoken until then.

I was pleasantly surprised by the number of friends who were interested and raised the topic themselves, particularly when Israel made international headlines with their attack on Gaza in 2008, and later on the Gaza Aid Flotilla. I also started slowly to get to know other activists—Jewish and non-Jewish—as well as Palestinians living in the diaspora and the Occupied Territories.

Having other people to talk to, and receive emotional support from, greatly accelerated my involvement. I have recently joined a peace activist group (Just Peace, Queensland), and participated in a Health and Human Rights delegation visiting the West Bank and East Jerusalem.

Vying equally with the feelings of shame and anger that I continue to experience, are my feelings of frustration and anxiety over the rifts that have developed with people I care about. It is like being yanked out of the Matrix and being unable to convince those inside that they are not, in fact, experiencing reality. I constantly struggle with trying to find better ways to communicate so that I can get through their dependence on the destructive mythology on which they have been brought up, and their profound fear of change.

As a social scientist I understand the inherent and powerful biases we all have in viewing the world around us. I genuinely do not think we have much conscious control over our reflexive filtering of information that is not in line with our beliefs, and the easy dehumanisation of the "out-group".

I remember experiencing some of the knee-jerk reactions myself, that I so regularly see in other Jews. I remember when even in my mind, the term "anti-Zionism" was entirely and immediately interchangeable with "antisemitism". I also recall, many years ago, after a congenial chat with a colleague at a conference, seeing his name on a petition to boycott Israeli products, and immediately thinking how racist he must be.

These experiences have led me to believe that when many (although certainly not all) Jews cry antisemitism, they are not trying to be disingenuous; they really believe what they say. As humans, we experience emotions first. We reason (or rationalise) later, to bring our thoughts and opinions into line with our gut reactions.

A huge emotional and intellectual chasm needs to be crossed, much more so for Jews who are more integrated in their communities than I am. Being able to internalise the immorality of a country that one has been taught is moral and good strikes very deeply at one's identity.

To my mind, it is analogous to spending years being married to a psychopath, having made a conscious decision to spend your life with them, and then finding out that not only do they have flaws that you may have been unaware of, but that they are committing crimes—

systematically and without remorse—beyond your worst nightmares. Not only do you need to be prepared to believe that you have been constantly lied to, but that you are—by association and ignorance—complicit in their crimes. And all the while, they staunchly maintain that they are the decent person you married, and indeed, sincerely believe that. It is not difficult to see why there is so much resistance to understanding the nature of Israel's crimes, and why convincing friends and family to recognise them is so difficult.

Despite many reasons to feel pessimistic, I do believe that the pace of change has quickened over the past five to ten years, and that justice and equality for the Palestinians is gathering steam. The world has been waking up—in no small part due to the role of alternative media that has been breaking down Israel's hold on the country's narrative, and the inability of the international community to turn a blind eye to Israel's increasingly desperate and audacious attacks.

I am convinced that when change does arrive, there are many reasons to think that the impact on both Israel and Judaism will be in a positive direction. I share the sentiment of Dr. Mustafa Bhargouti, who has stated that, "Israelis will never be free unless Palestinians are also free." It is time for a country that has been defined for almost the entirety of its existence by ethnic cleansing and a brutal occupation to find a new path. And similarly, when Judaism can let go of its profound fear of other humans—particularly of Arabs—and allow itself to move past its obsession with victimhood and exceptionalism, a far healthier and more creative chapter will begin. These are my hopes for a more united, tolerant and ultimately peaceful Middle East.

I am Now Again the Zionist I Once Was (But the Zionist Caravan Has Moved On)

David Langsam

Sitting in a black Mercedes in the driveway of PLO's [20] military commander Abu Jihad in Amman, Jordan, with another Merc blocking any exit and a clock ticking somewhere in, or under the car, I took the precaution of shoving my Sony tape-recorder between my legs and wondered how I got here, from thirteen years at Mt Scopus College and ten years at Habonim [21].

Three Mossad agents were killed in Larnaca the previous weekend. On my first trip to the Middle East in 1985, wanting to interview Arafat and settling for his military commander Khalil al-Wazir (also known as Abu Jihad), my PLO contacts told me that they were expecting an Israeli reprisal "at any moment". Great.

Escorted in by the guys with big lumps in their left armpits, I found Abu Jihad straight and business-like, rather than hospitable. When I asked (naïvely) how he would fare in a single state Knesset with Yasser Arafat, Yitzhak Rabin and Shimon Peres, he looked at me as if I was

---

[20] The Palestinian Liberation Organisation (PLO) was founded in May 1964. The PLO's current leader is Mahmoud Abbas and its headquarters are in Ramallah. The PLO is a multi-party confederation and its largest faction is Fatah. (AA)

[21] Habonim is a Jewish-Labour Zionist youth movement founded in 1925. In 1982 it merged with the Dror youth movement to form Habonim-Dror. (AA)

mad. "The Knesset? No. We shall have our own country and our own Parliament."

Speaking on behalf of the PLO, Abu Jihad told the Australian Broadcasting Corporation (ABC) and the BBC World Service in that interview that he would renounce terrorism and recognise Israel in exchange for "any piece of land where we can raise our flag".

I concluded that although he was then the world's most wanted terrorist, the military commander was no different to his Israeli counterpart, Yitzhak Rabin, a political moderate, tasked with the job of destroying the enemy.

On 16 April 1988, Rabin ordered the assassination of Khalil al-Wazir for his role in coordinating the First Intifada, thereby "removing an obstacle to peace", and at the same time ensuring there were "no Palestinians we can talk to".

In my 1985 trip, I conducted an informal survey among Palestinians. I asked, "Who do you support, Fatah's Yasser Arafat or PFLP[22] head Dr George Habash?" I scribbled the answers in a notebook and it was clear that an overwhelming majority supported Arafat and Fatah. The survey has been quoted back at me by Palestinians claiming it proves the PLO represents them, and by the late Rabbi Meir Kahane saying it proves they are all terrorists and should be "put on trucks" and deported.

I guess it was the piercing blue eyes against a clear white background that symbolised my thoughts on Israel and Palestine. The only problem was that Paul Newman had them in *Exodus* and Peter O'Toole in *Lawrence of Arabia*. Somehow the two melded into one for the Mt Scopus College student and Habonimnik.

On the one hand, I knew that Jews needed a safe homeland from persecution come the next Pogrom or Holocaust; and on the other hand, I wanted to ride a 1100cc Brough Superior to my death, having defeated the Turks with the assistance of a ragtag Bedouin army. I was also very partial to *Fiddler on the Roof* and knew there must be at least several other hands to be on.

---

[22] The Popular Front for the Liberation of Palestine (PFLP) was founded in 1967. It opposes the Fatah-led government in the West Bank and the Hamas government in the Gaza Strip due to the lack of new elections to the Palestinian National Authority since 2006. The PFLP takes a harder line on Palestinian national aspirations and supports a one-state solution in Israel-Palestine. (AA)

My parents immigrated to Melbourne, Australia, specifically the centre-of-the-known-universe, the inner suburb of Carlton (think Soho, UK; Greenwich Village, NY) in 1936 and 1937, thereby avoiding the annihilation suffered by the other 90% of my family. Carlton was, for two decades, the hub of the Jewish community.

Dad, Akiwa Majer Langsam, also known as Mark or Kuba, was a communist, a member of Hashomer Hatzayir[23], a politically-aware Warsaw student, denied any opportunity of becoming the lawyer or writer he should have been, by dint of his ethnicity and poverty.

Mum, Rachel Bak, was from a bourgeois Odessa family and had qualified as a dressmaker and teacher. I have a photo of Mum sitting at the knee of her childhood sweetheart Menachem Begin. Luckily for me (but not Benny[24]) Dad stole her away from the Revisionists.

Habonim, with its moderate Socialist policies, was a compromise for the six-year-old, sent off to youth camp a year or two early, so the folks could run their clothing factory. I loved Habo. Setting up the tents, digging ditches and dunnies (latrines) and stealing Bei'tar lamps at night from the neighbouring campsites.

Just about every *Erev Shabbat* (Friday evening) and weekend lunch we entertained scores of family and friends. The long table was always set with a white tablecloth and we would argue politics and social affairs. These arguments were often provoked by my father asking, "And what about the problems of the Jews in Russia?" and concluded with his long story about some poor person "who never had anything to eat or drink and would have died"—Mum runs off to the kitchen to put the kettle on— "if not for a cup of tea". Mum cooked the best King George whiting and the table heaved with the weight of her food, good times and bad.

My parents were followed by the internal spooks—the oxymoron known as the Australian Security and Intelligence Organisation (ASIO)—who concluded that they were not a threat because they argued against Stalin to my grandfather. (It was in fact the other way around.) ASIO seemed to spend nearly all its time performing a variation of train-spotting, listing Communist Party of Australia (CPA) members and associates' car number plates at public gatherings.

---

[23] A Socialist-Zionist Jewish youth movement founded in 1913. (AA)
[24] This is a reference to Benny Begin, Menachem Begin's son. (AA)

My earliest childhood memory is around the age of four, being held in my father's arms at Party secretary Ralph Gibson's home in Oakleigh, a middle-working class suburb, at a CPA meeting. My father's friend described his recent trip to the Soviet Union where tractor production was up 67%, agricultural output was up 45% and a bunch of other similar statistics repeated at every meeting for the next decade.

Around my *bar mitzvah*[25], I did what every good child of a Communist household did and became an anarchist. No god, no master. I remain an anarchist and an atheist and strongly believe all journalists should divest belief and also be anarchists and atheists.

 🙰

I was fifteen in 1968 and anti-Vietnam War sentiment was high. I was politically aware and just one year earlier was delighted to see the graceful delta-winged Dassault Mirage IIICs of the Israeli air force destroy the Egyptian Air Force on the ground. Australia also had the French fighter jets, and by July 1969 I had my student pilot licence. I wanted to fly Spitfires in the Battle of Britain and shoot down a lot of Nazis, but I was born thirty years too late, and my father kindly pointed out that if I did join the Royal Australian Air Force, I could enjoy napalming innocent men, women and children in Vietnam. Damn! End of that career choice...

At Mt Scopus[26] I always got into trouble for writing. In Grade six, I wrote an Elvis Presley-style love poem for the girl sitting in front of me, Josephine Rockman, who didn't know I was deeply in love with her.

But the Primary School headmaster Mr Kenny was looking through the classroom door's window and flew into the room slamming the desktop down on my fingers, hard. "May I ask what lesson you are teaching Mr Rothman?" "Maths." Mr Kenny then proceeded to read aloud my silly little poem, to my mortal embarrassment. With fingers

---

[25] *Bar Mitzvah*, roughly translated to "one who is responsible for his deeds", is a religious coming of age ceremony held in a synagogue or other place of worship (such as the Wailing Wall in Jerusalem), when a Jewish boy reaches the age of thirteen. It represents the completion of a required course of study, and its significance is that from now on the boy is considered a man before God and his community and is now seen as fully accountable for his actions. Before the age of thirteen the boy's father is accountable for his son's actions. A similar ceremony is available for girls and is called *Bat Mitzvah* (*Bat* is the feminine form of *Bar* in Hebrew), but it is a relatively modern development, and does not have the same religious significance as *Bar Mitzvah* does in Orthodox Judaism. (AA)

[26] Mt Scopus is a private Jewish school in Melbourne. (AA)

bruised and throbbing I realised that if you write the honest truth, you put your very life in danger. I didn't write another poem until second form (Grade Eight) and that was a tribute to the IDF (Israeli Defence Force), followed by one in support of the Viet Cong. This was a strange time when Israel was a Socialist country with kibbutzim and a Labour Government and was moving its alignment more closely with the US. I would be appalled in the 1980s to learn that Israel supported the US-backed Contras against the Nicaraguan Sandinista kibbutzniks. How could they do that?

I failed my way out of Mt Scopus, despite my parents' commitment to a Modern Orthodox Jewish education. I also got into more trouble for writing. Told to find another school, my parents enrolled me at Haileybury College next door to the Moorabbin airport, where I was taking flying lessons. While I failed art on my practical work (I passed theory), I have earned honours in everything else ever since. Funny about that. Mt Scopus failed a lot of its students back then.

I was a bit-part player in the anti-Vietnam War movement. As a sixteen-year-old I was pleased to be accepted to the après-demonstration parties of garlic bread and red wine and being treated as an equal by the luminaries of the draft-resistors, some of whom were my *madrichim* and *madrichot* (male and female guides) from Habonim.

I worked weekends in my parents' factory, earning money to pay for flying lessons. At the same time, I was running up Viet Cong flags, which I would give to Jill Jolliffe at Alice's Restaurant Bookshop in Greville Street, Prahran, a groovy San Francisco-like part of Melbourne. I know that ASIO bugged the place because one of two entries I have in my Dad's ASIO file is from the first conversation with Jill. The place was raided all the time.

But Israel and Palestine, that was difficult. At the University of Melbourne, I participated in the 1974 "Zionism is Racism" debate, having lent my watch with a stopwatch function to the moderator (now Professor) Simon Marginson, who didn't have a stopwatch, on the condition that I got to speak. He gave me a slot on the "Jewish" side of the debate against the Australian Union of Students.

I gave a half-baked King Solomon sermon on how we should all live together without cutting up the baby. This earned me the descriptor "renegade" from what I then thought was the Melbourne University Jewish Students Society, but in fact was just the brown suit, Michael

Danby, and the paid apparatchiks of the Australia Israel and Jewish Affairs Council (AIJAC). It all got too difficult, so I dropped talking about Israel and concentrated on South East Asia and Aboriginal issues instead.

As it recovered from the Holocaust, as the immigrants won better jobs and their children became professionals, the Melbourne Jewish Community moved from being politically 60% Labor and 40% Liberal (Conservative) to a conservative domination. Old Jewish socialist values were replaced by looking after "number one" and with it came a new brand of Zionism. It probably mirrored the rise of Likud in Israel. Melbourne Jews were overwhelmingly supportive of the State of Israel, right or wrong. They still are, but I think the support is falling away, not necessarily to opponents of Israel's policies, but to a new generation that just doesn't want to know.

The various pro-Likud lobby groups keep a constant pressure on the community, attacking anyone who dissents from the "Israel right or wrong" line. It is hard to be a public critic of Israel, even if the criticism is intended to make Israel a safer home for Jews, because the attack dogs of AIJAC and the State Zionist Council will be there attacking Jews more than they do anyone else. The British actor Miriam Margolyes has been singled out for their attention, along with Australian critics, especially the Australian Jewish Democratic Society and this writer. They love to hate Professor Noam Chomsky.

൞

In 1985 my niece, Naomi, was living in Jerusalem. She visited me in the country town of Albury, where I was a news and current affairs reporter for the Australian Broadcasting Corporation (ABC). She said that if she could come all the way to Albury, then I could visit her, too. By September, I was on my way and had a letter of support from the de facto PLO ambassador to Australia, Ali Kazak. The letter said something along the lines of, "David is my very good friend, please help him where you can."

When I returned, the AIJAC functionary Danby turned that letter into, "An ABC journalist, one David Langsam, who had his trip to the Middle East paid for by the PLO." Amusingly, in a court document one of the AIJAC directors Rabbi John Levy said Danby was able to make "amazing connections" that no one else had thought of—yeah, that was because he made them up!

But I digress…

I arrived at Ben Gurion airport and my most beloved nephew Jerome was there to greet me in his *tsahal* (the Hebrew acronym for IDF) uniform. We talked and drank and played with guns. I stayed at his sister's place, now in Tel Aviv, and planned my month in Israel, Palestine and Jordan.

Naomi's husband-to-be Arik was from a Likud family and was less than impressed. My sympathy for Palestinians as the equivalent to Australian Aborigines or European Jews was not reciprocated. But he has a wild sense of humour, so it was all a bit ambiguous. His questioning was a surprise. It was the first time I had debated the Israel-Palestine issue with an Israeli Jew, rather than Australian Jews. He was sharp, had a load of arguments and was not happy hosting or harbouring a journalist who could be perceived as a threat to a Likud Israel. It must have put Naomi in an invidious position as she partially agreed with both of us.

So why was a Jewish Australian on this mission to report on the plight of Palestinians, and in particular to conduct this survey that challenged Israel's claim that the PLO was not the Palestinians' representative organisation and hence there was no partner for peace?

There were a number of intertwining strings of thoughts. I had been brought up to value fairness and equality and had already been politically involved in the anti-Vietnam War movement. I had taken a very strong interest in the plight of the Australian Aborigines, and I had a world view that oppression of any people by another was not good and must be resisted. No one should treat anyone the way the Czars and the Nazis treated the Jews. The lesson I learnt from the Holocaust was that racism and oppression were evil. While I remain a strong advocate for the State of Israel as a bolt-hole for Jews from the next Pogrom or Holocaust, I think it is reprehensible that Jews or Israelis, of all people, should ever do to someone else anything remotely like what was done to us. When I see settlers rampage through Palestinian villages or cause trouble at Joseph's Tomb, it reminds me of the Cossack attack on the wedding in *Fiddler on the Roof*, except these Cossacks have *peyes* and *tzitzit*[27].

I headed off to the West Bank, Jericho and Jordan, without a camel, horse or Brough Superior and met Dr Nabil Hirsh in the Bakaa refugee camp on the outskirts of Amman. Confused by his surname I asked, "So what's a nice Jewish boy like you doing in a place like this?" He soon put me in my place. Hirsh is common to Jews and Palestinians, as well as Germans.

I guess what I have always tried to do as a journalist is disprove common currency lies. In 1989 the Israeli lie was that Palestinians children were only shot by the IDF when their parents pushed them forward to throw stones when the cameras were rolling. So, I secreted myself into Palestinian villages to observe without bringing attention to myself—a difficult, but doable job.

Meanwhile, Jerome, my nephew, had been trying to evade doing his annual military service in the Occupied Territories. He said, "Come along with us and with a journalist on board the hot heads hopefully won't do anything bad like shoot children."

Unfortunately, this story had already been done by my mate Danny Ben Tal, a paratrooper officer serving in Gaza. So, for a month I lived in the Palestinian villages where Jerome was on duty between Nablus and Jenin, as well as in Gaza and Jabaliyah refugee camps[28].

In 1988 I produced a forty-five-minute radio documentary on the Intifada Election for the BBC and ABC. It focussed on the divisions within Israel over the response to Arafat's Strasbourg call for dialogue, while the country concerned itself with tax cuts and hospital benefits. It was in this documentary that Meretz Knesset Member Deddi Zucker coined the expression that with a national unity government Israel would be "stucked", with its connotation of the double past tense.

Defence Minister Yitzhak Rabin told me that Israel would never give in, would never talk to "Palestinians from the outside". I questioned him repeatedly about the PLO accepting Israel and renouncing terrorism, and he told me a joke: "What if grandma had wheels? It would be a bus not grandma."[29]

---

[27] *Peyes* are the side curls and *tzitzit* are the visible fringes of the prayer shawl worn by religious Jewish men under their shirts. (AA)

[28] The story of waiting for an Israeli reprisal raid on the village of Kufr Rai is at: http://www.dingonet.com/casting.htm

[29] This expression is the Hebrew equivalent of "When pigs fly". (AA)

When I returned to Melbourne, my mother was using a motorised buggy to get around. I took a photo and sent it to Rabin's political adviser Eitan Haber with the caption, "Grandma has wheels!" He said the boss liked the humour.

It took another five years for Rabin and Arafat to shake hands on the White House Lawn.

ଈଷ

Living in London for a decade and visiting Israel frequently made me realise that I was not alone in my criticism of successive Governments of the State of Israel. While I may oppose some Governments, like the current Netanyahu-Lieberman coalition, or specific policies of a Rabin Government, I believe that constructive opposition is necessary to increase rather than decrease the strength of any democracy, Israel included.

An Israel perpetually at war with its neighbours is not what I call a safe haven for Jews. An Israel at peace with its neighbours building a strong collaborative economy with Palestine and Jordan, and eventually Lebanon, Syria and Egypt would be a great thing. And if it could export its secularism and science, we could even see a decrease in religious extremism.

Returning to Melbourne in 1995, I found the insular Jewish community happy to swallow all sorts of myths. Now the Labor member for Melbourne Ports, Danby was claiming that he had a right to comment on Israel because his electorate was 40% Jewish—a 'factoid' that successive Australian Jewish News editors could not believe was incorrect. Australian Bureau of Statistics data show that Melbourne Ports is 13% Jewish—and many won't ever vote for Danby because he is Labor. One old right-wing friend said he would, "Never vote Labor, not even if *Moishe Rabeinu* (the prophet Moses) was the candidate. Well, maybe if it was *Moishe Rabeinu*."

In Australia in the 1980s, I guessed that I was part of a 5–10% minority of Jews prepared to be publicly critical of Israel. (Today, that percentage may have crept up to 10–15%, but I believe there are far more that have become disengaged, partly because Israel does bad things and partly because of the bully-boy tactics of its Australian support groups, AIJAC, the State Zionist Council and the Anti-Defamation Commission.) In London in the late 1980s, I surveyed the

British Board of Deputies for *The Observer* newspaper and found one third of respondents opposed Rabin's 1987 policy of "break their bones". In Israel, I am not at all radical—I am mainstream Old Labor, maybe Meretz.

> I have not changed, Zionism has.

A Secular Jew From the End of the Earth

Vivienne Porzsolt

My parents got out of Prague the day Hitler marched in, on 15 March 1939. My father told me that when he was in the Czech army, my mother came to him at his barracks after the signing of the Munich agreement in September 1938. Through the iron bars of the barrack gate she told him, "They've sold us out—we're leaving!"

I asked my father once what it was like having to flee for their lives. He replied that it wasn't like that. It was just that there was no future for them in Nazi Europe. They were young, it was an adventure, he said.

My mother suffered intense alienation from what she described as the "cultureless desert" of New Zealand. She often recounted the conversation with the taxi driver on the way to the boat in Southampton that was to bring them to New Zealand. On telling him that they were going to New Zealand, the taxi driver said, "New Zealand? That's the end of the earth!" My mother always quoted these words in tones drenched with bitterness. For my parents, New Zealand of the 1940s and 1950s was a provincial, alien place. Seeing themselves as living in "God's Own Country", regular Kiwis looked askance at these "funny" people with their peculiar dark rye bread, (with salami, for God's sake!) and other "foreign" foods and mannerisms. How excruciatingly embarrassed I was by my mother's forthright manners and, above all, her foreign accent.

My father was much more sanguine than my mother about the migrant condition and described himself as "at home in homelessness". At home, very little was said about the world they had left behind, and

I found this deadly silence a significant burden and deprivation. For example, I did not even know my mother's parents' first names until long after my mother's death. My father explained that they did not discuss their lives before the war out of consideration for my mother's feelings because she had lost so many of her relatives in the Nazi Holocaust. (My father had lost many relatives too, but more of his family survived—the Final Solution did not reach Bratislava, his home town in Slovakia, until much later in 1944.)

My family background on both sides was of the newly emancipated Jewish bourgeoisie in *Mitteleuropa* [30]. My parents had both been Communists in pre-war Czechoslovakia, but they were purged from the Party as "bourgeois Trotskyites" in the late thirties. They were not at all Zionist, believing that socialism was the best hope for the emancipation of the Jews. However, they did keep loose contact with the organised Jewish community in New Zealand. For example, we received the *Jewish Chronicle* in our house.

Like many immigrants, they left their former world behind and focussed on making a new life in an alien land. My pre-school years were spent in the *émigré* world of *Mitteleuropa* Jewish refugees—afternoon parties with black bread, *liptauer* cheese (made with sour milk—yuck!), rich continental cakes and black coffee piled high with whipped cream.

My mother was by far the dominant figure in our household and her rage and depression, an amalgam of alienation, survivor guilt, and displacement, hung over us like a shroud. I found myself unconsciously wearing it and was completely unable to connect with the rough-and-tumble of a Kiwi kids' playground and neighbourhood. I experienced myself much more as a foreigner than as a Jew. The Jewish community in Auckland was so tiny, less than 5000. I was isolated and was picked on mercilessly. My schoolmates saw me as "different". One girl once pointed at me in the playground, taunting, "Vivienne's a Roman Catholic! Vivienne's a Roman Catholic!" I didn't even know what a Roman Catholic was, but obviously it was something undesirable, so I thought I must be one! That is the nearest I got to experiencing antisemitism. Growing up in an insular New Zealand I was far more aware of Protestant-Catholic tensions and "foreigners" than of Jews and antisemitism.

---

[30] A geographical and political German term for Central Europe. (AA)

The semi-bohemian, intellectual milieu of our home was very much what Isaac Deutscher called that of the "non-Jewish Jew": secular, rationalist, internationalist and critical. My emotional, intellectual and social roots are very much in this rich tradition and it still drives my political engagement.

Despite difficulties in adjusting socially, I was successful academically and went at a young age to Auckland University, where I eventually completed an Arts degree in languages. There I met my husband-to-be. I married young and moved with him to a provincial university town living the life of an academic wife caring for my two young children. I had trained as a teacher—my horizons were limited, typical of young women of the late fifties and early sixties—but had no great liking for it.

I remember around the time of the Six Day War (1967), members of the local Jewish community came to our house fund-raising to support Israel "fighting for its life". I had enough feeling of connection with Israel to give them my mother's old furs. But I felt alienated by the militarist triumphalism that succeeded that lightning victory.

I was engaged in Left politics generally for over twenty years before focusing on Israel and justice for the Palestinians. After the collapse of my marriage in the early seventies, I piled headlong into political activity—the anti-Vietnam War campaign, the feminist movement, the union movement, anti-Apartheid—all was grist for my mill. I went on one of the first student tours to the People's Republic of China as it opened up after Nixon's historic rapprochement.

Turning my back on the suffocating life of a 1960s middle-class housewife, I became a freezing worker in the male-dominated meat industry, working for equal rights for women there. I worked at all kinds of labouring jobs, often going for the less traditional ones for women: bus driver, deckie on prawn boats, factory hand and so on. At that time, forging a new single life after the break-up of my marriage, a polite little job was not for me!

Later I completed a First-Class Honours degree in Sociology and worked professionally in adult education, then as a public servant in equal opportunity and policy and planning. Now "retired", I do my political work and wonder how I ever found time for a paid job!

From my Jewish humanist background, I have drawn a deep sense of justice and of the rich potential of all human beings. I feel sadness at the evil and cruelty in the world but draw inspiration from those with the heart and strength to stand against it. Perhaps my need to make the world a kinder, more inclusive place comes also from my sense of being an outsider which was so much my experience growing up in little ol' New Zealand.

I have always been disgusted by the bystander to inhuman acts, even more than by the perpetrator who must be accountable for what he or she does. The bystander can daintily avoid the pools of evil and claim innocence. My mother always spoke out, often to my considerable discomfort. She spoke contemptuously of New Zealanders. "They have no civil courage", she would say, "They don't speak up."

While I draw enlightenment and inspiration from the Marxist tradition, I have never joined a Leninist communist party. I embrace the discipline of solidarity in a union or other general movement, but the intellectual constraints of such a party are not for me.

I had never had much impulse to explore my roots back in Europe. The world my parents had left behind was dead and buried, what was the point? It never seemed real to me. Nor had I taken much interest in Israel or my Jewish identity. What was real was the Jewish *émigré* community in Auckland which was my parents' milieu through the 1940s.

What an isolated, dysfunctional little family ours was! No wonder it left me wrestling with emotional demons. However, at a certain stage in my struggles, I could not ignore the impact of the Nazi Holocaust on me and my family. Also, around this time, I was interviewed by historian Ann Beaglehole for a book on children of Jewish refugees to New Zealand. This too focussed me on my Jewish background. So, I began to connect to my Jewish roots, those of Jewish secular humanism and *Tikkun Olam* (repairing the world)—Isaac Deutscher's "non-Jewish Jew".

I don't want to leave the impression that I experience the migrant condition as just a veil of tears. I find it very enriching to be able to drink at a variety of cultural wells. In this respect, I feel privileged compared with those of a mono-cultural background.

Since neither Zionism nor religious Judaism were for me, I have expressed my Jewish identity by working for a just solution to the Israeli-Palestinian conflict.

With the First Intifada, a group of Jews gathered "for peace in the Middle East" in Wellington, New Zealand. This was very much in the Peace Now paradigm, strongly Zionist and too limited for me. When I came to Sydney in 1991, I worked with other dissident Jews in Women in Black, the Sydney Jewish Left and Shalom Salaam. We established Jews against the Occupation Sydney (JAO) in September 2003, two months before the Jewish establishment set up a furore over the award of the Sydney Peace Prize to Dr Hanan Ashrawi. JAO presented Dr Ashrawi with a bouquet of flowers, which she placed on the stage when she gave her lecture. It was a powerful, poignant counter to the strident mendacity and hatred of the Zionists. The importance of a specifically Jewish voice speaking for Palestinian rights cannot be exaggerated. It challenges the restrictive definitions of "Jewish" and "community" that the official bodies try to impose. They seek to invalidate dissident voices, to place "beyond the pale" all those who oppose Israel's oppression of the Palestinians. Yet how important it is to demonstrate a diversity of Jewish perspectives. This suppression of debate with the implication that if one disagrees with the consensus on Israel you are "not a real Jew" is deeply unhealthy. Who are they to say who is really Jewish or who "belongs" to the Jewish community? What chutzpah!

But the responses from those within the fold can be confronting. I have received abusive phone calls, even a death threat. In Sydney, I have become one of those Jews that some love to hate. In particular, I experienced a specific rebuff from the circle of Jewish central European women, now widows in their eighties, from the days of my childhood. When in Auckland, I would join them at their weekly get together over lunch. I found the connection enriching and so I think did they. Once, when I rang one of them, she said "Oh, Vivienne, there has been a very unpleasant article in the paper about you." I worked out that a picture of me marching with Palestinians must have found its way across the Tasman Sea from Sydney to Auckland. I received a card from them. They said as Jews, they were proud to be Zionists. They could not abide that a Jew could march with those who were bombing Jewish children. I was entitled to my opinions, but they wanted nothing more to do with me. I have met with one or two of them individually since then, but I have never joined that lunch circle again.

I work with Zionist peace groups such as Jewish Voices for Peace and Justice and the Melbourne-based Australian Jewish Democratic

Society. While their positions do not reflect my own, these groups often do valuable work within the organised Jewish community. Despite their efforts to remain within the communal consensus, they too have been vilified in the Jewish press and official Jewish forums. For example, the AJDS came under heavy fire for their adoption of a limited policy to boycott goods from illegal settlements in the West Bank.

I think it is a particular responsibility of progressive Jews to engage with affiliated Jews as well as oppose them. Too many progressive Jews merely sneer at faithful Zionists, perhaps fearing contamination by their concerns. But it is irresponsible to avoid them, since most progressive Jews have come through the Zionist mill, and through a variety of countervailing experiences, have changed their views. If we can change, so can others.

The emotions surrounding Israel are immensely complex for so many Jews. The tragic experience of the Holocaust has been disgracefully misused by the Zionist movement. It has been keeping the wounds open and suppurating, feeding constant fear of ever-threatening antisemitism to provide emotional fuel for their project. There has been no chance to heal, a healing that is necessary for Jews to feel as strong in the world as in fact they are. Instead, they shield themselves with the illusion of an all-powerful Israel, which cannot long survive its current course. This spurious shield carries a great emotional, social, political and moral cost.

I have visited Israel-Palestine a number of times, connecting with peace groups such as Gush Shalom, Breaking the Silence, Machsom Watch and the Coalition of Women for Peace. I was on the 1996 International Vigil for Mordechai Vanunu, the 2003 Women's International Human Rights March through Israel and Palestine and the Gaza Freedom March in Cairo December 2009-January 2010. I have participated in demonstrations against Israeli encroachment on Palestinian land in Bil'in, Sheikh Jarrah and the South Hebron Hills. My most recent focus has been with the Gaza Freedom Flotilla group, organising an Australian contingent for the May 2011 Freedom Flotilla 2.

I mourn the occlusion of the rich progressive humanist Jewish traditions which were so strong among Jews before the Nazi Holocaust. These have been virtually banished by the shrill adherence to Zionism and preoccupation with Israel as the heart of Jewish identity. This preoccupation has drained Jewish culture worldwide of feeling, of humanity, of hope for a better world. It has been replaced by fear, by aggression and harsh ethnocentricity—a shocking and ironic posthumous victory for Hitler.

Yet progressive humanism has not disappeared, and already we see signs of a rebirth of that spirit. Peter Beinert's article in the *New York Review of Books* notes the alienation of younger Jews from Israel as a touchstone of Jewish identity. The recent demonstration by young Jews at the US Jewish General Assembly is a heartening harbinger of better times. The Jewish diaspora has a potentially crucial role in driving a genuine peace based on justice between Israelis and Palestinians—their support has, to date, been tragically vital in maintaining the impunity of the State of Israel from any kind of accountability for its lawlessness. Israel can only bring about its own destruction if it clings to its current path of colonial domination of the Palestinians.

I draw strength from my deep hope and belief in the possibility of a better future for both Palestinians and Israelis, where the past can be acknowledged and, where possible, remedied or compensated for, where reconciliation can occur on the basis of international law, justice and mutual respect and where the two peoples can flourish side by side.

A Troublemaker in Exile

Margot Salom
(1933-2016)

The starting point of my journey into Jewish activism was gradual. I have tried to remember those early vague realisations and steps along the way with little success. Those insights that eventually brought me to where I am now, were not accompanied by bells, whistles and emotional reactions such as denial, anger or even an "Aha" experience.

They were rather slow realisations that the Israel that had originally brought me into reclaiming my Jewish identity, did not in reality exist. There was no singular event that I can honestly say was the turning point when I left my earlier position as an ardent Zionist and a member of WIZO (Women's International Zionist Organisation) to become the committed activist for the rights of the Palestinian people that I am now.

Now in my senior years, I believe that reclaiming my proud Sephardic Jewish identity in my mid-thirties, coupled with an "Israel awareness", was for this very purpose—to eventually become a Jewish activist for the rights of an occupied and humiliated people.

Since my overt "coming out" point in 1991, I have accepted the title of "troublemaker", an epithet given by the mainstream Jewish community to Jews like me who reject the dominant Israeli narrative.

I confess that I much prefer "troublemaker" to "self-hating Jew", the alternative label. I strongly identify with the words of Marc Ellis: "I will always make trouble where trouble should be made to defend human rights." Ellis characterises dissenting Jews like me as "troublemakers in exile". Describing this as a "new diaspora", he adds that travelling this diaspora is a "spiritual vocation".

A 'Troublemaker's' Story: Searching for Jewish Identity and for Justice.

It was September 1991 and the Women in Black stood on the busy intersection at King George, Keren Hayesod, and Agron Streets in Jerusalem where they stood every Friday. As always, the women were dressed in black holding huge cardboard hands with the words, "Stop the Occupation" in Hebrew, Arabic and English. The Women in Black want an end to the occupation of the Palestinian Territories, and a just peace in Israel-Palestine.

Buses and cars slowed down as they passed by. Occasional abusive comments were hurled out of a car or bus window at the women as they stood silent and resolute. Every Friday since December 1987, Women in Black had demonstrated under the slogan "End the Occupation". In this year of 1991 I had joined their protest.

Before leaving Australia on long service leave, knowing I would be going to Israel for the first time, a Jewish colleague suggested that I should watch out for this group of courageous Jewish Israeli women.

The protesting women were not difficult to find on that sunny September morning in 1991. I needed to walk right past them at the intersection at Kikar Zarfat as I returned to my room in nearby Rehavia in West Jerusalem from a downtown shopping expedition. A week earlier I had taken a room in a nice apartment owned by an old lady of very *sabra*[31] credentials. As I stood with the silently protesting women, I idly wondered what my landlady's reaction would be if she knew that her lodger was standing in solidarity with this group of peace activists. Judging by some of her previous political comments, she would most definitely not have approved. Little did I realise as I stood in solidarity with the Women in Black for a cause I was only vaguely aware of back then, that the course was being laid for the years following my early retirement, two years later.

---

[31] A somewhat outdated Hebrew slang word for a Jewish person born in Israel. *Sabra* is the Hebrew word for the prickly pear, which was common in Palestine. Used to describe a person, it indicates how Israeli-born Jews thought of themselves: prickly on the outside but sweet and soft on the inside. To call someone a *Sabra* was a compliment because to be an Israeli-born Jew held a higher status than that of an Israeli Jew born elsewhere. (AA)

My colleague and I had frequently shared our concerns for the situation in Israel-Palestine during my supervisory sessions with her. This was at the time of a gradual growing awareness for me and it was good to find some Jewish support for my unease. I wish I could remember what we discussed in more detail. But I don't have a clear memory of those early revelations as I slowly started to accept that my former "Leon Uris"[32] attachment to Israel had been based on a myth that in turn had been based on a lie.

This was a time shortly before a review of the accepted Zionist narrative by several Jewish Israeli historians (Tom Segev, Ilan Pappé, Uri Davis, Benny Morris and Simha Flapan—the "New Historians") who told a different version of the 1947–1949 war based on the factual information that had been revealed when the mandatory 30-year embargo on the state's archival records was lifted.

One of the most contradictory revelations was the deliberate lie that the Arab population ran away to neighbouring Arab countries, when they had in fact been driven out, galvanized by fear because of massacres in villages such as Deir Yassin.

It was finding out about the April 1948 massacre at Deir Yassin that had the greatest impact on my previous loyalty to the state of Israel. Zionist forces massacred over 100 villagers in Deir Yassin, men, women children and old people. I felt betrayed. This was the point in my story when I started to face the reality that my former attachment to the Uris description of the "brave Jews" faced with overpowering Arab forces and the threat to "drive the Jews into the sea" was fictional.

There was a point in my life's journey when the early struggles of Israel and my Jewish identity intersected. It is difficult to remember exactly how and when these two strong identifying symbols impinged upon my role as young wife and mother. When did it start, the earliest search for my Jewish identity? Was it my Jewish father's death when I was twenty-seven? Had I really not thought of myself as a Jew until then? On reflection, it could be considered a gradual process of personal identity-seeking from a troubled adolescence to a more insightful young

---

[32] Leon Uris was the author of *Exodus*. The book, published in 1958, portrayed a fictional and romanticised Zionist version of the history of the creation of Israel and the 1948 war. In 1960 the book was made into an epic Hollywood film, starring Paul Newman. Both the book and the film had a strong influence on Western perceptions of the state of Israel and its history. (AA)

adulthood, and through my 20's that ultimately led to an interest in my Jewish ancestry.

But I do recall that it was on a flight home to Adelaide from Melbourne where I had met a senior Liberal/Progressive Rabbi, that I started to read *Exodus*. So, my first practical steps towards regaining my Jewish identity, and my introduction to the early story (albeit fictitious) of the State of Israel were virtually simultaneous.

I know now that we Jews had accepted the myth because in that brief time after the Holocaust, we needed to believe in the triumph, security and sanctity of the creation of a Jewish state. This was a time when the ethical traditions of Judaism were still important, and the truth of what was happening to the displaced indigenous Palestinians could not be faced. Had not the Jews of Europe just survived a horrendous annihilation? Were we not entitled?

These are the antecedents to my journey—a journey that ironically started out in a quest for recognition of my Jewish identity coupled with an enthusiastic support and pride for the state of Israel. Even now so many years later, I am not sure which came first, but I suspect that it was a mutual awakening experience.

This juxtaposition arises from the fact that since 1948, at the time when Israel was established, identification with Israel had been a fundamental hallmark for diaspora Jews. At that time leading up to 1967 when I entered the picture, the entire Jewish community shared pride in Israel's triumphs and fears for its possible destruction.

To reclaim my Jewish identity meant acceptance of a full and unquestioning support for Israel, which I had embraced. After all, Leon Uris' novel had been the sole source of my "factual" information at that early time!

My story as a Jew has ultimately ended with a questioning and an intense critique of political Zionism with its territorial oppression of another people.

By 1969 I had the breakdown of my marriage to deal with, a family to raise largely on my own, social work qualifications to acquire and ultimately a career to pursue. To some degree Israel's fortunes and misfortunes faded from my radar screen. My personal life took precedence, although I held on to the vague hope that one day I would go to Israel to experience the dream for myself. But gradually, event after troubling event, the brutal realities of the ongoing Occupation had begun seeping into my consciousness. The innocent idealism about Israel of my younger years began to crumble while I was absorbed in moving up the career ladder.

I wish that I could remember one defining experience that prompted the reversal in my thinking about Israel, but it did not happen that way. It was more a slow dawning of questions and answers and ultimately reading and becoming informed. Perhaps the accidental meeting with two Arab students at the Middle East University, whilst I was travelling in Turkey in 1989, served to obliterate the negative stereotype of Arabs that I had been unconsciously holding.

After all, don't stereotypes serve to protect one from fear? The "other" kept safely at a distance behind a label is manageable. What I experienced were two well-mannered and respectful young men who were no different from other polite young men of that age. I think that this rather banal but nonetheless defining experience was to have a greater effect on me than I could have imagined.

I was no longer able to demonise Arabs. I now had friends who were Arabs. Much later I discovered something of a synchronistic event when one of these young men, a Saudi, revealed to my American travelling companion that his father was a Palestinian refugee from Jaffa. Knowing I was Jewish he hesitated to tell me, until much later when trust had grown between us.

Early retirement in 1993 eventually allowed me the time to become more actively involved in protest against the injustices to the Palestinian people. I emphasise "eventually" as between my retirement and 2000, there was a book to be completed, published and launched. During those years of overseas travel, researching and writing the story of my Sephardic ancestors and their journey from *Sepharad* (Hebrew for Spain), the plight of the Palestinian people was on the edge of my mind. The somewhat parallel story of the Spanish Jews who were expelled in 1492, and their travels into the Sephardic diaspora, captured my attention and filled my life. This literary task also served to instil pride in my Jewish heritage. It was a different and more deeply personal pride than the "Israel factor" that it replaced.

The book focussed on the irony of the ultimate assimilation of my ancestral Sephardic line who had survived expulsion and exile, only to face the loss of their faith in the face of a benevolent integration process in their final Australian settlement—a land of "Sure Dwellings". There is little doubt that I was conscious of the irony of the loss of the Salom line to their proud Judaic history when I became the sole professing Jew in my family lineage.

My second trip to Israel in 1993 was a post-retirement journey to undertake further research of the Sephardim at the Mt Scopus campus of the Hebrew University in Jerusalem. It was by that time that the inequalities between Jew and Arab had strongly permeated my consciousness. Unlike my visit in 1991, this time I did not stand with Women in Black, but I very quickly grew aware of the essence of their protest. Now my involvement was closer to the "coalface".

How could I ignore the sarcastic remark from a ticket seller at the Jerusalem Central Bus Station, when together with two tourist friends we attempted to buy a ticket to Jericho on the West Bank? We were interrogated by the reluctant ticket seller as to our reason for going there, with a suggestion that surely there were better places within Israel for us to visit. Clearly, he had an issue with tourists who wanted to go to the Palestinian West Bank. I insisted that we wanted to experience the "oldest continuously inhabited city in the world" and demanded that he sell us the tickets. He did so resentfully and with much grumbling in Hebrew.

Undaunted by this experience, I resolved to speak with several residents in Jericho. I wanted to hear their reactions to the recent Oslo Agreement, and the highly publicised event on the steps of the White House when Yitzhak Rabin, Israel's Prime Minister, tentatively shook hands with Yasser Arafat. My tourist friends and I had avidly watched the event on the television in our hotel room just three days before. Like so many others I had hoped that this moment in history would be a defining point toward change and ultimate peace.

I was curious as to the reactions of Palestinians in Jericho. Previously, in Jerusalem, I was struck by the positive and hope-filled responses, youths joyously running through the Old City in Jerusalem with the formerly proscribed green, red and black Palestinian flag. The almost universal answer to my questioning had been, "We hope, we hope." These words of tentative optimism were repeated in Jericho. By contrast, reactions from many Jewish Israelis with whom I had spoken, tended to be rather negative and cynical. Despite the signing of a momentous and hopeful agreement toward peace, I found the mood in Jewish West Jerusalem to be largely sceptical.

I continued to receive warnings from my former landlady and others. I was not to travel in Arab taxis, identified by their blue license plates (a sort of identifying Israeli version of the notorious mid-twentieth century European Yellow Star, I thought), or to deal with Arab currency changers. Once again in a spirit of defiance and sympathy for the Arab Israelis, I ignored these cautions on that day trip to Jericho and we uneventfully travelled back from Jericho to Jerusalem in a shared taxi full of Arab Israelis and with the "dreaded" blue Arab license plates! We experienced only courtesy, and when one passenger heedlessly lighted a cigarette, the driver ordered him to extinguish it. Although I do not understand Arabic, I felt strongly that this was because of our presence and for our comfort.

There was no Separation Wall in 1993 as there is now. However, in many ways a type of wall did exist between the life of Israeli Jews and the life that Palestinians in the West Bank lived. There were no checkpoints then to hinder me going into Jericho on that day, but the attitude of a hostile ticket seller created a symbolic division between the two different realities, geographically close, but so very separate.

If I had not made a decision to go to Jericho and challenge the warnings regarding Palestinians and the West Bank, I would have lived my separate time as a visitor in Israel as so many others do, without any knowledge or insight into the other reality. I can see how tourists to Israel are able to enjoy the wonders of the Holy Land and its historic sites, and never have any contact with the dispossession of those who live so near, but so far away.

The finale of this story of personal revelations must surely be the drawing together of all of those slowly gathered fragments of knowing— the growing awareness that my early idealisation of Israel was largely based upon myths. It gradually dawned on me that the Jewish state, in its effort to maintain that racialist identity and to retain the Palestinian land taken in 1967, was unjustly dispossessing and dominating the indigenous people of that land. I left Israel with some understanding of the tension under which the entire population lives.

Both Jew and Arab are oppressed in different ways. Palestinians both in Israel and in the Occupied Territories are oppressed in overt and brutal ways, arising largely from a Jewish fear-filled agenda manipulated by geopolitics. On the other hand, Jewish Israelis are dominated and controlled by their memories and stories of past trauma and their inability to forget that past with its deep fears of, "if ever again". Perhaps this is another instance of, as eloquently described by Elkana[33], 'Hitler's tragic and paradoxical victory'.

I left Israel as a Jew with shame and bewilderment at what we Jews are perpetrating on another people.

This 1993 Israel-Palestine experience stayed with me until later when the book research was *fait accompli* and having returned from a long research sojourn in the United States, I took up residence in Brisbane in 1998. It was here in my new home that the book writing was completed and the finished volume was published and launched, first in Brisbane and later in Adelaide where my paternal grandparents had been early Jewish colonial settlers and many of their descendants (and mine) still live. The question then arose as we entered the new millennium, "What could I do to try to re-dress those injustices, now that I had settled in Australia and had the time to make a stand?"

My ten years of activism have been varied, from its starting point in 2001 when, determined to observe the thirty-fourth anniversary of the Occupation in my new home in Brisbane, I organised a very small vigil in King George Square together with a Palestinian man who was similarly motivated. From this inauspicious event many future activities arose. Most important was the creation of the group Palestinian and Jewish Unity for Justice and Peace.

During these last ten years of activism I experience the greatest personal satisfaction when I am invited to speak as a Jew at various rallies and vigils. Most memorable of these was when I spoke at a rally in January 2009 at the time of the brutal Gaza attack. I stood before what I would believe was an 80% Muslim audience and said, "I am a Jew. I and many Jews like me worldwide absolutely condemn this horrific act by Israel." I know with a deep conviction that it was for this vocation I was led to redeem my Jewish self, forty-five years ago.

---

[33] Elkana's article, "The Need to Forget", originally published in *Ha'aretz* in March 1988, is available at:
http://www.einsteinforum.de/fileadmin/einsteinforum/downloads/victims_elkana.pdf.

The Wicked Son: Hemlock and *Cherem*

Peter Slezak

I am a secular, atheist, assimilated, non-Zionist Jew. This is not a contradiction. There are lots of us. However recently I was disowned by two long-standing Jewish friends because of my political views and public activities as a critic of Israel. These public activities have also led to my being removed from the programme of an annual Jewish conference, after having been invited to make a presentation. To be sure, these experiences have not been quite as momentous as Baruch Spinoza's *cherem*, his expulsion from the Amsterdam Jewish community in 1656 for his "evil opinions and acts" and "abominable heresies." Nevertheless, there are interesting commonalities in virtue of universal features of human nature. Or perhaps just Jewish nature. The last straw has been my stand on human rights and international law on behalf of Palestinians.

Both my parents survived the Holocaust. Against the odds, my mother and grandmother survived Auschwitz together and regularly spoke of their experiences—for example, seeing Mengele with his riding crop, deciding which newly arrived Jews would go to the left or to the right straight to the gas chambers.

My parents always talked freely and frequently about their wartime experiences in the concentration camps—the improbable daily events that are the stories of any survivor. The message from my parent's stories wasn't explicit but rather a kind of humane, tolerant wisdom. However, the lesson I learned seems to have been quite different from the one drawn by other Jews. I thought the point was to understand the evils of racism and prejudice. It hadn't occurred to me that "never again" might mean only "never again to Jews."

My parents weren't political at all. And they weren't observant Jews either. As a result, the family environment was characterised by an absence of doctrine or dogma of any sort. The *laissez-faire* upbringing meant that I had no views at all about important matters and, therefore, no prejudices regarding politics or religion. Much later, realising the virtues of this accident of my upbringing, I resort to a rhetorical one-liner that conveys an important asymmetry in public debates with clergy about the existence of God. I suggest that I have an advantage because I don't care how the debate turns out. My religious interlocutor generally does not have the same luxury. Ditto for my political adversaries whose Zionism is not primarily a moral or political stance. Despite an intellectual façade, their position is a matter of emotional tribal allegiance and loyalty.

While there was no doubt about my parents' attitudes to the Germans or their visceral reaction to the German language, there was no sign of the kind of ethnic prejudice that has been widespread—the notorious Goldhagen thesis that Germans are uniquely, congenitally evil. My mother tells of one Wermacht soldier who showed some human kindness to her in Auschwitz and at the first chance when the Russians were near, abandoned his post, discarded his uniform and caught the first tram to Breslau. For very many years a young German woman, Gertie, was our house cleaner and my mother was very fond of her. I learned implicitly that people were not tainted because of their national origins—and, in this case, their quite recent history.

My attitudes were undoubtedly influenced by the fact that my parents had a distaste for the self-important, self-aggrandizing Zionism in their own community—the ostentatious largesse in public donations to Zionist causes such as the JNF[34] (of which my mother's cousin was Federal Director in Australia). For reasons that were not political, my mother avoided the WIZO activism of her circle of friends. Although

---

[34] The JNF, the Jewish National Fund, was founded in 1901 for the purpose of buying and developing land in Ottoman Palestine. The JNF has been raising funds using tin collection boxes called *ha'kufsah hakchulah* "the blue box", which were distributed widely in Israel and among Jewish communities around the world. The JNF has been accused of planting forests to obscure the sites of Palestinian villages that were deliberately destroyed during the ethnic cleansing of Palestine in 1948. (AA)

her closest family are in Israel, the Jewish state was not a political cause or an answer to the Holocaust.

Most of my friends were sent to summer camp when we were kids, and I thought I was missing out on their holiday fun. Their experiences forged life-long bonds that are evident among them today. Of course, these were Zionist youth camps, Be'itar, Habonim etc. I felt left out, but it meant that I missed out on the Zionism that they acquired in their formative years.

By contrast with the undeniable centrality of a secular Jewishness in our lives, one pair of my parents' friends converted to Christianity and didn't reveal their background to their son. Similarly, one of my mother's uncles, Paul, had become a Catholic. These conversions were always frowned upon, but in retrospect they appear to be a perfectly understandable response to events at the time. It was Jack, the brother of this Catholic uncle, who held the Passover *seder*[35] each year. As a result, Paul and his wife would always arrive at the *seder* late, for coffee and cakes with the family when the traditional ceremony had concluded.

My parents were steeped in the Jewish tradition of their origins in Europe, but they had no trace of any commitment to Judaism as an exclusivist ethnic metaphysic that overrides a shared humanity with others. This was not explicit doctrine or ever spoken, but clearly implicit in their attitudes and clearly quite different from the attitudes of others in my group.

My father was a decent human being and a wise, cultivated and learned man with a warm, easy-going tolerance for other people, including the non-Jews who became partners in his law firm. This was

---

[35] The *seder* is the traditional, highly ritualised Passover family or community dinner. It is organised around the *Haggadah shel pessach*, the "Telling of the Passover", which is the *seder*'s order of service. The oldest complete manuscript of the *Haggadah* dates back to the tenth century, but it could have been written earlier. It is a collection of passages from the book of Exodus, prayers, songs, morals and other narrative in Hebrew, that together tell the reason for the celebration of the Passover. The Passover dinner focusses on telling the story to the children in order to make sure that it is passed on and remembered. For this reason, children play a central part in the celebration.

The *seder* is a substitute for the original ritual of sacrifice at the temple in Jerusalem, the centre of Jewish religious life and ritual. A few generations after the destruction of the Second Temple, there was growing anxiety among Jews that their origin story would be forgotten, and that Jews might end up losing their identity. The *seder* ritual was therefore devised as a substitute for the temple celebration, to ensure that the story of the exodus and its meaning for Jewish identity would be preserved. (AA)

an example that I must have absorbed unconsciously. When I started to go out with a non-Jewish girl, I instinctively knew it wouldn't be an issue at home. It came as a surprise many years later when friends of my own generation raised severe objections to their own children "marrying out." My mother, too, was self-educated and widely read in the best English literature which she still reads avidly in her eighties. She always had a tolerant liberal outlook and it was undoubtedly these qualities that led to my own attitudes that placed being human above being Jewish.

Calling for an even-handed human-rights approach to the Israel-Palestine question hardly seems to warrant being called "*kapo*[36]" or "Jew for genocide". Accordingly, the experience of becoming a pariah in my own community prompts the question of how I got into this situation. It goes back to primary school. I felt ashamed for having bread sandwiches during Passover, when all the other Jewish kids had *matzo*[37]. I knew then that I was an outsider. I felt the same sense of not really belonging at the *seder* in my uncle's house each year. I could not read the required passage, the *Mah nishtanah*[38], although it was my duty as the youngest boy. My older cousin, a "mere girl", read the traditional question, "*Ma nishtana ha-laila ha-zeh mi-kol ha-leilos?*" in fluent Hebrew. "Why is this night different from all other nights?" The annual implicit reproach was an early lesson in ethnic community disapproval.

My cousin had a children's picture-book *Haggadah* that had little cardboard tabs protruding from the side of some pages. These tabs moved parts of the illustrations to create an animation effect. One of these tabs slid back and forth to make the Egyptians pursuing the Israelites disappear beneath the waves of the Red Sea. This mass

---

[36] *Kapo* was what the Nazis called a camp prisoner who worked for the Nazi camp administration. *Kapos* received some privileges for their services and were often brutal to the other prisoners. As a result, they were despised and seen as collaborators. To call someone a "*kapo*" is the same as calling them a "despicable Nazi collaborator". (AA)

[37] *Matzo*, (plural form of *matzah*), is the unleavened bread eaten during the Passover festival instead of ordinary bread, in compliance with Passover's dietary laws. According to the Bible the Israelites were in such a hurry to leave Egypt, that their dough didn't have time to rise. Eating *matzo* is also a symbol of humility, eating "poor people's bread" rather than the leavened bread that symbolises excess and pride. It's supposed to be a reminder of the harsh conditions that the Israelites suffered in Egypt. (AA)

[38] The *Mah nishtanah* is a part of the traditional Passover liturgy. It is usually sung by a child during the *seder*. It explains, in the form of questions and answers, how the Eve of Passover is different from all other evenings, giving an opportunity to retell the Passover story. (AA)

murder by a loving God, and the pleasure we were to derive from it, did not bother me at the time. The service has been solemnly intoned and imbibed by Jews throughout their history, but the ongoing situation in the Middle East gives certain passages a chilling relevance to attitudes evident today:

> *"Blessed are You, G-d, our G-d, King of the universe, who has chosen us from among all people, and raised us above all tongues...*
>
> *For not just one alone has risen against us to destroy us, but in every generation, they rise against us to destroy us; and the Holy One, blessed be He, saves us from their hand!*
>
> *...Pour out Your wrath upon the nations that do not acknowledge You... Pursue them with anger, and destroy them from beneath the heavens of the L-rd."*

The remnants of my family at the seder table were mostly survivors of the Nazi concentration camps. For my generation, the Holocaust and the personal stories of our parents' experience were sufficient evidence of our lot as perpetual victims.

Admittedly less important, but equally incomprehensible to me at the time, was the practice in such English texts of hyphenating the words "G-d" and "L-rd". Does the omniscient creator of the universe not know we are referring to him? And why would an omnipotent deity care? My puzzlement concerning such official doctrines was undoubtedly early evidence of delinquency. In this regard, of course, in retrospect, one passage of the Passover liturgy takes on special significance:

> *"The Torah speaks of four children: One is wise, one is wicked, one is simple and one does not know how to ask. The wicked one, what does he say? "What is this service to you?" He says "to you", but not "to him!" By thus excluding himself from the community he has denied that which is fundamental.*
>
> *And therefore, be honest with him and tell him: "This is because of what the L-rd has done for me, when he took me out of Egypt." Emphasise you and not him, because even if he had been there, he would not have been worthy to be redeemed."*

I would not have been redeemed. Recently, a Jewish acquaintance came across to my tennis court from the adjacent one where he had been playing, in order to abuse me loudly. Among his insults, the worst thing he felt he could say was, "I hope you realise that the whole Jewish community hates your guts." Instinctively, he knew that this was the worst fate of all, to be loathed by one's community.

This minor episode in the overall scheme of things sheds light on the mechanisms for enforcement of tribal loyalty. This acquaintance had clearly internalised the lesson of the *Haggadah*. I may have been too preoccupied with the fate of the nations upon whom G-d, King of the universe, was to pour out his wrath and indignation, to destroy them from beneath the heavens. Actually, to be honest, I don't remember being disturbed by these passages until recently at the *seder* at an old friend's house, where others noticed my raised eyebrows as we read the words, knowing exactly what I was thinking.

My apoplectic tennis acquaintance couldn't imagine that I might have become immune to his own fear of being loathed by Jews precisely because I am no longer in the ghetto that he lives in, whose walls are psychological rather than physical, but no less real for that.

I still live in Bellevue Hill, but I had long ago left the security of a tight-knit community for a wider, more inclusive one. However, in the Eastern Suburbs of Sydney, the friends of my teenage years still socialise in the circle that comprised the crowd at Central synagogue dances in the 1960s.

My break with them came at a self-conscious moment one Saturday night around 1965. The school friends with whom I partied on Saturday nights kept together when they entered Sydney University in 1964. A long table on the second floor of Manning House was occupied exclusively every lunch time by this circle of Jewish friends. Unusually, one Saturday night, a non-Jewish student in our chemistry class invited us to a party in Jannali, far from the Eastern Suburbs. As I was enjoying the discovery of new, non-Jewish people, I was forcibly struck when I noticed my friends huddled together in one corner talking amongst themselves. I felt disapproval of their discourtesy and in particular, disdain for their complacent insularity. Fifty years later, their dinner parties are attended by the same Manning crowd.

For my part, I met a cute blue-eyed, blonde *shikse*[39] from the chemistry class, a Catholic girl living at Sancta Sophia College, now my wife. My parents didn't sit *shiv'ah*—the traditional mourning ritual—to pronounce me dead, as Jews are required to do on such occasions according to Jewish law. Of course, learned rabbis had warned that by "marrying out" I would be "completing the work of Hitler", but this weighty consideration failed to have the desired moral effect. I didn't go on to murder my parents or their friends with Zyklon-B[40], but clearly, I had strayed from being a good Jew since the *Pesach* episode with bread sandwiches in primary school. And then at university I encountered an even more corrupting influence: not only the *goyim*[41] (Hebrew for non-Jewish people) in Jannali, but the philosopher Bertrand Russell.

It was only much later that I learned that Russell's works were charged with being, "lecherous, libidinous, lustful, venerous, erotomaniacal, aphrodisiac, irreverent, narrow-minded, untruthful, and bereft of moral fibre". Russell was described as, "a recognised propagandist against both religion and morality", a "philosophical anarchist" and "professor of immorality", "the devil's minister to men" who poisoned the minds of the youth. One educator wrote,

> *"Mr. Russell is unmistakably a dangerous person. He is subversive; he is the spirit that denies... Whether the theme of his discourse be religion or patriotism or citizenship or capitalism or matrimony or education or some other phase of our social order is a secondary matter."*

I hadn't yet discovered the small book *Marriage and Morals* that was to elicit this storm of denunciation and that caused him to be prevented from teaching logic at City College in New York.

In that first year of university in 1964, on the shelves of Fisher Library I found Russell's *Religion and Science* in the brown Home University Library edition. Together with Russell's writings on politics and morals this was a heady, liberating mix for a seventeen-year-old. I would write out his aphoristic remarks in a journal. The most exhilarating feature of Russell's writing was its articulation of heretical

---

[39] A Yiddish and Polish word for a non-Jewish woman. It refers in particular to attractive blonde women and can be used in a humorous or derogatory way depending on context. (AA)

[40] A cyanide-based pesticide used by the Nazis for mass extermination of human beings during the Holocaust. (AA)

[41] Hebrew for "nations", the term for non-Jews. *Goyim* is the plural of *goy*. (AA)

thoughts that I had vaguely entertained, but which were expressed so eloquently and persuasively by the most famous philosopher of the twentieth century.

Of course, these were not Russell's technical ideas that I only studied much later, but popular reflection on questions of universal interest written in a style reminiscent of Francis Bacon's essays that I had read at school. However, the greatest impact of Russell's thinking was due to the obviousness of what he wrote, combined with its being, at the same time, contrary to accepted, conventional thinking. It seemed clear to me that he was the only one marching in step. I had the feeling of sharing a terrible secret and joining a special club of independent and, therefore, subversive thinkers, the path towards radicalism, dissent and *cherem*, if not hemlock—the fate of another dissident philosopher charged with "corrupting the youth."

Much later I recognised that Russell had set me on an inevitable path to Chomsky. Long after having become an acolyte in linguistics and politics in graduate school at Columbia University, I would learn that Chomsky has a large photograph of Russell on the wall of his office at MIT—a mark of admiration for Russell's towering intellectual achievements and for his activist engagement in the political and moral issues of his day, beyond the ivory tower.

Of course, Chomsky is the most proximal cause of my excommunication as a "self-hating Jew". When I first had occasion as a university lecturer to write a professional letter to Chomsky, it was entirely formal and stilted, but as a personal post-script I ventured to express my admiration and to say that he was to blame for my having spoiled many dinner parties defending his political views. I was touched by his reply in which he said in his own post-script simply, "I apologise for the dinner parties." Recently, when I had the privilege of visiting Chomsky in his office at MIT with Russell looking down at us from the wall, I reminded him of that first letter thirty years earlier and said that he has a lot more to apologise for now. Russell too.

Russell had explained the roots of deviance and dissidence. He wrote: "A certain percentage of children have the habit of thinking; one of the aims of education is to cure them of this habit." It follows that the well-educated become the most conformist, as Orwell noted when he remarked, "One has to belong to the intelligentsia to believe things like that: no ordinary man could be such a fool." He was talking about nationalism. As a consequence, a proper system of education should protect children from their teachers and to develop what Chomsky has referred to as "intellectual self-defence", namely critical thinking along the lines of the scientific outlook. For this reason, he suggests, if conducted properly, the role of education should be subversive in a healthy society.

It's of some relevance that I was a near-failure throughout my career as a student. Although I'm a more-or-less respectable professor of philosophy today, I had been at the very bottom of my classes in the final years of primary school and performed in the middle range at high school with a mediocre Leaving Certificate pass in 1963. My Jewish friends achieved the highest possible grades with maximum distinguished honours. Their brilliance led them to outstanding professional careers mainly in medicine and law. I enrolled in a science degree with no career ambitions and was finally kicked out after four years for failing the most allowable number of subjects.

I enrolled at the University of New South Wales in an Arts degree taking "useless" humanities subjects such as philosophy and sociology as a way of learning something interesting while I figured out what to do with my life. I didn't learn much, perhaps because I spent a great deal of time smoking dope (by now it was the late 1960s). I recognise that it sounds silly, but this was part of a morally and politically uplifting, transformative experience—not so much the smoking, but the entire syndrome of the counter-culture and anti-Vietnam War protests, of which marijuana was such a symbol.

It may have been an adolescent gesture of defiance, but smoking marijuana and, indeed growing it, was an expression of dissent from pointless, repressive authority and a criminal government. The gesture was based on an important, subversive insight. It was not difficult to discover that the pharmacologically active ingredient THC (Tetrahydrocannabinol) in cannabis is not addictive and less harmful than coffee. The lesson was that authorities lie, conventional doctrines are often false, and official power is used to suppress the truth and punish "deviants".

This was, after all, an important idea I did learn in sociology from the fashionable writings of R.D. Laing among others: Deviant behaviour may reflect a pathology of the society rather than of the individual. The lessons of the Vietnam War and world affairs were the lessons of pot smoking writ large. In his first political essays of the late 1960s Chomsky asked, "Who was really crazy: the kids behaving unconventionally in the streets or those responsible for mass murder in Washington against whom they were demonstrating?" I still have my Penguin copy of Chomsky's 1969 book, *American Power and the New Mandarins*, which has a "Moratorium" sticker pasted on the first page.

I'm pretty sure my Jewish friends who were now beginning their professional careers didn't smoke dope and missed out on these lessons of being a hippy. Besides beards, bandanas and tie-dye shirts, the sixties generation has laid the foundation for the peace movement, civil rights, feminism and environmentalism. I realised how far our paths had diverged since lunch times at Manning House, when one of those Jewish friends recently confessed that he doesn't know anyone who is not a Liberal Party[42] voter.

Among Jewish friends, we joked that none of our fathers had a shed or even a toolbox, the way that "real" Australian men do. The first proper toolkit in my family was a handsome red fold-out metal box filled with essential equipment—a twenty-first birthday present to my younger son from a close Aussie friend, and a fitting symbol of having reached adulthood in Australia. Neither I, nor any Jewish friend, would have thought to give such a wonderful gift. With my Jewish friends, we swapped anecdotes of paternal incompetence in the handyman department of domestic life. Growing up in the 1950s, I recall the oddity of Australian neighbours near our mainly Jewish-occupied flats, who wore overalls and tuned their car engines on Sunday mornings. So not Jewish. When we finally owned a car much later, my father barely knew how to open the bonnet. And, of course, he had never set foot inside a pub.

As a Jewish boy from Bellevue Hill, I never knew a typical Australian working-class guy. However, my intellectual and moral journey from Bertrand Russell to Chomsky was decisively abetted by one of my sociology lecturers with whom I felt privileged to become friends, and who had a deep and lasting influence on me. My lecturer had the "Marlboro Man" rugged good looks and was the stereotypical Aussie bloke, perhaps the first one with whom I went to have a beer in the pub.

---

[42] The Liberal party in Australia is not liberal. It is the equivalent of the Conservatives in Britain or the Republicans in the US. (AA)

I never quite got the hang of it. Years later, my father-in-law diplomatically stopped inviting me to join him at the RSL club where I clearly didn't quite belong. I drank my schooner of beer too slowly while, according to the custom I hadn't known, others had to wait for me to finish before drinking the next round.

Besides knowing about handy things like tools, materials and building an entire mud brick house, Bill was the antithesis of the stereotypical bookish Yid, but also paradoxically, the antithesis of the stereotypical Australian male. He embodied intellectual, moral, aesthetic and emotional qualities that made him deeper and more sensitive than the average Australian male, or for that matter, the Jews I had grown up with. Bill was a kind of bushie Bertrand Russell. Unlike those in my Jewish circle and unlike the stereotypical Aussie bloke, Bill had an acute social conscience that I had not encountered before except in Russell's writings—a sense of outrage at the world's injustices large and small.

The universal, ineradicable conviction among Jews is that, deep down, everyone is an antisemite. It is universally held that, in the heat of an argument, the dark truth will emerge in some insult that reveals that your closest friend, or even your wife, perhaps unconsciously, harbours antisemitic feelings. After a weekend away with Bill and a couple of other guys in a tin shed on a remote beach near Wollongong, I confessed, to their surprise, that even though I am more assimilated than most Jews, I am always aware of being a Jew among gentiles. Their indifference to these questions and my hang ups was a salutary experience that removed a barrier that other Jews cannot overcome. I felt a mixture of "anthropological strangeness" together with the pleasure of belonging in an alien culture. These are feelings that I have had in a more pronounced form recently among Muslims at a banquet to which I had been invited, celebrating the end of Ramadan. The persistent thought during that evening was, "I wish my Jewish friends could experience this." Apart from the absence of alcohol and the separation of men from women, who were dressed in beautiful scarves and full-length skirts, it wasn't too different from a Bar-Mitzvah party.

On this topic of Jewish identity, I began a recent essay by citing one critic who protests at Russell's disavowal of his own religious tradition in his famous essay, *Why I am not a Christian*. Russell explains that he cannot rationally accept the central dogmas concerning God and immortality. However, the critic complains of Russell's attempt to "define himself out of Christianity" on "narrow grounds" that are purely intellectual and rational and, therefore, not based on thinking culturally. The complaint is revealing about the topic of belonging and tells more about the author than about Russell. The critic points out that Russell was:

> "... after all, the product of Christian society, Christian history, Christian morality, Christian literature, and Jesus Friggin' Christ!—even Christian language. His national anthem was "God save the King". He matriculated at Trinity College. Bertrand Russell wasn't a Muslim, a Jew or a Hindu. He wasn't a Trobriand Islander or a Khoe bushman... he was inescapably in a global sense a Christian, albeit one with some doctrinal issues."

In my essay, I noted that this is the sense in which I'm a Jew—albeit with some doctrinal issues. The models of Jewish identity I cited: Spinoza, Freud, Einstein, Arendt and Chomsky, are Jewish in one characteristic sense. They are what Isaac Deutscher called "Non-Jewish Jews", like himself, in that they seek to transcend their narrowly conceived ethnic identity while remaining attached to it. Such Jewish thinkers embrace a wider, universal, Enlightenment outlook—the tradition of secular liberalism and humanism.

We need not be surprised that, where ethnic, patriotic and tribal sentiments are involved, even exemplary intellectuals may lapse. For example, we can perhaps understand Albert Camus' admission when asked about his failure to protest against French actions in Algeria: "I believe in justice, but I will defend my mother before justice." Of course, the French colonial enterprise in Algeria was not his mother.

In a famous reproach, Hanna Arendt was said to lack love for her own Jewish people, *ahavat Israel*, as a consequence of her universal stance on questions of justice. Her reply is apt also in response to Camus' personification of France. Arendt said, "Love is not a collective matter: I indeed love 'only' my friends and the only kind of love I know of and believe in is the love of persons." The demand on Jews to show the patriotic state worship of *ahavat Israel* has had a long tradition of critique. In Plato's *Republic*, Socrates admonishes his interlocutor Callicles: "We are both lovers... Besides the person I love, I am also in love with philosophy, while besides your lover, you are also in love with the state of Athens."

Arthur Koestler explained this kind of love in his famous account of abandoning a secular religion—Communism. Koestler writes: "A faith is not acquired by reasoning. One does not fall in love with a woman, or enter the womb of a church, as a result of logical persuasion."

Edward Said has indicated the challenge posed by loyalty since "no one... is above the organic ties that bind the individual to family, community, and of course nationality." However, he said:

> "...loyalty to the group's fight for survival cannot draw in the intellectual so far as to narcotize the critical sense, or reduce its imperatives, which are always to go beyond survival to questions of political liberation, to critiques of the leadership...the intellectual's loyalty must not be restricted only to joining the collective march."

The preponderance of a particular belief in a particular locality suggests that religious and political commitment are akin to allegiance to football teams—their determinants not being reason based on evidence. In my talk to the Limmud-Oz Conference 2009, I asked the audience: "Are you proud of being Jewish? What have you done to deserve the credit for Einstein or anyone else?" As Hume says of those who hold religious beliefs based on irrational, superstitious principles, "They are never led into that opinion by any process of argument." The question is as much ethical as intellectual or psychological, as W.K. Clifford's essay argues in support of his famous principle: "It is wrong always, and everywhere, and for anyone, to believe anything upon insufficient evidence." This might be enough of a truism to not merit discussion if it were not for its widespread violation and even explicit denial by philosophers such as William James.

Around the age of ten I had suggested to a very Orthodox Jewish friend that he was committed to Judaism only because he had been raised in an Orthodox Jewish family. His answer stumped me at the time. He responded, with some justice, that I was an atheist only because I have been raised in a non-religious home. It was only much later that I recognised the fallacy in this rejoinder. Our circumstances were not symmetrical, because I didn't go to atheist Sunday School or learn to recite Bertrand Russell by heart.

Ditto for my political views. When we were in high school having lunch under a tree in the schoolyard, apropos of nothing, the same Jewish friend asked me whether I was a Zionist. I was embarrassed at having no idea what the question meant. I mumbled something to hide my ignorance. Fifty years later, I have figured it out. The answer is, "No." His *bar mitzvah* gift for me was a biography of David Ben Gurion. I still have it on my shelf, next to a biography of Yasser Arafat.

I spent one *seder* evening with his family. My friend tried to show his fortitude by taking a very large spoonful of horseradish into his mouth at once and nearly exploded. His mother had encouraged me to learn more *Yiddishkeit*[43] but, again, I had no idea what this meant. Though it was not the sort of thing she had in mind, one example of *Yiddishkeit* became revealing only in retrospect. It was only recently upon reading Israel Shahak's book *Jewish History, Jewish Religion* that I was suddenly struck with the meaning of a long-forgotten incident. We often walked home from school together past a house on the corner of Ebley Street and Hollywood Avenue that was used as a Baptist Church. The minister was the father of another schoolmate. As we walked home one day, to my surprise, my friend uttered a curse and spat at the church. Shahak writes of the long-standing practice according to which, "it became customary to spit (usually three times) upon seeing a church or a crucifix..." Shahak writes:

> *"These customs cannot be explained away as mere reaction to antisemitism or persecution of Jews; they are gratuitous barbarities directed at each and every human being... Without facing this real social fact, we all become parties to the deception and accomplices to the process of poisoning the present and future generations, with all the consequences of this process."*

My mother confirms that this was a standard practice in her town, just as Shahak notes. He also spells out the evident bearing of such practices on the current problems concerning Israel and Palestine.

Our Baptist schoolmate invited me to a lecture at his church one day after school. My mother had allowed me to attend his church hall, where someone explained the essential tenets of Christianity with colour slides. The only thing I remember clearly of this lecture was a picture depicting someone with a heavy burden, a large bag, on his back, trying

---

[43] Yiddish for a "Jewish way of life". (AA)

to carry it up a steep hill. I think the burden represented his sin that was thrown off in the next slide when he discovered Jesus. My mother's easy-going attitude to my attending the Baptist church brings into sharp relief the attitudes of my Orthodox Jewish friend.

We were the only Jewish family I knew who didn't have a *mezuzah*[44] on the doors of our house. I have a vivid memory of the first time I saw the father of the girl next door with leather straps around his arm and a funny box strapped to his head—the daily ritual of *tefillin*. I was too embarrassed to ask what it meant. To be honest, I still have no idea. The feeling of seeing an alien tribal ritual has stayed with me—an anthropological perspective on the customs of a culture to which I don't belong.

Halper notes that today an "unreflexive, self-celebratory group affiliation" is deep in the heart of Jewish identity, but mainly among diaspora Jews. The charge that Arendt was lacking *ahavat Israel*, love of the Jewish people, arose from her complaint that the Eichmann case was presented as a crime against Jews, and that the prosecution refused to identify Eichmann's crime as a "crime against humanity—committed on the body of the Jewish people". The failure to make this crucial distinction continues to disfigure the remembrance of the Holocaust and the true meaning of "never again", which is taken to mean only "never again to Jews". The influential Jewish community and its leadership were invisible during the twenty-four years of near genocide of the East Timorese next door to Australia, in which our government was deeply implicated. Those who have been preoccupied with the lessons of the Holocaust remained silent when they might have exercised their unique moral authority.

I felt the need to draw on this experience when I was invited by Palestinian friends to address the large protest rally held in Melbourne on Sunday, 18 January 2009 as the Israeli attack on Gaza raged. In my mind, I was speaking as much to other Jews as to the audience of

---

[44] The *mezuzah* is a decorative case containing a parchment with the sacred "Hear oh Israel" prayer and verses from the Torah. On the outside it usually displays the Hebrew acronym for "Keeper of the Doors of Israel", *SHADAI*. The *mezuzah* is placed in the doorways of Jewish homes (sometimes also in the doorways of bedrooms) and it represents protection. It is a reminder of the part in the exodus story about the mark that the Hebrews were required to make on their doorways with the blood of the Passover lamb, during the tenth plague. When the spirit of God was passing through Egypt, killing the eldest sons of the Egyptians, it "passed over" the dwellings that were marked with the blood, thus avoiding killing the eldest sons of the Hebrews. Hence the word *Pessach* in Hebrew, which literally means to "pass over". (AA)

Palestinians and others. Someone asked me how long it took to write the speech and I answered: "About thirty years." Parts of my speech were as follows:

I am one of many Jews—here today, in Israel, and around the world—who are distressed and shamed by what Israel has been doing in our name...

I am proud to join you today to express our anguish at this carnage and our anger, and to express our solidarity with the people of Gaza... So, I am here today because I share a motivation with many Jews here and around the world. My eighty-three-year-old mother is a survivor of the Nazi concentration camp at Auschwitz. I grew up with her questions: Why didn't anyone help the Jews? Why didn't anyone else care? Why did the world allow it to happen?

These are the same questions we must ask today about the crimes against the Palestinians.

So, I'm here because the State of Israel does not represent all Jews. If we have learned the real meaning of the slogan "never again", we can't remain silent when the crimes are being committed in our name. We must universalise the lessons of our own tragedy to include others in our moral universe...The Nazis made Jews wear a yellow Star of David to stigmatise them. I grew up with the immensely moving image of others, non-Jews, like the King of Denmark, who showed their humanity by wearing the yellow star to symbolize their solidarity with the Jewish victims of persecution.

This is the spirit in which I wear a Palestinian badge today and the spirit in which very many Jews and others around the world stand with Palestinians.

It is the spirit captured by an Italian volunteer working in Gaza right now, called Vittorio Arrigoni[45]. I would like to conclude by reading an email from him, sent over a week ago on Friday, 9 January. He wrote:

The Italian Consulate has just contacted me, saying that tomorrow they shall evacuate a fellow Italian, an elderly nun...The consul gently urged me to seize this last opportunity to escape this hell with the nun.

---

[45] Sadly, Vittorio Arrigoni was murdered in Gaza in April 2011 aged only thirty-six. He was an Italian reporter, writer, pacifist and activist. He worked with the pro-Palestinian International Solidarity Movement (ISM) in the Gaza Strip from 2008 until his death. Arrigoni maintained a website, *Guerrilla Radio*, and published a book of his experiences in Gaza during the 2008–2009 Israeli attack. His murder was condemned by a number of Palestinian factions.

I thanked him for the offer, but I'm not moving from here—I just can't. For the sake of the losses we endured, before being Italian, Spanish, British or Australian, right now we are all Palestinians.

Canada

The Courage of My Convictions

Lesley Levy

I have been actively involved in the Palestinian rights, anti-occupation movement for the past nine years. There are times when I wonder why I am spending so much time and energy on this issue when there are so many other desperate causes in the world. At those times, I am reminded of the outrageous human rights abuses perpetrated on the Palestinians by the Jewish people, and I immediately re-experience the strong feelings of outrage and injustice that drew me into this in the first place.

When mainstream Jews insist that Zionism and Judaism are synonymous, I cannot help as a Jew but to feel tarred with the same brush. There is a yearning to cry out, "Not in my name!" I cannot remain informed of what Israel is doing to the Palestinian people and at the same time continue to be a silent bystander.

Ever since I was a teenager I have had confused thoughts and feelings about Israel, but I haven't felt that I had permission to express them. I was made to believe that I didn't know enough facts or history to have a valid opinion. I was also told that as I didn't live in Israel, I had no right to express such thoughts. As the years went by and the Occupation grew worse, I was afraid to share my "naïve" point of view, and I was easily intimidated, silenced and shamed if I dared to express my opinions. I didn't have the courage to trust in my own intuitive sense of right and wrong.

I grew up in the north of England in Hull, a town with a small Jewish community. I went to shul three times a year, and *cheder* (Jewish Sunday school) on Sunday mornings. There were quite a few Jewish social events, but I felt some uneasiness in these environments. They seemed so very separate and different from the rest of my life, in which I went to a Church of England girls' school and played with local kids on the street. Somehow, I felt more comfortable in this reserved, quieter world; the dinner table scene in the movie "Annie Hall" portrayed this dichotomy perfectly!

My grandparents came to England from Latvia around 1900 and my parents grew up in Hull. My mother was more involved in Jewish life than my father. She was active as a volunteer with Hadassah (a Zionist women's organisation) and WIZO (Women's International Zionist Organisation). Sadly, she died when I was ten years old.

My father had turned away from the strict Orthodoxy he was brought up in and became very secular. He was not an ardent Zionist. He wanted to integrate into English society and not stand out as a Jew, especially following the Second World War. We even went on vacation to Germany when I was about six years old as my father was curious to see post-war Germany

In 1966 when I was sixteen, I went with my cousin on a six-week trip to Israel with a group of peers from all over England. It was quite an eye-opening adventure to go rambling all over the country in rickety buses, stay on kibbutzim, learn Israeli folk dancing and see explicit footage of the Holocaust. I was told that the minute my feet touched Israeli soil I would feel this deep connection, and would be amazed that everyone was Jewish, even the bus drivers and garbage collectors! But I never did feel that connection to a homeland. It felt quite foreign, and as much as I enjoyed the vacation, I did not have a desire to go back.

I left home at seventeen to study in London, and then left England at twenty. From the time I left home, I don't think I ever went to shul or had anything much to do with my Judaism for another twenty years. I enjoyed meeting people from all over the world, the more exotic and different from myself, the better.

However, in the 1970s I was drawn into a Jewish world. I had a job in a Jewish hospital in Montreal and I was married to a nice Jewish doctor (a peace activist). Gradually I found myself settling into a Jewish community and belonging to a somewhat progressive shul. When my two children were born, I felt it would be wise to give them the benefit of a Jewish education and let them decide for themselves as they grew up. I was also ready and curious to explore my own identity as a Jew. I learned to read Hebrew, did a *Shabbat* dinner every Friday night, and I was even on the board of the shul and active on many of their committees. As the children grew up and moved away, I realised that the Jewish identity I was searching for was not to be found at the shul but in the world in general.

I did go back to Israel in 1995 for three months, when my husband had a mini-sabbatical in Be'er Sheva in the south of Israel. We had time to travel all over the country and spend time with my husband's family on a kibbutz. They took us to meet Arab friends in a nearby Arab village where we were treated to a typical warm Arab hospitality, and a wonderful Friday night dinner. Our kids immediately went off to play with their kids like old friends, and we listened to the story of what had happened to this family and village over the years. When my husband's mother called from Montreal during dinner to wish us *Shabbat Shalom*[46] and asked where we were, we were afraid to tell her! It was interesting for us to see that just one or two kilometres from the kibbutz was a village so very different, with dirt roads and poverty.

A significant turning point for me was a presentation about nine years ago by an Israeli activist who was on a speaking tour of North America and Europe. He met with a small group of us at a *Succoth*[47] event in our shul, and passionately expressed his disillusionment with the state of his country. He believed that it needed to be rescued from itself. He saw how disillusioned his son was, who had just finished his service with the IDF (Israeli Defence Force), and who along with his friends was planning to leave the country.

The speaker believed that because we, diaspora Jews, were so deeply involved in supporting Israel morally, financially and with frequent visits, we had every right to criticise Israel's policies; that we should and must speak up about this. He reminded us that we were privileged in Montreal to have very large Jewish and Palestinian communities, and that there was no excuse for us not to make the effort to meet and get to know each other.

---

[46] Shabbat Shalom, "Peaceful Sabbath", is a traditional Hebrew Sabbath greeting. (AA)
[47] The Festival of Tabernacles. (AA)

His talk validated what I had been feeling for a long time. I was moved, excited and inspired. I had finally been given the permission I needed to "come out of the closet". Along with Ronit, an Israeli-Canadian woman, and Nada, a Palestinian woman I had just met, who were part of Women in Black, I arranged for a small group of Jews and Arabs to get together at my house, and the Montreal Dialogue Group[48] (MDG) began.

This is a dialogue group for Jews and Palestinians that meets regularly to learn more about each other, to invite guest speakers, read books and see films about the Middle East. It was a wonderful opportunity to meet real live Palestinians here in Montreal, where I have been living for thirty-five years. I quickly realised that for me, "the other" was not defined along ethnic lines but along the lines of ideologies and values. It became clear that we also needed a dialogue group for Jews with divergent opinions to talk about these very emotional and divisive issues, as there is rarely a safe forum for this to happen.

I learned so much in those early, coming-out days. I heard first-hand narratives of Palestinians, where they came from, how they became refugees, what happened to their families. As I developed close friendships with them, I felt much more validated in my own beliefs.

A documentary called *Checkpoint* made by the Jewish Israeli filmmaker Yoav Shamir, had a profound effect on me. The two gruelling hours of humiliation at checkpoints of men, women, children and the elderly were unbearable to witness. Witnessing this abuse, hearing the sexual harassment of young girls, seeing people kept outside for many hours in cold rain or scorching sun, and denying children the right to see a doctor filled me with sadness, outrage and anger. If I felt that way just watching the film, I could hardly imagine what the Palestinians must feel, experiencing this day after day for years, with no end to the Occupation in sight. I agree that Israel is entitled to its security, but why does no one question what causes people to become terrorists in the first place? The type of collective punishment that the film is showing only breeds new generations of terrorists.

The MDG taught me so much, but after a few years I was ready to be more of an activist. I was excited when Independent Jewish Voices

---

[48] See: http://www.dialoguegroup.org.

(IJV)[49] was formed in Canada, with a Montreal chapter. Although, as its name suggests, the organisation represents a range of views, the mainstream Jewish establishment in this country considers IJV an extremist, anti-Zionist organisation. Intellectually I understand this predictable response, but at a heart level it saddens me and I think it is illogical. I do not perceive myself as extremist, naïve, or self-hating. I'm just a person who cares deeply about human rights, justice, equality for all, and adherence to international law. As Canadian author and peace activist Margaret Laurence said, "If peace is subversive, in God's name what is war?"

So many Jewish people are extremely generous and active in causes all over the world, but when it comes to Israel, there are different values. Many Jews feel threatened by antisemitism. They are fearful and perceive themselves as victims, as was so well portrayed in Yoav Shamir's recent film *Defamation*. The desperate need for a Jewish homeland seems to allow for endless human rights violations, but it is not making us safer, far from it. It has become idol worship and an unquestioning mindset that Israel can do no wrong.

Another turning point was my involvement with the McGill Middle East Programme in Civil Society and Peace Building[50]. This initiative brings people from Israel, Palestine and Jordan to Montreal for a year to do a Masters in Social Work. We hosted two Palestinian women from Nablus at our home, until they found their own apartments. I wasn't sure what to expect. Being so influenced by the media, I half expected women in *chadors* and *hijabs* to arrive from the airport. I was surprised to see two completely Westernised women: one, an art therapist in jeans, a T-shirt and a ponytail, the other a doctor in high heels, a pink suit and long blonde hair.

We hit it off from the word go. All the stereotypes and prejudices vanished as my two guests buzzed about helping me in the kitchen, while we chatted about the latest Oprah show. We soon felt like old friends. A few weeks later their husbands and children arrived, so we had a year to get to know them. It was an amazing opportunity for my family to hear first-hand about living in Nablus under occupation, about curfews, tanks rolling in every night, regular dealings with tear gas and being unable to travel a few short kilometres to work.

---

[49] See: http://www.independentjewishvoices.ca
[50] See: http://www.mcgill.ca/mmep

Was this supposed to be my enemy? How could it be? I wanted to tell the world that if only we could hang out together instead of ghettoising ourselves, we could dispel the myths and the fears, see all that we have in common and celebrate our differences. Friendships are not necessarily based on shared ethnicity but rather on shared values.

In the past few years, the main part of my activism has been selling Zaytoun[51] Fair Trade Palestinian products such as olive oil, soap and *za'atar* from the West Bank, and embroidery from Gaza. After being part of so many committees and board meetings over the past eight years, I really enjoy this hands-on form of peace activism. As I sell the products, I have the opportunity to speak to a lot of people about the issues. It's about supporting the farmers whose trees are being destroyed, it's about education and consciousness raising, and it is the other side of the coin to boycotting.

When my activism began and I started to speak out, I could see that some of my Jewish friends were uncomfortable with it. Some of these relationships ended. I had been naïve about this. I discovered how emotional and deeply visceral Zionism is for many Jews. Instead of the old joke that if there are ten Jews in a room, there are eleven opinions, only one opinion seems to be allowed on this issue.

To my family in Montreal, Israel is sacred and is their most important concern. There is an understanding that we avoid the subject of my activism, and we never talk about it. As a result, there is always the proverbial "invisible elephant" in the room. I sense that I am disapproved of and that they feel that I have betrayed them. In the past this made me feel self-doubt and guilt. But as time goes by, especially as the peace movement is gaining international momentum, I feel more and more validated and trust my instincts. In family situations I work hard on being respectful and compassionate. I try to transcend any need I might have to express my opinions and prove my point, but it's challenging!

Meeting a whole new group of like-minded Jews through my activism has been invaluable, and the solidarity and support amongst us is important. My husband Michael shares my feelings and opinions on these issues and he is supportive of my efforts. I certainly couldn't do

---

[51] See: http://www.zatoun.com

this work if we didn't share these values, especially given that the basement of our house is packed floor to ceiling with cases of olive oil!

I still find my identity as a Jew quite confusing. In a recent conversation I was discussing my many identities: I am a woman, a mother, a wife, a Montrealer, a Canadian, a peace activist, an educator, and yes, a Jew. I felt that my Judaism was pretty low down on the list. My friend inquired how that could be when I spend hours every day on this activism precisely because I am Jewish. This is true. My sense of outrage, guilt, and shame about the treatment of Palestinians clearly demonstrates that I do identify strongly as a Jew. I can disagree with the Zionist ideology and the policies of the State of Israel and still be proud of my Jewish heritage.

One advantage of being in my sixties is that I have much less to lose by speaking out. I no longer worry about what others think, or whether it will ruin my chances of getting a job. I have earned the courage of my convictions.

The Hole Truth

Ronit Yarosky

Whenever I talk about my experience with the Palestinian-Israeli conflict, people always ask me: "What was your turning point?"

There are two incidents in my life that were truly life-changing, one that I was not aware of as I was living it, but that became a huge transformative force later in my life, and the other, the actual turning point.

I was born in Montreal and raised in a "typical" Jewish family. My family moved to Israel when I was fourteen and I lived there for nearly ten years, more than two of which were as a soldier during the First Intifada.

I always tell this story because it truly seems impossible that it could be. I spent more than two years in the Israeli military during the First Intifada, much of that time in the West Bank, and I did not know there was an occupation going on. I was a soldier in an occupying army, serving in the Occupied Territories, and was not aware that there was an Occupation. The territories were not called the Occupied Territories, but were referred to as *EYOSH*, a Hebrew acronym for Judea and Samaria.

I knew that somehow those Arabs in the West Bank were different than those within Israel proper, that I had a blue identity card and theirs was orange. The only reason I knew that was because when I first arrived in Israel, before I became a permanent resident, I had an orange ID card too, and the kids at school used to tease me, "What, are you an Arab?"

I knew the Arabs in the West Bank were throwing stones and making trouble but I did not know why, nor did I particularly care. We stayed in many Arab cities and towns when I was in the army, all of which were nameless to me because they were "only" Arab towns, and therefore of no significance in my life. They did not make it onto my "radar screen".

I was brought up believing in "A land without a people for a people without a land"[52]. I was in Jewish school all my life—in a private parochial school in Canada and in a Jewish Israeli high school when my family moved to Israel. My father was the Executive Director of *Keren Kayemet* (the Jewish National Fund, JNF) in Canada, and many other Jewish agencies.

My parents moved to Israel because they—well, mostly my father—was a Zionist, and they loved Israel. His two brothers who had already moved there twenty-five years earlier, were *moshavnikim*[53]. My father's parents moved when we did, and thus his whole family was there.

In 1986 I finished high school and went to the army. The Intifada started in 1987. We were called *"yaldei ha-intifada"*, children of the Intifada. I didn't have a clue. I didn't know anything. I didn't know what the Green Line was. I didn't know what the settlements were. I didn't know what the Occupation was, or that there even was an Occupation. I didn't understand about Palestinians or "Israeli-Arabs", except that they were all Arabs and all to be feared. I was totally disconnected from Palestinian reality during my army years, even though I was physically living in the midst of it all.

In one instance my unit had taken over a school and were living in it. There were no toilets at the school and I remember thinking how inconvenient this was for *me*, never thinking of how inconvenient this must be for the hundreds of children who attended the school. In fact, it was not until many years later that it occurred to me to wonder where

---

[52] The phrase "A land without a people for a people without a land" started to be used by Zionists and Christian Zionists in the late nineteenth-century. It is associated with the denial of the existence of the Palestinian people, and the erroneous but convenient claim that the land of Palestine was unpopulated when the Zionist programme began. (AA)

[53] Hebrew for *moshav* member residents. The m*oshavim* (plural of *moshav*) are a form of Zionist rural settlement usually based on agriculture. They were traditionally different from the kibbutzim because *moshav* members own their property. The *moshav* is based on the principle of mutual assistance and support, with the members acting as an organised community. Palestinian-Israelis are not accepted as *moshav* members, although many *moshavim* have traditionally used Palestinian labour. (AA)

the hundreds of children were, who should have been attending the school. But back then it was of no importance to me.

Once when I was hitchhiking as a soldier[54], I was standing on a road far out from the base, which was North of Zichron Le'zion (within the Green Line). Suddenly a car with Arabs—it probably had the typical blue license plates from the Occupied Territories—came down the road. I was positively terrified. Mind you, that was a period when there were incidents of kidnapping and killing of soldier hitchhikers, so it may have not been a totally baseless fear...but I was beside myself, certain I was about to be kidnapped.

I remember standing in my home base in Beit Sahour near Bethlehem in the occupied West Bank. It was *Yom Ha'atzmaut* (Independence Day). We were all in *madei aleph* (dress uniform), standing at the flag singing *Hatikvah*[55]. Tears were streaming down my face because I couldn't think of anything more incredible and moving than serving my country and singing *Hatikvah* as a soldier. I could see nothing amiss with the situation—a soldier singing her national anthem, but on occupied land.

A couple of years ago I was going through my photos from the army and was looking at pictures from my home base in Beit Sahour. To my absolute astonishment, right next to the parade grounds, I noticed a number of Palestinian homes. I have absolutely no recollection of these homes. I don't remember ever seeing them before. Here are homes of Palestinians who literally have Israeli soldiers parading through their backyards, and they were not on my radar screen. They were invisible.

Once we were on a bus going from one base to another in the Occupied Territories. We were called to some demonstration. I served as a *pkida plugatit*[56] with the paratroopers at that time. I remember two things about that day. One was that there was one soldier who refused to get off the bus, because he was objecting. I remember thinking, "What the hell is wrong with him?" I never realised that there was such a thing as refusing, as conscientious objection. I just thought he was weird and had no idea what he was objecting to. The second thing I remember about

---

[54] Hitchhiking was a common way for Israeli soldiers to move around, especially if their bases were remote and not easily accessible by regular public transport routes. (AA)

[55] *Hatikvah* means "The Hope". It is Israel's national anthem. (AA)

[56] A military unit's administrative assistant. (AA)

that day was when the bus stopped and it was time for the soldiers to get off. They didn't just get off the bus, they tore off it, like dogs after foxes, thirsty for blood. When they returned, one of them said to me with great pride and excitement: "Look, look, I hit the mother-fucker so hard he broke my watch." The soldiers brought back with them five Palestinian youths, blindfolded and cuffed. They were shoved to the back of the bus, and I never gave this a second thought. I never thought how terrifying it must have been for these young kids to be taken prisoner by a busload of armed soldiers. I never gave a second thought to what happened to them. I don't even remember what we did with them. (I knew they were trying to harm us, and maybe would try to kill us if they had the chance—but did we ever ask, "Why"? Did anybody wonder why they hated us?)

Once I had to go to a Military Police base, I don't remember where, maybe Jenin. When I walked in, there were maybe five young Palestinians crouched on the floor, blindfolded and cuffed. When I walked out, they were still there, in the same position.

That was the whole of that episode. Nothing more happened. But years later I remembered it, because I realised that I had walked past those kids without seeing them, as if they were chairs. I noticed them in the same way I would notice a piece of furniture. What if someone saw my son like that and didn't do anything?

Most of these memories from my military service only came back to me after some ten years. They were transformative events, only I did not realise it at the time. The change within me began when I started to question and think and ask, while I was doing my MA research.[57] This is astounding in and of itself; that I could be at the level of a graduate thesis and discover that I knew so little. While reading Benny Morris' *The Birth of the Palestinian Refugee Problem*, I discovered that my uncle's *moshav*, Kerem Maharal, once had a different name, Ijzim. It used to be a Palestinian village. The village down the road, Geva Carmel, also used to have another name, Jaba. And Ein Ayala used to be called Ein

---

[57] Incidentally, my MA thesis, which dealt in part with the dissonance between Israel as a Jewish and democratic state, was given an F (fail grade) by one of the three examiners at McGill University, a Jewish professor with conservative views. The other examiners had given it an A– and a B. This had never happened before at McGill and the department wasn't quite sure how to handle it. After challenging this grade, and having five additional professors read it, it passed with a B and I graduated.

Ghazal. The three villages formed an alliance during the war. The building where the kids sometimes had bonfires used to be the mosque. My uncle's very house was a Palestinian house. How did I not know?

When I told my mother she said, "Well, obviously." How come she knew and I didn't? Was I just stupid? I felt stupid, and very confused. I felt like my world had been shattered into smithereens; that everything I knew and thought to be true was, perhaps, not true. What was I to believe? Who was I to believe? Was everything I had learnt my whole life a lie? Was it me? Was it a *chor bahaskala*[58] that only I had? A hole in my education—a hole in the truth.

This was the beginning of a total, albeit slow, metamorphosis for me, my turning point—the realisation that there is more than one story in history. There are multiple stories. And I grew to realise that we cheat ourselves as human beings by telling only one side.

In 2001 I returned to Israel for a year. Two months later the Second Intifada started and I became involved in what is called the "radical left"—a term that I find funny. What's so radical about people fighting for justice for all? I went to numerous demonstrations in the Occupied Territories. I remember one time when the army was firing tear gas at us and the Palestinians were offering us shelter. I was thinking, "This is my army attacking me, and my 'enemy' helping me!" Seeing (really seeing—not like when I was a soldier and was "blind") the behaviour of the soldiers for the first time was revelatory. How can we treat people like this? Maybe we don't really think they are people. Not as much as we are. Can you truly believe someone is your equal and treat them like this?

When I returned to Montreal I became involved with "anti-occupation" groups. But I was always uncomfortable with the "anti" slant. It seemed to me that it pitted people against each other rather than bring them together. It was also always the same small group of people—the typical preaching-to-the-converted experience.

I realised that without more people changing, change would never happen. I knew that I had a story, a message, and I knew that it was possible to change if the message was heard in a way that resonated.

---

[58] A common Israeli expression meaning, "A hole in one's education". It refers to something that someone should know, but for some reason doesn't. (AA)

I was one of the founders of the Montreal Dialogue Group (MDG) in 2004. The MDG was founded as a politically neutral organisation, with board members from both communities and always Jewish Israeli and Arab-Palestinian-Muslim co-Vice-Presidents. There was no political platform, no taking sides, no trying to convince each other that, "I'm right and you're wrong." It was a forum for people concerned about the situation in the Middle East, to come together and hear and be heard, in an environment free from aggression and judgment (to the greatest degree possible!). We hoped that people might come to acknowledge that there can be a different side to the story they knew as *the* truth.

Now when people refuse to acknowledge the existence (or even the possibility) of another side to the story, I ask, "Why are they so defensive? What are they hiding?" Or, perhaps even more significantly, "What is being hidden from them, that they are not even aware of?"

I'll be honest, it's not easy. I have been told that it is too bad that my children have not been killed in a suicide bombing. I have been spat on. I have been roughly handled by the police and detained. (I'm four feet ten inches tall— not such a big threat!)

I have been fortunate to find myself in situations that have allowed me to open my mind. I am sure that I had to go through everything I've been through to get to where I am. If I didn't have the benefit of hindsight, I would never have known that I had been blind, and I would never know that others are blind too. Having had the opportunity to see both sides first hand (as a soldier, and as an activist), and to get a better understanding of the Palestinian side, has made me more aware of the injustices, the propaganda, the distortion of truth, the inability to see. This exists everywhere, all around us, and the solution is only within us, not within the "other".

The challenges are huge. But there are also examples of change. A few months after a fire-bombing at a Jewish school here in Montreal, one of the Jewish members of the Dialogue Group was talking about her fears. Unexpectedly, one of the Palestinian members said, "I suddenly *get* that you are really and truly afraid. I always thought that you just all *said* you were afraid as an excuse to do bad things to the Palestinians. But now I get that you are really, actually afraid. And even though I don't understand this, given that you are so much stronger, I get that you are afraid." This was an amazing moment. Another was when a Jewish member said to a Palestinian, "But Barak offered to give you so much land." The Palestinian turned to this gentleman and said, "Excuse me, this is *my* land that you are generously giving to me!" There was a flicker of "penny dropping" in the Jewish man's eyes as he realised that he had just heard a perspective that he had not considered before. Maybe he didn't agree with it, but he heard it.

A number of years ago I was presenting at a conference at Concordia University. A well-known local Palestinian activist stood up and said that he is against dialogue because dialogue requires you to explain your perspective, and he felt that he did not owe anyone an explanation, he was sick and tired of explaining himself. "Why do I have to apologise over and over for who I am?" he asked.

I take his point. It must be horrible. But what is the alternative? I answered by saying that if only I had had the opportunity when I was seventeen or eighteen to speak to him, or his friend or his uncle or his cousin, and hear their perspective, hear their story, hear them, who knows what sort of difference that might have made in my life?

The truth is that if I did have the opportunity for dialogue with Palestinians when I was younger, it would not have changed the fact that I was serving in an occupying army, in occupied territory, and that the soldiers on my base were parading through Palestinian backyards. But it might have changed something in me.

To quote my favourite phrase, "You have to be the change you want to see in the world."

Israel

Comprehending Oppression, or How I Came to Understand Occupation and Resist It

Jeff Halper

I first became aware of being an "Israeli in Palestine" on 9 July 1998, the day my friend Salim calls "the black day in my life and in the life of my family". On that day the bulldozers of Israel's Civil Administration, its military government in the West Bank, demolished his home for the first time.

It was an act so unjust, so brutal, so at odds with the ethos of the benign, democratic, Jewish Israel fighting for its survival, that I had absorbed on "my side" of the Green Line, that it was inexplicable in any terms I could fathom. It had nothing to do with terrorism or security. It was not an act of defence or even keeping Palestinians away from Israeli settlements or roads. It was purely unjust and brutal.

As the bulldozer pushed through the walls of Salim's home, it pushed me through all the ideological rationalisations, the pretexts, the lies and the bullshit that my country had erected to prevent us from seeing the truth: that oppression must accompany an attempt to deny the existence and claims of another people, in order to establish an ethnically pure state for yourself.

If, as the popular saying has it, "a conservative is a liberal who has been mugged", then a post-Zionist is a Zionist who has witnessed a house demolition. My conversion experience was unplanned.

Demolitions are normally done early in the morning, just after the men have left for work, and with no prior warning. It was only through an unusual constellation of factors that day that I happened to be on the scene.

The Civil Administration officials who had already demolished five homes in the Anata area, thought they could squeeze in one more. They did not start with Salim's house then, until late morning. Salim's resistance—he had rushed home when he heard of the demolitions—delayed things even longer. At noon he heard the dreaded knock on his door. Opening it, he saw his house surrounded by dozens of soldiers and Border Police.

Micha Yakhin, a heavily armed inspector of the Civil Administration, stood menacingly before him. "Is this your house?" Yakhin asked brusquely. "Yes, it's my house", Salim replied. "No, it isn't", said Yakhin. "It is our house now. You have fifteen minutes to remove all your belongings. We are going to destroy it."

As Micha and the soldiers pushed their way into the home, Salim argued and pleaded with them. When, however, he touched Micha as the latter advanced on him in a threatening way, Salim's protestations turned instantly into "resistance", triggering a full military response. He was beaten, handcuffed and thrown out of the house.

In the pandemonium, Arabiya, Salim's wife, managed to quickly slam the door shut and lock it with her and her six children inside. She then got on the phone, calling frantically for help. One of the numbers she called was ours. By chance we happened to be close by, preparing for a demonstration against the policy of demolishing Palestinian homes. The demonstration, initiated by our Israeli Committee Against House Demolitions (ICAHD), was to be held at the Civil Administration offices in the West Bank, not far from Salim and Arabiya's home.

As I rushed to the site, I crossed the membrane few Israeli Jews ever cross, running right through the lines of Israeli troops that surrounded the house. It was so unheard of that any outsider should show up on the scene, let alone an Israeli Jew, that I took them by surprise and ended up at Salim and Arabiya's door before they could stop me.

When Micha's workers had emptied the house of most of its contents, he ordered a waiting bulldozer driver to finish the job. As it passed by me, I did almost instinctively what I have done many times since: I threw myself in front of it to try to stop the demolition. After trying to coax me to get out of the way, the soldiers brusquely (but not too roughly) pushed me down the hill, where I found myself lying in the dirt and dust next to Salim.

As we lay together on the ground, guarded by soldiers whose guns pointed at us menacingly, watching helplessly as the bulldozer proceeded to demolish his home systematically, I watched Salim's face contort in pain and disbelief. "But I didn't do anything wrong", he kept saying. "I'm not a criminal. I'm not a terrorist. I tried to get a permit for the house. Why are they doing this to me?" Occasionally I heard him gasp and sob, as when the antenna and water tanks on the roof collapsed. These poignant moments brought home to him the reality of what was happening. At one point, when the bulldozer emerged from the ruins of his home through his children's bedroom, I saw him raise his arms high, as if beseeching someone to intervene. Wiping the perspiration from his pained face, awkwardly trying to find consoling words, I promised Salim that the world would hear his story.

On that day, lying on the ground at gunpoint with a Palestinian innocent of any wrongdoing, witnessing one of the most wrenching experiences that can ever happen to a person, I found myself in another country I thought no longer existed: Palestine. I was amongst people who were supposed to be my enemies but who shared with me their suffering at the hands of what could only be called Israeli state terrorism.

Nothing could reconcile what I was witnessing and experiencing with the Zionist narrative I had learned. No, something else was going on here, something of fundamental importance that I had to understand and grapple with. I could not go home as if nothing had happened except yet another atrocity of the Occupation. Only by understanding what had transpired that day would I truly grasp the nature of the Israeli-Palestinian conflict and, perhaps, how to get out of it.

From Ethnic Jew to Jewish National to Israeli

Until that July day in Anata I suppose you could have called me a "Zionist". I was a Jew who had immigrated to Israel from the United States twenty-five years earlier. I generally subscribed to what may be described as Zionist principles, if not to the full-blown ideology. I acccpted the idea, fundamental to Zionism, that the Jews constitute a nation in the political sense of the term, based upon their national existence in Biblical times, a kind of religio-nationality maintained throughout the centuries of exile/diaspora, and a revived national identity emerging with other nineteenth century European national movements. I accepted the notion that the Jewish nation possesses the right to self-determination in their historic homeland, just as any other nation does. It seemed self-evident to me that the homeland was the Land of Israel.

As a Liberal-Left Zionist, I of course accepted the Palestinians' right to self-determination as well, but only in a state alongside the state of Israel. When pressed, even by my own doubts, I would invariably fall back upon a conviction that for me trumped all the problematics of Zionist claims and excesses: the Jews were truly a persecuted people who needed, and had a right to, a state of their own. That seemed enough to justify the existence of Israel as a Jewish state, while subordinating Palestinian claims. The Palestinians had to fit into the nooks and crannies of my national existence in "my" country. Like other Israeli Jews, I did not press the issue any further.

Why did this ideology speak to me? What led me, a normal secular middle-class Jewish kid from a small town in the Midwest to adopt a radically different identity from the ethnic Judaism characteristic of my family and the American Jews among whom I lived? Why did I adopt the identity of a Jew in the primary, national sense—the first step toward becoming an Israeli?

In fact, I came to my Israeliness easily, almost naturally, without any need for a Zionist ideology or even close contact with a Jewish community. It all began in my hometown of Hibbing, Minnesota, where I grew up. The experience of immigration was still strong. Hibbing was still populated by migrants from Scandinavia, Croatia, Serbia, Poland and Italy and their children, my friends. The immigrants' languages were still fresh, their food and traditions still permeated local life, rather than being packaged into ethnic "fairs". This was true of the small Jewish community as well. Composed of about fifteen families, it had a small wooden synagogue but no Rabbi. Despite their thoroughly secular Americanism, my parents very much wanted their children to "remain Jewish", or at least to preserve a modicum of "Jewish identity".

Thoroughly melded into Hibbing's mix of ethnicity and small-town America, the Judaism I grew up with was defined by its ethics. I am still guided by the definition of Judaism propagated by the official textbooks of the Conservative Movement that I used in my Sunday school teaching: "Ethical Monotheism". Perhaps that spoke to me because of the general ethos that I absorbed in Hibbing, plain old Midwestern fairness. My moral position in the world was defined by that down-to-earth, rock-solid sense that if the people are simply fair and nice, we'll all get along fine with each other.

It was that deep sense of elemental unfairness and outrage that welled up in me as I witnessed the demolition of Salim's house and propelled me in front of the bulldozer; outrage at the plain unfairness that underlies the much bigger concept of "justice".

Hibbing was perhaps the closest America has ever gotten to a classless society. Labor was glorified. Most of the town's bread-winners still earned their decent wages as skilled miners in the vast open-pit mines. Two of the town's finest sons were Gus Hall, long the head of the American Communist Party, and Woody Guthrie's *protégé*, Bob Dylan.

In that thick ethnic environment, American-ness was thin and unfulfilling. Like many third-generation Americans, I sought a return to my ethnic roots, but Jewish life in the Midwest resembled nothing more than warmed-over Protestantism. I even enrolled in the Hebrew Union College, the Reform rabbinical seminary in Cincinnati, but to no avail. The only meaningful connection I could forge between my Jewish identity and American life took the form of my involvement, as a Jew, in the civil rights and anti-Vietnam War movements that I associated with the value Jews placed on social justice.

The actual event that pushed me into Israeliness took place in 1966 when, as an undergraduate student, I won a scholarship to study the Falashas, the Jews of Ethiopia. As I was booking my ticket, I found out that going through Tel-Aviv was as cheap as any other route. So, I decided to make a brief stopover.

Landing in Tel Aviv that summer, I found my way to a youth hostel run by an old man named Joseph, who took a liking to me. Soon after I arrived he invited me to travel with him to Jerusalem for the day. About the only thing I remember clearly is standing in an observation tower looking out over the Old City, which was still under Jordanian rule.

That was it. On the surface nothing dramatic had happened. I did not change my views in any way, I was not "transformed", and I still knew nothing about Zionism. But those few days in Israel had touched me. If, over the years my Jewish identity was steadily overtaken by an American one, I was now moving beyond Jewish ethnicity towards a kind of proto-Israeliness, with Israel itself entering the equation unintentionally, almost accidentally. Yet I was able to take on "Israeliness" without sacrificing my political or ethical principles. That meant keeping a loathing of Israeli policies of displacement, segregation, occupation and oppression deriving as they did from an insular and exclusivist national narrative.

From Israeli to a critical Israeli

By the summer of 1973, at the age of 27, I was finally ensconced in Israel. My transition to life there was smooth and happy. As a PhD student in anthropology, I had a professional agenda. My fieldwork, for which I had a generous fellowship, involved research into the ethnic identities of working-class Kurdish Jews in the inner-city neighbourhood of Jerusalem, where I still live. Interviewing elderly Jews from Kurdistan, Iraq, Iran and Yemen, as well as their children, I had connected to the "real" Israel. The "Jewish" part of my identity melted away in favour of an Israeli one upon my arrival in Israel, and it has never returned.

My work among those *Mizrachi*[59] Jews grounded me solidly in Israeli society. The other community with which I was involved, the Israeli peace camp, continued to be important to me. No sooner had I landed in Jerusalem, that I attended a meeting of *Si'akh* (Hebrew for dialogue), the Israeli New Left, where I met my future wife and partner-in-crime, Shoshana. While I engaged in activist peace work over the years, it was by no means my main preoccupation. I even mentioned to Shosh a few times that we should try to have more Arab friends. But like other Israeli Jews we had few opportunities to even meet Arabs, let alone socialise with them.

The Arab-Palestinian element of Israeli life started to break through only when I took over the Middle East Centre of Friends World College, an American college associated with the Quakers. I then hired as a co-faculty Nabila Espanioli, a Palestinian citizen of Israel who lived

---

[59] Hebrew for Eastern or Oriental Jews, meaning Jews from Arab countries, as distinguished from Ashkenazi Jews who are from European background. (AA)

in Nazareth. As we travelled with the students through Israel, the Occupied Palestinian Territories, Jordan and Egypt, Nabila—a keen critical thinker and the first Palestinian I had really spent time with—opened my eyes to Palestinian realities.

I remember in particular one of our first study trips together, when Nabila took the students and me into a Jewish National Fund forest planted over the remains of the Palestinian village of Saffuriyya. She began to explain the history of the village of 4000 inhabitants, their expulsion in 1948, the ethnic cleansing of the Galilee by Israeli troops, massacres, and how Jews had been allowed to take over Arab lands. Like many other places Saffuriyya was replaced by a Jewish town called by the Roman-era name Tzipori.

When we returned to the minibus I began to "correct" Nabila gently. Not that the facts weren't true, mind you, but that the tone was one-sided. As an Israeli Jew I didn't feel that "my side" had been fairly presented: that Tzipori had once been a famous city where part of the Jewish Talmud was codified; that the city had been taken in 1948 in the context of a war; that Jews had "returned" to the city as part of their own national revival.

The more Nabila insisted on her version, the more defensive I became. Our voices rose to a shouting match. I told Nabila that as educators we had a responsibility to present our facts in a balanced way, that as an anthropologist I wanted to understand both sides, that we couldn't just propagandise our students. And here's where the students stepped in.

"Wait a minute," they told me, "Why are you getting defensive?"

"We haven't heard anything from you that contradicts what Nabila said."

"Tone?! What do you expect from a Palestinian standing at the site of a demolished village? How many times did you talk about persecution of Jews in your lectures to us—and with a definite 'tone' of sympathy? Why should your voice, your narrative, your 'tone' be privileged over Nabila's? Don't bullshit us about critical thinking and then pull rank as a professor and a Jew. And a man! We resent your using your louder male voice to drown out Nabila's."

They were perfectly right, of course. That interaction was a turning point in my life. For the first time I confronted the hidden reality on the "other side" of the Israeli-Palestinian membrane; that porous, transparent filter that defines and envelopes Jewish space and turns everything "Arab" into mere background, that separates "us" from "them".

But I also confronted the uncompromising demands of intellectual honesty. Without the benefit of a classroom where I controlled the discussion, without the safe distance between teacher and pupil, my students compelled me to adhere to the very intellectual standards I demanded of them. I learned that defensiveness is not an honest intellectual position. Quite the opposite. It obfuscates. It is employed when a strong argument is lacking, or when you know the other side has a point.

Nabila and the students did not offer me the luxury of staying comfortably within self-imposed parameters, using sophistic intellectual devices to avoid going where I didn't want to go. What I learned that day proved crucial to my ability to deal with such a charged, emotionally-laden issue like Israel-Palestine. One of the hardest parts of critical thinking is the ability to detect in yourself elements of irrationality, prejudice, fear, peer pressure and social conditioning—and to confront them.

Israeli Committee Against House Demolitions

In 1997, in the wake of Binyamin Netanyahu's election, a number of us in the Israeli peace movement met and decided that it was time to re-engage in resisting the Occupation. The Oslo "peace process" was in an obvious state of collapse, the Occupation was brutally reasserting itself, and the peace movement had become dormant during the Rabin and Peres years. But what to do? We sought the views of Palestinians we knew, asking them, "What issues do you consider of greatest priority? In what ways could we best work together?" The bottom line, of course, was—-and still is—bringing about a total end of the Occupation.

One issue arose repeatedly: Israel's constant demolition of Palestinian homes. Several members of our political circle had become involved in efforts to save the home of Ata Jabar and his family near Hebron, which the Israeli authorities threatened to demolish due to the lack of a building permit. Although long-time peace activists, we did not know much about the phenomenon, but it galvanised us into action and ICAHD, the Israeli Committee Against House Demolitions, was founded.

I wish I could say that we had chosen the issue of house demolitions consciously and strategically, out of a well-informed assessment of the political situation and a clear notion of where we were going as a political action group. We didn't. We backed into it without fully appreciating how powerful a vehicle of resistance the issue of house demolitions would turn out to be. Only gradually did we discover that Israel's policy of house demolitions constituted the very essence of the conflict: Zionism's programme of dispossessing the Palestinians altogether.

After decades of life in Israel, learning Hebrew, raising a family here, serving in the army, involving myself deeply in academic work as well as in political activity, having run (unsuccessfully) for the Jerusalem City Council, and participating in all the myriad experiences that are part and parcel of daily life, I can say that I had become an Israeli. Yet, if my "Israeliness" had supplanted my Jewish identity, in the end it also superseded Zionism. Now, as I became involved in ICAHD activities with the Palestinians in the Occupied Territories, I saw how important it was to go beyond Zionism, to approaching Israel as a real country and not as some ideological construct.

છ⋑

"Are you a Zionist?" I'm often asked. Or a post-Zionist, a neo-Zionist, an anti-Zionist? The question, for me, is irrelevant. I am an Israeli living in a real country called Israel. That means, for me, that Israel is a fact of life. No matter whether Israel should have been established, the crimes committed in 1948, Israel's deplorable forty-year Occupation and its ongoing persecution of the Palestinians, Israel is a political fact that cannot be simply erased, even if one feels all the moral justification to do so. This is the starting point of my political work. But only the starting point. Israel, like all colonial regimes who managed in the end to redeem themselves from their oppressive pasts, must traverse a long and painful trail from decolonisation through reconciliation, to a new form of political life that is just and inclusive of all the country's inhabitants, before it can expect security and normalisation.

Conversion

Dorothy Naor

I am seventy-eight years old, which would not be remarkable except that it identifies me as being a member of the Holocaust generation. No, I did not experience the Holocaust. I was born and lived comfortably in the United States (in California) until the age of eighteen, when I took my first trip abroad for six months. That trip, in 1950, took me to Israel.

While I had not personally experienced the Holocaust, I met people my age who had, and whose stories I heard. I saw pictures of the camps and their skeleton-like inhabitants on cinema news clips. This was also the period when the state of Israel was born. I met Israeli Jews who had come to the San Francisco Bay Area to study at one or other of its universities. My future spouse was among them.

The long and the short of it was that although I grew up in a Left-wing family, like many on the Left in the US, including my own parents, I was led to believe that Jews who had suffered so disastrously during the Nazi era needed and deserved a country of their own. All that I knew about Palestinians was that they killed Jewish farmers who were innocently tending their fields.

Today, over sixty years later, I think very differently from then. My father changed his views much sooner than I did—about a year or two after Israel became a state. But he was an unusual man who devoured books on politics, economics, and history.

Back then, having been affected on the one side by the stories of Holocaust survivors, and on the other by the Israeli Jews I'd met, I believed the popular mantra, "A land without people for a people without a land." I knew nothing about the *Nakba*.

When in 1950 I was invited to spend six months on a leadership training programme in Israel with Young Judea[60], I jumped at the opportunity. We had barely landed in Haifa when I fell in love with the country.

But I remained blind. During much of the course, we lived in Jerusalem in houses that when we arrived were in various states of damage and disrepair, but that were clearly once sumptuous homes. It never occurred to me to ask, "Where are the people who used to live here?" I accepted the "fact" that the Palestinians had run away, leaving the entire country to the Jews.

I recall meeting a Palestinian only once during that entire six months. He accompanied us on one of our side trips.

I returned to the United States more convinced than ever that Israel was an amazing country, and that given the suffering that European Jews had undergone, it was just and right that they had a country to call their own.

My conversion took years.

My spouse, Israel[61] and I married in 1952. After he completed his MSc in Civil Engineering, we returned to Israel in November 1958 with three small children: a five-year-old, a four-year-old and a six-month-old baby. Israel would have been content to stay in the United States, but I urged that we should raise our children in Israel. It was not difficult to convince him to go back. He had parents and also younger siblings who were born here after the family had escaped from Nazi Austria.

Israel, his parents, and a younger brother came to Palestine in 1939. His mother gave birth to two more children here, partially as therapy for her deep depression at having left her parents behind. The remainder of Israel's extended family in Austria and Hungary perished in the extermination camps, except for one uncle who survived and subsequently came to Israel.

---

[60] Young Judea is a Zionist youth movement in the United States. It was founded in 1909 and according to its website, it "seeks to build Jewish identity and Zionist commitment in American Jewish youth and young adults". (AA)

[61] Israel is also a man's name in Hebrew. (AA)

The first years here were busy ones for me. I was raising three children, teaching English at a hotel-training school, attending evening school to learn Hebrew and caring for the house. I liked my neighbours and felt happy in our small house, even though it was much smaller than the one we had left behind in California. In later years we expanded it, and Israel and I still live in it today. Most important for me in those early years is that we had a large yard for our children to play in. The fact that we were cramped into two rooms in the early years did not bother me at all.

Our children now have their own homes and families. Our eldest lives with his wife in the United States and their children are grown up.

At some point I began to feel uneasy about certain things happening here. I don't remember exactly when. But I do recall that after the Six Day war in 1967, when Russia declared an embargo on arms to neighbouring Arab countries, it upset me greatly that the United States did not declare a similar embargo on arms to Israel. By that time, I had had enough of wars. Also, when the Russian Jewish immigration began to flow, I was upset by the Israeli propaganda that coaxed Russians here.

When the colonisation of the West Bank began, I joined in with Peace Now (still in its infancy) demonstrations in the West Bank against colonisation. But I still hung on to the rightness of a Jewish state. I was not a Zionist. In fact, I knew nothing about Zionism. I just felt that this was home. Although I had problems with some government policies, this would probably be true of any country that I lived in.

Beyond feeling uncomfortable and being opposed to colonising Palestinian land, I did nothing political. My spouse's work for an Israeli company took us to various countries in which we stayed a year or two. This always demanded a period of acclimatisation for the children and learning a new language for all of us. I spent most of those periods abroad teaching English in local schools. When our older children reached high school age, I decided that for their sakes the time had come to stop moving around. Israel continued to work abroad much of the time, but the children and I remained at home.

My uneasiness increased.

I do not recall exactly when I began to question the rightness of a Jewish state. But I clearly recall the three events that drove me to begin seeking answers to my questions.

The first was on 25 February 1994 at dawn on a Friday during Ramadan, when Baruch Goldstein slaughtered twenty-nine Palestinians praying at a mosque, and spraying the worshippers with bullets, wounded 125 more. As horrid as the massacre was, I was yet more shocked when the government instead of locking up the Jews in the Hebron area, enforced a month-long curfew on the Palestinians there. Families of the wounded were kept from visiting loved ones in hospitals.

And yet, beyond feeling intensely angry, I still did nothing.

The second incident was on the eve of *Rosh Hashanah* (Jewish New Year's Eve), on 30 September 2000. Our family members had left our home following a pleasant dinner. My spouse left to drive his elderly parents back to the nursing home. I was alone in the final stages of cleaning up when I turned on the news on the TV. I remained rivetted to the screen, watching over and over again the scene of a Palestinian father and a child behind him. They were both on the ground shielded in part by a concrete wall, bullets flying all around them, the father attempting to protect the child, but failing. In the end, both appeared to be dead. This was the story of twelve-year-old Mohammed al-Dura and his father. The father survived, though badly injured. The child did not. The Intifada had broken out a day earlier.

The third incident began a day later, on 1 October 2000. Palestinians began to demonstrate in Wadi Ara, South of Haifa, and other areas. The Israeli police came out in force and over the next few days killed thirteen Palestinians, twelve of whom were Israeli citizens.

I could not believe that Israeli police would open fire on demonstrators. They never did so with Jews, no matter how violent the demonstrations or the riots. But the fact that the police had opened fire on Palestinians showed me how racist Israel is. I felt ill.

My naivety ended in almost a split second—following Mohamed al-Dura and the thirteen that were shot by the police—and my search for answers began.

A few days following the killings, someone told me that a group of women were planning to pay condolence visits to the families of the murdered Palestinians and suggested that perhaps I join. I did. That was my introduction to New Profile, a young organisation at the time. I have been with it ever since.

That evening we visited three homes. The visits were traumatic. The families received us politely. But the pain of losing their loved ones and the racist acts of the police hung in the air as we listened to their stories. In one home the eighteen-year-old son who was subsequently killed, had been watching the demonstration from up the hill rather than participating in it. He had a scholarship to the Hebrew University, where he planned to study physics and another subject—I don't remember which, except that it was from the humanities. His father pointed out over and over again that his son had been sitting under a tree on the hill, and that the police had targeted him intentionally. His mother and grandmother wept the entire time that we were there, repeating over and over, "My flower, my flower." It was heart breaking.

I'm sad to think that after forty-odd years of living in Israel, this was the first time that I had visited Palestinian homes, the first time that I had spoken to Palestinians except for the occasional handyman or gardener who would come by our house looking for work.

I was unable to accompany New Profile activists to additional condolence visits. Israel and I had plane tickets to visit our son and his family in the United States. But when we returned, I began studying Zionist philosophy and acts in earnest.

Along with studying Zionist sources, Israel and I began taking part in an Israeli Jewish-Palestinian organisation called *Ta'ayush*[62]. We joined its attempts to bring humanitarian supplies (mainly cooking oil, sugar and flour) to Palestinian villages in the Occupied Palestinian Territories (OPT). We also participated in demonstrations against the Occupation, and later against the wall.

By chance I had heard a group of Palestinians speak at an Israeli home one evening on the subject of the two-state solution. They were very Western in their manner. I thought to myself, "Wow! They should be able to convince every Israeli that Palestinians can be trusted." I became friends with two of them, Diana Buttu and Michael Tarazi, and

---

[62] Arabic for "living together". (AA)

began to organise meetings for them to speak at. But the miracle did not happen. They were unable to convince Israelis to believe in Palestinians. This was not the speakers' fault. No one could have surpassed their endeavours. Except for the minority that questions, Israeli Jews just believe what they want to believe.

Israel's and my first baby-steps on our own into the OPT began at the time of the construction of the Wall. We went several times a week to Mas'ha, which was the first village to organise against the use of the wall to steal the village's land. Unlike the subsequent means of opposition, the Mas'ha camp was less a hands-on activity and more a learning experience: studying the Wall, how it would steal Palestinian land, and how to oppose it. Mas'ha was where the organisation Anarchists Against the Wall was born.

Unlike most visitors, Israel and I did not sleep overnight in the tents. But we returned around three times a week, and each time remained for the entire day. For the first time in our lives we met and spoke to Palestinians as friends and worked with them in a joint endeavour.

Subsequently Israel and I participated in a good many demonstrations against the wall in various villages. We learned how to deal with tear gas and other crowd dispersion methods popular with Israel's military, which now has no problem shooting also at Jews and internationals who come to help Palestinians protest against the theft of their land.

We also took part in olive harvests. We felt more and more at home among Palestinians. We became close friends with some, whom we continue to visit, although we no longer attend the demonstrations in the villages or the harvesting of olives. Both of us have knee problems, and my back also does not allow me to walk long distances, or to run. I guess we have to realise that age also takes its toll.

But we have nevertheless gained. Like most Israeli Jews, we knew no Palestinians for the better part of our lives in Israel. This has now changed. And this change has impacted as much on my thinking as did my research. I can't believe that I could have lived here so many years and not have had a single Palestinian friend! Few Israeli Jews apart from activists against the Occupation have Palestinian friends.

We continue to be active against the Occupation, which I now consider as having started in 1948, if not earlier.

My main activity now is informing, and I do this in several ways. As a member of New Profile, I contribute to its Alternative Information email list[63] as well as to other email lists. I also contribute one day a week to an on-line journal, the *Occupation Magazine*[64]. I conduct day tours of the Salfit area of the OPT to give those who come with me an intimation of what it is like to be a Palestinian living under occupation. When I'm abroad, I do presentations.

In these activities I urge people to engage in BDS (Boycott, Divestment and Sanctions), and to press their governments to do the same. BDS are nonviolent means of pressuring governments. In my email messages and in my presentations abroad I show that Israeli Jews pay a high price for occupation. The price they pay is less than that of the Palestinians, but they nonetheless pay a price. It seems to me that now, finally, some Israeli Jews are beginning to realise that while so much is spent on expansion, ethnic cleansing, and wars there is no money for education, health, or social welfare.

Today I realise that Israel is not the haven that Zionists had intended it to be. To the contrary. I realise that it is one of the worst things that could have happened to Jews who live here. No country grounded on a single race, religion, or ethnicity can be democratic. There is no difference between a "pure Aryan state" and a "pure Jewish state". Nowhere else in the world since WWII, have Jews been subjected to twelve wars and military campaigns in less than sixty-two years. Nowhere else have so many Jews been killed since WWII. Nowhere else do so many Jews suffer from post-traumatic stress symptoms, and nowhere else are all Jewish eighteen-year-olds, male and female, required by law to enlist in the military. Yet, notwithstanding all of Israel's wars and military might, Jewish Israelis are not one iota more secure today than they were in 1948. In fact, they are less secure in Israel than anywhere else in the world (except maybe in war zones like Afghanistan). Lastly, there is at present no silver lining in sight. I can't see a glimmer of the day when all the peoples of this blood-soaked area who love this land, Jews, Muslims, Christians, seculars, and others, will have a future to look forward to, a future of justice and peace.

---

[63] To subscribe send a message to newprofile-subscribe@googlegroups.com.
[64] The *Occupation Magazine* can be found at: http://www.kibush.co.il.

I believe in not doing unto others what I would not want done unto me. Therefore, I feel that any solution to the Palestine-Israel issue must include the Palestinians' Right of Return.

Other than that, while I will accept any just solution, my dream is of a single state for all who love this land, with equal rights for all its citizens, be they Muslim, Jewish, Christian, secular, or other. I hope for a country where access to the beach does not depend on one's religion or race or on a military permit, a country where my Palestinian friends can visit me as readily as I can visit them.

The chances are small that I will live to see my dream fulfilled, but the wonderful thing about dreams is that so long as I live, they give me hope.

Eucalyptus Tree

Maya Wind

There is something Israeli within me. The familiarity of the white stone walls reflecting the colours of the sun, the dust that settles everywhere, the smell of pine trees and the warm dry breezes that sweep through the city—all leave me knowing that I have no other home but here in Jerusalem, where I was raised. The only other place that ever came close was my grandparents' kibbutz where my father grew up. We used to drive up north almost every weekend to visit my grandparents on the kibbutz they helped build, at the foot of *Mount Gilboa*.

My grandparents were my role models ever since I was old enough to hear their stories. Survivors of the Holocaust, they were left alone in the world. What kept them going was a sense of mission, something greater than themselves—a dream of making a new home for the Jews in Palestine. After the war they travelled through Siberia and Uzbekistan all the way to Italy, gathering Jewish orphans, to make the trip to their new homeland. My grandmother would tell me of the first time she could make out the sunny shores of Haifa in 1948. This was her last chance to leave death behind. Here, in the swamp and malaria-ridden wasteland, she would make a home for herself, for my father, and for me.

Tirelessly she worked as a schoolteacher in the kibbutz while my grandfather laboured in the groves harvesting olives, the indigenous tree of Palestine. Coming to the kibbutz from Jerusalem always felt like going back in time, like understanding where I came from—walking beneath the Eucalyptus trees that they planted to dry up the swamps;

along the Assi River, where my grandmother threw her *Shabbat* silver candlesticks, her last remaining item from home, in order to be equal to everyone else in the kibbutz. She was a socialist and was willing to drown her past, so that I would one day have a home and not be afraid. But her dreams for me took some unexpected turns.

December 2008

I come to visit her in her modest one storey home and sit in her mustard-coloured kitchen. I meet my cousin Ayelet there, who is three weeks older, and who was raised alongside me. Ayelet had just enlisted in the IDF. For the first time my grandmother and I saw her in her olive uniform and brown high boots. My grandmother's eyes glisten, and she disappears into her bedroom. When she emerges, she holds my grandfather's old shoe polish and brush.

"Here", she says, "He would have wanted you to have it."

She turns to me, with disappointment and asks, "Well, wouldn't you want this too?"

I look down, avoiding her stare. Didn't I want to continue her legacy of selflessness and giving, that I so admired? Any desire I had to give to something greater than myself culminated in this one great act that I had been bred and educated to achieve—to join the IDF. This was my chance to give back, not just to my people, to my country, but also to my grandmother. This was my chance to show her how much I appreciate her sacrifice and everything she has done for me. In just two weeks it would be my turn to carry out this great tradition, to do as my father had done, and as my children would surely do one day. In two weeks' time is my draft date. Ayelet looks at me and states matter-of-factly, "The army is the last station to board the train to Israeli society."

I too wanted to make that sacrifice. It had always been clear to me, as it had been to my classmates, that we would one day join the army. We were also very certain about why. The same October I turned twelve, the Second Intifada broke out. Buses, cafés and crowded market places were blown up, leaving us frightened and in constant mourning. Our fears soon ripened into anger, that was turned towards the Palestinians, whose bombs took our childhood's innocence along with their victims.

And then, just three years before my enlistment, I met a Palestinian for the first time. It was in a dialogue group that was formed in Jerusalem for youth from both sides of the Green Line. Several days into our summer camp we are sitting in a circle, and everyone can tell one story about their experience of the still ongoing Second Intifada. One Palestinian girl speaks softly, "When I was twelve, Israeli soldiers entered our house in the middle of the night and took my father away." She chokes, "I never saw him again. They told us he died in prison from disease." Her body shakes as she begins to cry, and I feel her words hang in the air between us. Never before have I experienced such guilt in my entire life. Stunned, I look at her and blurt out the first words that come to my mind, "I'm so sorry." Surprised, she answers, "It's all right, it's not your fault."

But it was. It could have been. Was one of those soldiers my father? My friend? Could it be me in a few years? Could such a story even be true? My mind races with questions. I cannot understand how a moral and strictly defensive army, made up of all the good people that I know, could possibly do such a thing. Could I, knowing what I do now, take part in it? This question would only open many more. It would lead me to venture tentatively into the West Bank, a formerly frightening and unknown territory to me, in an attempt to find those answers for myself.

Two years later, on a Friday afternoon in early November, I find myself with a group of Israeli Jews from Jerusalem who joined Palestinians in their olive harvest. It would be my first visit to the West Bank village of Ni'lin. I am told that the residents of this village have difficulty accessing their olive groves because of Jewish residents from the nearby settlement of Hashmonayim. We arrive at a checkpoint at the entrance to the village. The IDF soldiers inform us that we cannot enter the village, as it is a closed military zone. We get off the bus and walk away but meet a resident of the village who shows us another entrance. Walking through Ni'lin I feel very self-conscious. The Arabic graffiti on the walls and spoken all around me, scares me a little. So, do the flat-roofed grey houses and winding, poorly paved streets. Everything feels so foreign.

We then split up into groups, and I accompany Ahmed and his family to their olive groves outside the village. It is then that I learn that because of the settlement of Hashmonayim, the separation barrier is being built so that it separates half of the villagers from their olive groves. We make our way to Ahmed's grove that is still accessible. We just begin to harvest, when I hear shouting and look toward the village.

Marching toward us is a group of residents of Ni'lin along with Israeli Jews shouting and chanting. Apparently, there are weekly demonstrations against the barrier in Ni'lin, and unknowingly I was caught in the middle of one.

Before I can make sense of what is happening, two army jeeps come racing toward us, sirens wailing. The armed soldiers jump out and begin firing tear gas everywhere. The crowd scatters and chaos breaks out. Frightened, I begin to cry even before the tear gas reaches me. Suddenly four soldiers come running toward us with their rifles drawn and pointed right at us. They draw near and warn us that if we do not clear out within five minutes, they will shoot tear gas grenades at us. Ahmed loses it and comes right up to one of the soldiers yelling, "You have a gun, just shoot me!" One of his daughters, who is about my age, becomes hysterical. Fearing for his life, she screams at her father to stop provoking them. She begins running toward him sobbing, so I grab and hold her, and try to calm her. But I am scared and unsure myself. For the first time in my life an IDF rifle is pointed at me. I am there with the Palestinians being shot at.

That afternoon in Ni'lin the "us" were the Palestinians and Jewish Israeli activists, and the "them" were the IDF soldiers. That afternoon the IDF soldiers were not protecting me against violent Palestinians. They were shooting at us and demanding that farmers not harvest their own land.

Things started turning upside-down for me. I had to re-examine my reality as I knew it, because it was fraught with contradictions. If we were the peace-seeking people, why did we build settlements in the West Bank and take over Palestinian land? If we were only after terrorists, why did we jail non-violent protestors in Ni'lin and shoot at their demonstrations? If we were the ultimate victim, why were the Palestinians the ones behind the high walls?

I soon began going places and doing things I never imagined I would. Acts that were illegal, dangerous and unthinkable began feeling natural. At the same time, what had always been true, what had always felt like home, began to feel absurd.

I decided not to enlist.

I joined a group of ten other Jewish Israeli high school seniors who planned to go to the induction base to refuse military service, knowing we would be sentenced to military prison for civil disobedience. We wrote a letter that we sent to the Minister of Defence, the Chief of Staff, and the Prime Minister. We circulated the letter widely in the Israeli media and abroad and gave interviews about our collective decision not to serve the Occupation of Palestine. We called our action the *Shministim* Letter as *shministim* is the Hebrew word for students in their last year of high school.

14th of January 2009, 7:30 AM.

My draft day. As we pull into the parking lot outside the white metal gates of the induction base, my heart pounds and my stomach turns. I look out and see proud and teary-eyed parents escorting their sons and daughters to the gate; sending off their children into the great unknown of the base, as did generations of parents before them and as many more would do after them.

My mobile phone vibrates in my pocket. It is a text message from Ayelet: "I think you're making a big mistake, we should talk about this."

My friends from the *Shministim* group, media and other activists with banners, drums and megaphones have already gathered, and we begin to march towards the main gate shouting and carrying signs, "We refuse to serve the Occupation!" Stunned parents and their children stop and stare. And then, in a moment, a wave of anger washes over them, and they encircle us yelling, "Traitors!" "You don't deserve to live here, you are putting us all in danger!" Political arguments break out, and shouting erupts all around us.

Amidst the chaos I look around at all the young men and women my age, all staring at me either in anger or bewilderment. And suddenly I feel guilty. I know how long they have all waited for this important rite of passage, and I am ruining it for them with my protest. I stand there and for a moment I feel deeply proud and terribly ashamed at the same time.

"You are doing the right thing," I whisper to myself as I walk forward, and show the guard my ID card and draft papers. With one final glance at the commotion behind me, I enter the induction base, heading for prison.

Military Prison 400, Tzriffin Base. 2 February 2009. Twenty-second day in Prison.

I feel that I have been reduced to my most basic, biological self here. I think of food, showers, sleep. The only topics I seem to think about are things like how often should I wash my undershirts? How many hours did I sleep in the last twenty-four? How many hours separate this meal from the next? These little calculations and useless ponderings somehow make me pass the time. This place seems to lead even the most cheerful people into a state of gloomy, energy-less despair. I find it hard not to get sucked into it myself.

And suddenly I understand how the Occupation works. The good people that I know join an army that keeps them at a basic level of existence. They in turn keep the Palestinians at a basic level of existence. And instead of living, everyone is struggling to survive.

November 2010

Muhammad looks intently out of the window as we drive down the familiar streets of Jaffa. It's Friday afternoon traffic. Everyone is agitated and restless in the car seats. We take a slight right off the main road that starts at the old clock tower, past all the upscale restaurants that now neighbour designer chain stores. We go on past the many juice sellers with their oranges, carrots and pomegranates on display, past the Middle Eastern sweet shops and the Christian schools, shutters closed for the weekend. We head west on a road that follows the cliffs bordering the Mediterranean. Charming villas stand in orderly rows, their earthy colours suggesting the Middle East.

Muhammad pulls over. "Here it is", he announces. He looks back at me triumphantly.

"You see, when you know where it is it takes five minutes to find. Didn't I tell you?"

I smile at him as I step into a breeze that reminds me of late summer, not the end of November. The building has been repainted. But the shape is still the same, he explains. I circle the cream-colored, modest one storey house. The sign on the door discloses its current identity, a synagogue. I feel a pang that only intensifies as I realise where I am. I look below me at the waves of the sparkling blue sea rolling noisily onto the rocks below. The horizon is a single golden line where the radiant blue of the sea and the warm yellow of the sky meet. It is stunning. Probably among the most expensive real estate in the country.

"Come", he urges me back into the car. We are driving to his modest house in East Jerusalem where he was settled as a refugee of the 1948 war, after being evicted from this house in Jaffa.

On the way back, I look out of the window at the fields on the side of the highway and think aloud "This country was built on the pain of the Palestinians." Muhammad laughs, a strange half smile emerging beneath his white moustache.

"This, everyone knows", he says.

"I didn't" I almost whisper.

To me my grandparents were heroes, the foundation of my proud heritage. Did they too displace Palestinian families from their homes? They had always been the reason I had felt so proud to be Israeli. They were the reason I felt I had belonged here in the first place. They had built all this for me. They came and dried up the swamps, planted fields and built houses in their place. Suddenly I felt betrayed by them, confused by the gaps in their stories and wondering where all this left me.

But I do belong here

I belong here because I was brought up here, and because Hebrew is the first sound I heard. As a child, I played both under the Eucalyptus that my grandfather planted and under the olive tree that a Palestinian farmer once harvested.

As a young woman, I came to understand that many of the roots that nurtured me were using someone else's water, and that I have grown strong, tall and proud at their expense.

Today I stand opposite the majority of Jewish Israeli society and am called a traitor. At times it is hard not to believe that I am. But then I know that there are times in which we must ask ourselves honestly what is right by humanity, not by the people closest or most similar to us. It is up to me to struggle to disrupt the power structures and artificial divisions that have maintained the Occupation. Through my struggle I will sow the seeds of equality, in the shade of which we might all one day sit together in peace.

United Kingdom

Leaving Israel

Avigail Abarbanel

One day in November 2000, my husband Ian burst into the house and asked me to come outside quickly to listen to something on the car radio. It was an ABC[65] Radio programme featuring an interview with Avi Shlaim about his then newly published book, *The Iron Wall*. I don't remember anything Avi Shlaim said, but I remember feeling troubled, writing down the title of his book and resolving to order it, while at the same time wondering if I was going to regret it.

I usually attribute my "conversion" from Zionism to anti-occupation, pro-Palestinian and ultimately to anti-Zionism, to reading *The Iron Wall*. I now think that the book was a catalyst rather than the cause of my shift. There have been a series of almost insignificant experiences in my early life that I believe are responsible for my present position. Avi Shlaim's book provided a context for these experiences and helped me make sense of them. It also provided vital "missing pieces" to fill in the gaps in my perception of the history of Israel and its relationship with the Palestinian people.

But the most important thing that the book did for me is plunge me into a painful and uncomfortable process of soul-searching and a review of my identity, my values and my belief system. I often say that it caused my brain to turn upside-down and inside-out because that is exactly what it felt like.

Two months earlier, in September 2000, Ariel Sharon marched to Haram Al-Sharif, the Temple Mount in Jerusalem, under heavy guard. This was the catalyst both for the Second Intifada and for my decision

---

[65] Australian Broadcasting Corporation, the Australian equivalent of the BBC.

to renounce my Israeli citizenship. When I watched the images on the TV screen, I saw the arrogant pushiness, the entitlement and the callousness that I have always associated with that man. I felt sick with rage. I felt that what he did was disrespectful, unnecessary and clearly deliberate.

I was furious with Sharon but it wasn't because I was politically enlightened, or because I understood anything much about what was going on in Israel-Palestine. I just hated the man in a personal kind of way, without much insight behind the feeling[66].

It wasn't until March 2001, after I had read a few chapters of *The Iron Wall* that my rage translated into action, and I decided to contact the Israeli Consulate in Sydney and apply to renounce my citizenship. It felt like a huge step and I was not sure of myself. But I could no longer justify to myself being a member of a "club" whose history, values and behaviour I was beginning to question.

Some time later my mother cut off all contact with me, and I eventually found out that it was specifically *because* I renounced my citizenship. Only then I began to understand that my parents were in fact Zionists, and that I grew up in a Zionist home. Prior to that, it never occurred to me to think about us as Zionists. We were just Israelis, and we took that identity for granted.

It appeared that my mother's loyalty to her country, her 'tribe', was stronger than her loyalty to me. This was a big eye-opener. It made me think of Tevye, the milkman in *Fiddler on the Roof*, who had to pretend that his daughter Chava was dead because she married a non-Jew. He was required by religious law to perform the mourning ritual of *Shiva* and never ever speak to his daughter again.

Tevye was a fictional character but he obeyed a very real religious Jewish law intended to deter members of the group from converting or 'marrying out'. By expelling the 'offender' from the tribe — the biggest punishment you can inflict in tribal societies — you both warn others from doing the same and avoid 'contaminating' the purity of the group. It is a similar rule to the Catholic excommunication, expunging those who do not conform. Although my mother's decision had nothing to do

---

[66] I should really be grateful to Sharon because he played a central part in my decision to leave Israel in 1991 and move to Australia. Back then I believed that he would one day become Israel's Prime Minister. The thought of living in a country under his rule filled me with indescribable dread.

with religion, I could see how an old religious edict can still resonate in the reality of a secular society. This is probably because religion is a product of natural human tribalism and not the other way around.

I grew up in "downtown Israel"— downtown not only in terms of the physical conditions, but also the culture and the atmosphere. I was born in 1964 in the industrial south of Tel Aviv and spent the first four years of my life in a grey and dry urban desert. After my brother was born in late 1968, my parents moved to Bat Yam, a satellite town of Tel Aviv, just South of Jaffa on the Mediterranean coast.

Our flat was new and slightly more modern and spacious than the previous one. But it was not a good place to grow up. Our small family was one of sixteen occupying a noisy, square, featureless block, in a noisy street. People yelled, tooted their car horns all day and all night, played loud music, shouted over the verandas, spat and littered — and we did it too. This was an environment governed by survival, low levels of education and low aspirations.

My family was troubled, as were many of the working-class families around us. There was violence and abuse in my family, which I can't blame entirely on the trauma my Holocaust survivor grandparents had inflicted on my mother. My father's parents were spared the Holocaust. They came from the Middle East but from deprived backgrounds with poverty, homelessness, alcoholism and violence, and these do tend to get passed on through the generations. If it wasn't for my excellent schooling and for the caring way in which my teachers treated me, I don't know where I would be today.

The experiences that led to my "conversion" were not remarkable in any way. They mostly involved me feeling or sensing something I couldn't quite define and wondering quietly in my head. I had no one to talk to, to ask about or make sense of these experiences, and I kept them to myself.

One of those was during primary school. For several years as I walked to and from school, I would pass by building sites where more apartment blocks like ours were being built. The labourers who built them were all "Arabs". I knew they were Arab from the derogatory comments that I would frequently hear about them. I was told that they hated us and that they did *avoda aravit*, meaning "Arab labour", a common phrase meaning poor quality workmanship.

I didn't know who these "Arabs" were but I knew that they weren't like "us" and that they were somehow dangerous. They wore shabby clothes covered with dust and lime, woollen beanies (skullcaps), and worn, dusty dress shoes that didn't look right for the work they were doing. I remember a few times when I dared to look up at the scaffolding and my eyes would briefly meet the eyes of one of the men. I saw something in those eyes that bothered me, something like anger mixed with insult[67].

Occasionally one or two of the men would smile at me as I walked past. I never smiled back because I knew that I wasn't supposed to. So, I would just lower my eyes and hurry along in horror. Many years later I began to wonder what these men felt when I did that, how hurtful it must have been that even a little girl couldn't acknowledge them as human beings. I wondered whether they had children my age back home and what their real occupations might have been.

When I was about thirteen, there was a recruitment drive at our school. A friendly, cheerful man came to our class to invite us to a meeting; something to do with volunteering for our country. I couldn't quite get what it was all about. When I tried to ask, I was told that I should just come to the meeting and all would be made clear.

At the meeting I found out that the recruitment was for HAGA,[68] that there was something new called 'Young HAGA', and that they wanted young people to volunteer. I still couldn't understand what it was about exactly, but I was also flattered and excited that they wanted us. I don't remember much more except that one evening I had to go on my first "patrol" in a van with some other children my age and three armed men. Being around armed men wasn't unusual. We always had two armed male parents or teachers accompany us on school excursions, and I was also used to seeing armed soldiers in the street or on the bus on their way to and from their bases. Not only did it not feel disturbing, it made me feel safe. That evening, I felt like I was part of something important made all the more exciting by the mystery surrounding it.

---

[67] Many years later I read a description of the exact same experience in "A Room on the Roof", a short story by Savyon Liebrecht in her book *Apples from the Desert*

[68] A Hebrew acronym that stands for *Hagana Ezrachit*, or Civil Defence. I don't know if it still exists, but back then HAGA was responsible for keeping order on the home front in wartime.

When the van stopped, I was disappointed to discover that we were not far from where I lived, at a building site much like those in my own street. Then someone opened the van door. All I remember was seeing a man, an Arab labourer, covered with lime and wearing the typical knitted beanie. He was sleeping. One of the men from the van woke him up with a kick and yelled something. The man seemed confused and disoriented and then the van door closed and we weren't allowed to see anymore.

I don't know what happened to this poor man, but afterwards someone finally explained that the purpose of our patrol was to look for Arab labourers who stayed in building sites overnight. They were considered a security risk and weren't allowed to stay there. I don't know what I thought, but I remember feeling let down and disturbed and that it was wrong somehow. I never went back and I never spoke to anyone about it. I also felt like a quitter, like I was not brave enough and that I should have continued in this "volunteering". The face of that labourer, the way his body was curled up on the ground, surrounded by building materials haunts me to this day.

Much later in life I learned that these labourers came from the Gaza strip, about fifty miles away. They'd have to stand at the Gaza border crossing before dawn every morning, hoping that Israeli contractors in search of cheap labour would pick them for that day's work. It was like a slave market. These men did hard physical labour for less than the minimum wage, and with none of the conditions afforded to Jewish workers. These were not proper jobs, and work was not guaranteed from one day to the next. When they stayed in the building sites overnight, these men slept in appalling makeshift conditions with no proper shelter or sanitation. But they had to provide for their families in Gaza, and this was the only way to guarantee another day's work. It is not unusual for settler-colonisers to exploit the indigenous people whom they pushed to destitution and economic desperation.

When I was in seventh grade, we were one day told that we were going to start studying Arabic. Two male teachers from Tayibe, in the Triangle [69] area came to teach us. I'm guessing that it was an experimental programme by the Department of Education. The teachers were what we called "Arab-Israelis". The word "Palestinians"

---

[69] The "Triangle" is about twenty-five miles north-east of Tel Aviv, near the Green Line. It has a concentration of Palestinian-Israeli towns and villages.

didn't exist in my world then. They were qualified teachers employed by the Education Department as were my Jewish teachers except they were Palestinian citizens of Israel.

I loved my Arabic lessons and did well in my studies, but the atmosphere in class during those lessons was different to the usual. It was tense, almost explosive. I thought I noticed the same disturbing look in the teachers' eyes that I saw in the eyes of the Arab labourers. My friends and I talked about these teachers behind their backs. The fact that they were "Arab" caused a big stir. I liked them both but I knew that I wasn't supposed to and ended up colluding with my friends although it felt uncomfortable. These teachers were Israeli citizens but, in our world, they were alien.

I felt like crying when one day we were told that they wouldn't be coming back to teach us anymore. We later found out that some of the parents complained because they didn't want their children to be taught by "Arabs" and they didn't see why we needed to learn Arabic at all. I remember not understating why and feeling that it was unfair.

Throughout my childhood, my father and his workmates — all bus drivers and members of the Egged cooperative, Israel's largest public transport company — would sometimes organise a bus to take the families on Saturday excursions around the country. These excursions often took us through Arab towns and cities, and we would sometimes stop to buy sweets in the local sweet shop. My absolute favourite were the noodle cakes filled with pistachios. Back then you couldn't get them anywhere else, and they were an extra special treat to my sweet tooth.

Somehow, I knew that it was dangerous to be in those places, and that we mustn't linger, which made the trip across the road to the sweet shop even more exciting. There were always arguments between the adults about whether we should stop at all. The adults seemed tense, and there was a clear sense of relief when the bus moved on.

I didn't understand what these places were, why they were so different from our cities, who these people were, and why their children were wearing funny clothes. I remember the smoky smell in the air, which was so alien to me. It felt as if we were in a completely different country with no similarity to our own, although we were within Israel and not particularly far from Tel Aviv. When I tried to ask questions to understand what these places were and who were these people, I was dismissed and told, "They are just Arabs." I felt a peculiar sense of loss every time we left. I wanted to stay longer, find out more, but it wasn't possible. There was a palpable silence around all of these issues, the kind of silence children always notice.

My mother was born at the end of the War in Europe and grew up in Yaffa. When I was quite young, she once told me that when she was a teenager she briefly went out with an Arab boy. She said that "he didn't look Arab" because he was blonde, and that he was "not like other Arabs" because he was "nice and polite"...

One day she brought him home, but when my grandfather, the Holocaust survivor, realised that the boy was Arab, he yelled at him never to show his face there again, and threw him out of the house, a house stolen from a Palestinian family only a few short years earlier.

This story always made me feel sad. I didn't understand what was wrong with the boy being an Arab, and my grandfather's behaviour seemed horrible and unfair. But my mother seemed to think that her father was right, and that she should have known better than to go out with an Arab. Only many years later when I started to learn the truth about the establishment of Israel and about the *Nakba* I suddenly registered that my grandparents lived in a house that used to belong to a Palestinian family.

Although I was quite small I still remember that house. When the Palestinians were driven out of Yaffa (and many other places), their houses and property were handed over to newly arrived European Jews. That's how my grandparents came to live there with their children in 1948 when they arrived in Israel from a British detention centre in Cyprus. The painful irony was suddenly so clear. As my own family ended their refugee status, a Palestinian family just started theirs. I wonder what that boy must have felt being kicked out of a house that probably belonged to neighbours, relatives or friends of his family.

My grandmother Rivka, my father's mother, was from a Jewish Greek family, and grew up in Palestine. Her family did not go through the holocaust. They were already settled in Tel Aviv prior to the Second World War. My grandmother was an abused child. She was illiterate and was rejected by her family.

When she divorced my alcoholic and violent grandfather, whom she was forced to marry, she already had a three-year old child, my father. Her divorce brought 'shame' on the family and she was not allowed back. She was reduced to homelessness and to wondering the streets of

Tel Aviv trying to earn a meagre living to feed my father. The British mandate of Palestine did not include social services for the indigenous people, nor any help for destitute and abused women and children.

My grandmother told me that she had many Arab friends who took her in when she had nowhere else to go, and that they taught her to speak Arabic. She taught me a few Arabic proverbs like *Bukra fil mishmish*, "Tomorrow when the apricots bloom", similar to "When pigs fly". When I complained about something bad that happened to me, she would say in Arabic, *Yum assal yum bassal*, "One day honey and one day onion", meaning sometimes things are good and sometimes bad. I loved my grandmother and felt safe with her.

She always told me her stories in secret because my parents didn't want her to talk to me about these things. My family and everyone else around me saw Arab culture, language and people as inferior and primitive, and my grandmother seemed to be a source of shame to my parents as well.

She always spoke about her Arab friends with love and respect. I sensed that she was sad and distressed about something bad that had happened to them, but I didn't know what it was. I didn't understand where her friends went, and why she couldn't see them anymore. I don't remember if I asked, and even if I did, I don't know what she would have told me. I believe that she had sown a seed in me. These seeds germinated later in life and helped me to begin to see Palestinians as human beings like me, feel empathy for their suffering and outrage about the fact that it was my people who caused it.

One day during my military service in the early 1980s, I caught the bus to Haifa from the centre of Tel Aviv to meet up with my boyfriend. Shortly after I took my seat on the bus, three armed Military Police soldiers came on and marched straight to the back. I was curious so I turned my head and saw an elderly Arab man in traditional dress, sitting in the middle of the back row with a shopping bag in his lap. The soldiers demanded his ID and he gave it to them submissively, eyes cast down.

I felt a pang of pain and sympathy for the man. He was clearly harmless and was being singled out for no other reason except that he "looked Arab". No one else on the bus was asked for their ID. I wanted to offer him some sympathy, a kind look, something, and I glanced in his direction again. At that moment it hit me that I was wearing the same uniform as those soldiers who picked on him. I knew then that no matter how nice or kind I tried to be, to him I was "one of them". The uniform was getting between us. I felt ashamed, trapped and powerless, and I wished I could disappear.

There are more stories I can tell. Many of them involve people close to me making racist comments about Arabs in my presence, sometimes to people's faces sometimes behind their backs. I remember the smugness and sense of superiority and entitlement on the part of my fellow Israeli Jews, and the humiliation and hurt they caused on the other. I rarely spoke up. It was as if I was just observing in a kind of a mute dream state, taking it all in.

This might be a good place to mention that I did not become aware of the word 'Palestinians' until I went to University at age twenty-five and attended classes run by Professor Yoseph Hodara. He was an excellent lecturer who was considered subversive and controversial. He subsequently had to leave the University and Israel because of his political views. To this day Israeli Jews still talk about 'Arabs' and not 'Palestinians'.

None of the experiences I recalled are remarkable and it doesn't seem like much to go by, but they did something to me. The picture I am trying to paint is of a life in a deeply racist country where the Palestinian people are worse than invisible. They are the inferior "other", the one we had full control over, the ones who depended on us for a meagre existence, the "primitive", those we had permission and were even encouraged to hate. I felt something about it, a sense of wrongness that comes out of simple human empathy, but it was vague, uninformed and mostly unconscious. I was supposed to be faithful to 'my people' and this loyalty kept me silent.

Despite my vague discomfort I was a Zionist without knowing it. I knew what Israel wanted me to know, and I thought it was all true. I believed what I learned in school and it never occurred to me to question anything, especially not that we had a right to have our own country and the right to defend ourselves.

At the same time, I sensed that there were holes in the story that were never explained. At school we were taught Zionist history separately to general history. Even when we learned general history the focus was mostly on how events have affected us, Jews. I have always felt that there was an intensity and an insistence about the way Zionism was taught, that I instinctively disliked.

Like everyone else I needed to believe that we were good. I couldn't imagine in my wildest dreams that we did anything wrong. We were a people who have always been persecuted by others. Surely that made us innocent, didn't it?

We learned about the Holocaust repeatedly at school. I was acutely aware that I was the same as those who were murdered by the Nazis; that if I were alive during the War the Nazis would have captured and killed me too. This is part of what made the history of my people feel so personal.

The question of whether another Holocaust was possible was repeatedly raised and debated throughout my education. I now realise that it wasn't about finding a definitive answer to the question, but rather a tool intended to keep the possibility alive in our young minds. I was taught that everyone in the world, including Arabs, hated us *just because we were Jews*. There was nothing we could do about it, except guard our country, that we had earned with blood, sweat and tears, and that was the only safe place for us.

By the time I was in my twenties, my abusive and traumatic upbringing started to catch up with me. Life became very hard and I was barely coping with my daily life and my job. I was deeply depressed, even suicidal, and plagued with chronic anxiety and a host of other symptoms. I had no energy to spare for my country's troubles or for its complicated politics. It all seemed like an unbearable burden when all I craved was peace and quiet and some relief from my suffering. But there was no peace inside me and no peace around me. Israel was a pressure cooker with widespread anxiety, and an ever-present sense of urgency and emergency.

I resented the Arab countries around us and our "enemy from within"—or the "fifth column" as the Palestinian citizens of Israel were sometimes called—that I thought wanted to "throw us into the sea". I resented the world that didn't seem to understand us and was against us all the time, for what I thought was no reason except our Jewishness. I didn't understand why "they" couldn't just leave us in peace. I thought the reason for our suffering, anxiety and insecurity was *out there*. Together with everyone else I felt hard done by, hassled and unsafe.

Years later when I read the *Iron Wall*, my whole world turned upside-down. Everything I thought I knew about Israel's history, its relationship with the Palestinians and with the world turned out to have been based on half-truths or outright lies.

The feelings I had are hard to describe. I desperately wanted to accuse Shlaim of being some kind of a lunatic, someone with an "agenda", and for everything he said to not be true. But everything he claimed in the book was backed with documented evidence, most of it from Israel's own official state archives.

I was overwhelmed, devastated. I felt intensely angry, betrayed and used. I also thought I was stupid because my feelings seemed out of proportion. The feelings I had were comparable to the feelings of a woman who was married to a man for many years, only to discover that the entire time they were married, he was having an affair with another woman. Can you imagine the sense of betrayal?

I wondered if there was anything in what I was taught that was at all true. I realised that I was exploited in the service of deceit and propaganda when, as a naïve and eager-to-please child and teenager I sang nationalist songs or recited lies in our many school ceremonies. The country I thought was good was in fact criminal and its birth was in sin.

But it was the intensity of my feelings that I noticed more than anything. I knew that there was something peculiar about them, that they weren't "normal". I haven't met anyone who felt feelings like these about Australia, or any other country for that matter. How can a person feel the same depth and intensity of emotion about a country that they do in personal relationships?

It gradually dawned on me that there was something special about my relationship with Israel. I realised that I was brought up to think of Israel not merely as a country, an organisation of people. I was brought up to see Israel as a living breathing entity that was inseparable from me, and with whom I was required to have a deep, intimate and symbiotic relationship. I was supposed to give myself to my country, and in return it would protect me and keep me safe from all those who wanted to kill me — from the next Holocaust…

In the late 1990s in Sydney Australia I was studying for my degree in psychotherapy and was introduced to the work of Murray Bowen on the "differentiation of self". To differentiate from our family of origin means to learn to stand in the world as a person in our own right with our unique values and beliefs.

To be well-differentiated it is necessary to develop a sense of self that is separate from the collective identity of our primary group. My course required us to apply Bowen's theory to ourselves and work consciously to increase our level of differentiation. In our second year we had to document our effort in a written thesis. My teachers rightly believed that it was necessary for psychotherapists to be committed to an ongoing process of differentiation. They believe that therapists have no business sitting in front of clients unless they are committed to their own ongoing process of development and differentiation.

A few years later it became obvious to me that differentiating from my family of origin wasn't enough and that I needed to differentiate also from the country and the society I grew up in[70]. It wasn't just my family of origin that shaped my identity. I realised that my enmeshed relationship with Israel had affected my identity much more than I had originally realised. I had to find out who *I* was and find a way to leave Israel not just in body but also in soul.

I didn't want to live in fear any more. I didn't want to be forced to believe that everyone hated me and that this was my lot in life. I didn't want to believe in lies, and I especially wanted to make it right with the Palestinians. I felt guilty and personally responsible for their suffering. I grew up benefiting from their slave labour, and from everything we took from them. I know there are degrees of culpability and that I never harmed a Palestinian personally. But by living in Israel, serving in the army and being a loyal and patriotic citizen, I harmed generations of Palestinians and actively helped Israel's settler-colonial machinery.

It's hard to describe the turmoil that all of this caused me. I felt like a traitor to my people and I felt deeply guilty. I also became aware that I harboured a deep, mostly unconscious, fear of antisemitism although I have never encountered an antisemite in person. I feared that by being an activist, by writing and speaking publicly, I was "giving ammunition to the antisemites", as someone once accused me of doing.

I was frightened that it was true that as a Jew I didn't have a right to see myself as an equal member of the human race. These feelings were

---

[70] I wrote about this journey in my paper "Differentiating from Israel", which was published in 2003 in the *Australian & New Zealand Journal of Family Therapy*. The paper is available at: http://www.avigailabarbanel.me.uk/diff_from_israel.html.

reinforced by hate mail, death threats, accusations like the one above, curses (someone once wrote to me to tell me they put a curse on me), phone calls in the middle of the night with voices whispering, "You are Hitler", and labels like "Nazi", "self-hater" and "traitor".

I was afraid, but it was a case of "feeling the fear and doing it anyway", as the title of a famous self-help book. I could neither betray myself nor the Palestinian people who have been betrayed and violated long enough. Fear or not, I had to live with myself and be true to my values. More than anything, I couldn't now pretend that I didn't know what I knew.

Back then I believed that it was my destiny to always feel this turmoil, that I would never be free from it. I resigned myself to it thinking that it was a small price to pay compared with the hell the Palestinians were living. I didn't understand back then that I was on a journey, and that the stronger I became within myself the more peaceful I would feel. I no longer need an identity other than my own, and I experience myself more and more as a member of the human race rather than of a particular tribal group.

※

I sometimes think I am the laziest activist on the planet. Most of my work so far has consisted of writing, maintaining a website, signing petitions and public speaking. I am conscious that I have never been on a flotilla, never helped Palestinians harvest olives, never demonstrated near the separation wall, never stood in front of a bulldozer, never accompanied Palestinian children on their way to school to protect them from attacks by fanatical settlers, and never stood alongside Palestinian families while their homes were being demolished.

I am filled with admiration for my fellow activists who are involved in these, and many other creative and courageous ways to make a point and to offer support to the occupied and oppressed. I may still have a way to go as an activist, but emotionally I am at peace with my support for a single state in Palestine with equal rights to all its citizens, support for a full right of return for the Palestinian refugees and with my anti-Zionist position.

Perhaps it's selfish of me, but I want to make sure that when the terrible saga in Israel-Palestine is finally over, and when Israel and its society are called to account for their crimes against the Palestinians, I will be on record as someone who didn't keep quiet.

Journey Out of Zionism

Susan Nathan

I know for sure that the journey into Zionism was a very marked experience in my childhood that remains distinct to this day. Equally, the journey out of it was memorable and traumatic.

A very British childhood spent in boarding schools, where I was often the only Jew amongst several hundred children, helped to mark me out as somehow "not belonging"—included on one level but excluded on another.

I now recognise that this feeling was inculcated into me by my father. He came from a poor Jewish family that fled the pogroms in Lithuania and Latvia to settle in South Africa. If I ever asked my father about his childhood he would endlessly recite the lasting trauma of having parents who never quite fitted in, who never had enough money, and who could never speak the new language fluently.

My first taste of antisemitism in Britain was when I applied for and passed the required exams to a well-known girls public boarding school. The headmistress wrote to my father to say that although I had obtained the required academic level, she would not be able to give me a place as the "Jewish quota" was full. In an effort to appease me, my parents tried to join a country club in north London where I would be able to swim, only to be told again that "Jews were not allowed".

All of this of course helped to solidify in my mind the concept that Israel existed so that should we Jews find ourselves in further difficulties in Europe, then we could always move to Israel. This belief followed me through most of my adult life. The wars came and went in the Middle

East, but the predominant theme in all of them was Israel's victory over those "primitive, marauding" Arabs that threatened our very existence.

On reflection, I find it shocking that we never questioned the media reports. I never wondered about the "other side", the death or destruction of their families or way of life. It just didn't enter my head. So entrenched was I in my Zionist viewpoint—celebrating Israel's Independence Day with the local Jewish community, observing all the high holidays and more minor festivals—that Palestine or Palestinians were a total non-issue in my home and psyche.

Even in 1982, when Israel invaded Lebanon and the horrors of Sabra and Shatila took place, we as a family somehow justified these massacres. It was acceptable for anything or anyone that was a threat to us, to be eliminated.

My father, a well-known surgeon, was renowned for his humanity and decency. He was a person who was never intimidated by governments or institutions, and who exhibited exemplary behaviour towards all his patients, and towards other human beings in general. He was never unable to cross over barriers of class, colour or ethnicity. There is no doubt that his passion was social justice, and yet I realise now that this did not extend to Palestinians or Arabs in general.

It is this point about my upbringing, centred around the importance of Jewish ethics and what it meant to be a Jew in this world, that I now understand as a key point on my journey. It later became a point of conflict for me in relation to Israel, my relationship to it and to the Palestinian issue.

Our home was avidly involved in everything to do with Israel. The Hebrew University in Jerusalem greatly benefited from my parents' generosity. They made regular donations to help support Israeli scholars and their families to visit London. My father would hear no criticism of Israel. I can remember him cancelling our subscription to *The Guardian* newspaper, which he considered to be "definitely on the way to antisemitism".

All of this now reveals itself to me as some sort of bizarre puzzle of the mind. Why do I say this? Because in 1960 my parents took a lengthy holiday in Israel from which they returned with a distinct mindset. Their take on Israel changed from being one of great hope to one of doom and gloom.

I say doom and gloom because I can never forget my father's miserable predictions for Israel. The visit seemed to have troubled him deeply. As a South African he knew only too well the problems of Apartheid and the reasoning behind it. The Israeli visit showed him another kind of Apartheid, against Jews from Arab countries, the "Arab Jews" (*Mizrachi* Jews) who were being discriminated against and marginalised by the dominant Ashkenazi[71] elite. He returned feeling horrified that Israel could adopt this policy. He had toured extensively in the south of Israel and had witnessed the transit camps for Jews from counties like Yemen, Libya, Tunisia, Iraq and Morocco. He predicted then that they were to become the "black slaves" of the "white" Ashkenazi Jews.

Yet despite all of his misgivings, I cannot remember my father speaking openly about his new point of view on Israel. It was as if to do so publicly, and he was a highly respected public figure, was to be a traitor to a country that essentially was there to protect us. For me this was to be the root cause of a serious identity crisis once I reached Israel.

I made the decision to live in Israel when I was around eleven years old and was feeling particularly on the outside of my school community. The desire to move there never left me. When later in life I finally found the opportunity to make *aliyah*, I left for Israel with a sigh of relief and a feeling that it was right for me.

My arrival in Israel fulfilled me as a secular Jew. I no longer had to make excuses for my name, my religious holidays and my desire to rest from Friday afternoon to Sunday morning. There was a sense of peace within me. Few Jews acknowledge that there is a sense of power that comes from knowing that you are in the majority for a change, and that the country is designed for you and your needs as a Jew.

My difficulties with my identity began with the Second Intifada that started in September 2000, during which, in April 2002, the Israeli army invaded the west bank and perpetrated a massacre in the Jenin refugee camp. My nationality was not "Israeli" as you would expect, because such a nationality does not exist in Israel. My nationality was now "Jewish". It began to dawn on me that the policies of extreme brutality against the Palestinians were taking place in my name as a *Jew*, and allegedly for my own good. How could I be a Jew who believed in

---

[71] Ashkenazi Jews are Jews from European background. (AA)

a certain ethical code of behaviour towards mankind, at the same time that I was using my religion as my nationality?

This proved to be the separation point for me. I had to decide if I was inside or outside the camp. It was a time of intense deliberation, which I kept entirely private. Having understood and seen by this time the immense amount of discrimination against the Palestinian citizens living within Israel, having witnessed the brutality of the Occupation, the wall, the settlements and of course the barbarity of Israel's treatment of Gaza, the decision I had to make became very clear and logical to me.

How could a Jew with a South African background, who had witnessed the evil, cruelty and deprivation of Apartheid allow herself to live in Israel with closed eyes and ears? The comparison was overwhelming. The deeper moral issue was identical. It was the issue of inalienable human rights. This troubled me enough that I decided to move to Tamra, a Palestinian town in the lower Galilee. There I found myself to be the only Jew amongst 30,000 Muslims.

This move to Tamra proved to be one of the best moves in my life. I learnt intensively about the "other", and in so doing, freed myself from government and Western propaganda. Never had Edward Said's book *Orientalism* rung so true. It sprang to life in front of my eyes. It is impossible for me to impress upon the world the sense of emotional, spiritual and physical liberation that I experienced, freeing myself from political propaganda, and seeing the harsh reality through un-blinkered eyes. That is true people power, and we can all have it.

Once I had published my book *The Other Side of Israel*, my London Jewish friends, ardent supporters of Israel right or wrong, all dropped. However, they were all ferociously English and found themselves faced with serious loyalty and identity problems once Israeli politics began to threaten their values.

I can never forget that first meeting with Dr As'ad Ghanem, a Palestinian academic and community leader, in which the subject of *aliyah* came up. I found it hard to be honest with him and hard to be honest with myself. It was a confusion that began the collapse of my world and life values, the collapse of everything I had believed in with regard to Israel and the Zionist project. From that moment on, every stone had another history underneath it and it wasn't mine.

I read everything I possibly could about 1948. One of the very best accounts of this period is offered in a PhD thesis by Efrat Ben Ze'ev from the Hebrew university in Jerusalem. For her thesis she interviewed the former inhabitants of the Palestinian village of Ein Hod. Ein Hod is now a fashionable Jewish artists' village, where the true history is eradicated or ignored. The precious mosque is now a restaurant flaunting a naked woman on the awning. The shocking thing about this thesis is the way in which the former villagers relate the story of the surrounding land. Their minutely observant detailed accounts of the tree growths, the fruits and vines and the herding of sheep take one back to an idyllic life that has been shattered forever. It has been planted over by the Jewish National Fund with its relentless "Plant a Tree for Israel" programme.

When one reads an accurate account of the area and its vegetation one can begin to take in the enormity of the falsehood that is Israel today. It is to behold a country that is geographically engineered to help with the forming of the Jewish ethnocracy. This artificial planting and the obfuscation of all Palestinian life in former Palestine, is something that to this day is the source of great sadness to me. I carry it like a sword in my back.

Many Palestinians who have heard me speak have said that I have entered into their lives so completely that they could not express their pain any better. It is a great honour to be accepted into the world of the "other", to experience life through the eyes of the "enemy". This experience has liberated me from government propaganda against the Arab world, not only in Israel and Palestine but within the wider context of the Islamic world. I have become a traveller. I am free, and I have insights that have enriched my life tremendously.

Knowing the truth about the founding of Israel has taken me on a voyage to hell and back. I have experienced moments in which I thought I would never recover my equilibrium. I have seen my health nosedive, yet out of all this I have found a new way of being and relating to our fellow humans that I have never experienced before.

The painful question that remains constantly in my mind is this: Why is it that we Jews have learnt nothing from the Holocaust other than how to continue perpetrating what has been done unto us? Have we learnt no mercy, no compassion for our fellow humans? Is it to be our legacy that we know only repression, murder, occupation, home demolitions, child imprisonment, settlements, checkpoints, closures, siege, night time raids and terrified traumatised children? Is it not enough that we come from terrified and traumatised families ourselves? Do we have to make this our legacy to the world? If the answer is "Yes", then we have political Zionism and its fanatical followers to blame for the monstrous creation we have made.

Out of the Frame: The Journey Out of Zionism

Ilan Pappé

I was born in Haifa on Mount Carmel in 1954 to a German Jewish family. My parents immigrated to Palestine in the early 1930s, my mother from Hamburg, and my father from *Lignetz* (now *Ligneza* in Poland). My mother's family was a typical Orthodox Eastern European family that resided for a year in a small Jewish township before moving to the north of Germany. Out of eight sisters, only three survived the Holocaust by immigrating to Palestine. My father was a scion of a well-off German Jewish family with a long history of wealth and political clout. This family too was obliterated by the Nazis. It is this history, more than anything else, that disallowed me to be silent and complacent about the events in Palestine in the past, and in Israel in the present.

After a relatively "normal" Israeli Jewish childhood on Mount Carmel, life became somewhat more realistic when I joined the Israeli army at the age of eighteen. Normal in this respect meant a life sheltered from meeting anyone who was not like me, namely Palestinians or Mizrachi Jews. I did encounter the latter group eventually in the army. Significant meetings with Palestinians however, only happened after I went to university. My army service was eventful. It included the 1973 war, during most of which I was stationed on the Golan Heights. I had little actual fighting experience compared to others, but I had enough to turn me forever into a pacifist of a kind. Politically, I still had a long journey ahead of me.

As many Israeli Jews do, I went to university straight after the army. In those days, the faculty of the Humanities at the Hebrew University in Jerusalem was in Giv'at Ram, on the Western side of the city. It was quite a pleasant place to study, compared with the monstrous labyrinth built later on Mount Scopus, where this faculty is now located. I read the history of the modern Middle East as my major subject, and International Relations as my minor. I chose Middle Eastern studies as a major field of interest because already in high school I was attracted to Arabic and the history of the region surrounding Israel.

The army encouraged Arabic studies. Occasionally, intelligence officers would visit my school trying to ensure that we would opt to serve in their units once we graduated. I was probably one of the few, if not the only one, who *because* of serving in intelligence was pushed in precisely the opposite direction to the one planned for me by the authorities. My close, intimate relationship with the Arabic language, culture and history, kicked off a journey outside of Zionism, rather than a career in the community of Israeli security or civilian experts on Arab affairs.

Very early on at university I was drawn to political activity. I was recruited by members of *Mapam*, the Left Zionist party, at that time in alliance with the Labour party. I served both as an advisor on Arab affairs to their Knesset delegates, and as a national coordinator of their student cells.

The first doubts sprouted not so much due to the political activity that was within the Zionist frame of mind, and irrespective of the fact that it allowed me to develop more intimate relationships with Palestinian students. It was the experience of being a student in Middle Eastern studies—and a very involved and industrious one—that bred the first profound questions about the Palestinian story, and about the influence of Zionism on the way Middle Eastern studies were taught at the university. It was a narrative that portrayed Israel as an island of enlightenment and progress in a sea of barbarism and backwardness. But I would have to leave the country for a while to be able to articulate these views more clearly and forcefully.

I left because I wanted to pursue my postgraduate studies abroad. After weighing several options, I decided to study at Oxford University. As often happens in life, I was entrusted by chance into the hands of two supervisors who would have a profound influence on my career later on. I had what I termed elsewhere a "dream team": the late Professor Albert Hourani, and Professor Roger Owen, may he live long. Hourani brought the wisdom of someone who was part of the history I intended to write about, and Owen the updated scholarly methodology and approach that helped revisiting and contextualising that history in our time.

No less mundane was the decision to choose the events of 1948 as a topic for my doctoral studies. As a typical student in modern history, I was looking for a topic for which there could be new, and previously unseen, documentation. The secrecy laws both in Israel and the UK meant that the 1948 documents became available when I commenced my studies in Oxford. I understood the significance of 1948 as a pivotal year in the history of the country but was not as yet aware of how significant such research would be for my own life.

From then on, I think there was a clear trend in both my professional and public life. The documents I found in the archives told a story of which I was previously not aware. More importantly, it exposed the Israeli historiography to which I belonged, as having been developed by a fraudulent group of experts. In time I would come to treat this historiography as a straightforward fraud.

After immersing myself in more philosophical and theoretical literature, enhanced by a close friendship with the late Edward Said, I recognised the powerful way in which nationalism and settler colonialism have affected the professional historiography of the Zionist movement, and later the state of Israel. But on a very personal, almost emotional level, I had a sense of betrayal. Wondering how I could have been misled in such a brutal manner about my own history, is the best description of this experience. The gap between what I knew— remember I was a history student with a particular focus on my homeland's history, as well as that of the region around it—and what I found, was so wide, that it did eventually produce deep mistrust on my part in the Zionist ideology and the state it created.

The research I conducted was part of what became known as the "new history" in Israel: written by a group of professional historians who debunked Israel's foundational mythology. The most important point in this mythology was the claim that the Palestinians left Palestine in 1948 voluntarily. We have proven that the Zionist leadership ethnically cleansed Palestine, and by that we have reaffirmed important chapters in the Palestinian narrative.

For me it was more than just a historical revelation. It became a journey outside of Zionism and it was caused as much by the reality around me as by the historical findings of the past. The defining moment for me, I think, was the 1982 Israeli invasion of Lebanon. I was then a postgraduate student in Oxford and was called, as many other Israeli students in the UK, to help defend Israel's policy publicly. For me it was not only difficult to justify a war of choice of the kind the Israeli government conducted. It also shed light on the history of the state since 1948. The war was mainly an assault against the PLO, and it closed a long history of Israeli attempts to take over as much of Palestine as possible and leaving in it as few Palestinians as possible.

I came back to Israel in 1984, still uncertain of how to translate a burning desire to "do something" for the cause of peace and reconciliation, without losing my place in my own Jewish society. In 1992, I came to the conclusion that it was impossible to work towards these goals from within the Zionist mindset or political structures. I have tried that for several years but to no avail. As I mentioned earlier, I was part of Mapam. Then when I came back from Oxford, I joined for a short while the Left wing of the Labor party, through a think tank called *Mashov* (Hebrew for feedback), headed by Yossi Beilin. In a way I took part in the preliminary negotiations leading to the Oslo Accord. But even before the signing of this accord, I felt that unless Israel is de-Zionised there is no chance for peace.

As a first step in this direction, I joined Hadash, the Democratic Front for Peace and Equality, with the communist party as it main component (although I did not join the party itself). It was a non-Zionist, Arab-Jewish, party and there for a while I found my ideological home. Increasingly, without any other reference group, I have also found my social home and comfort zone there. My membership of Hadash helped to remove any remaining barriers between me and my Palestinian friends and milieu.

My contacts in, and visits to, the Occupied Territories intensified as well. The more I went there, often with my own car, the more I became convinced that there was no difference between Haifa and Jenin. Historically they were part of the same country. Ethnically and culturally they were populated and surrounded by the same groups. The same colonial and apartheid policy affected life all over what used to be Palestine in a similar way: allowing the Jews to live as a *herrenvolk* (German for master race) democracy, and the Palestinians in Bantustans. The solution became clear in my mind, as it did in the eyes of many at that time: a democratic state for all.

In the second half of the 1990s, I also began a series of meetings with refugee communities around the world. It already started in 1993 when I was invited by the PLO to Tunisia and continued in other encounters in the Arab world and beyond. It coincided with my involvement with the internal refugee problem inside Israel. These were Palestinians who were kicked out of their homes in 1948 but were allowed to stay within the Jewish state. By the 1990s they were more than a quarter of a million, experiencing probably the worst trauma of a refugee: seeing your house, neighbourhood, field or village looted and then taken by someone else. In addition to the idea of a single state, these contacts with the various refugee and exilic Palestinian communities brought home also the issue of the refugees' Right of Return. I became convinced that without it there was very little chance for peace and reconciliation in Israel and Palestine.

Support for one state and a commitment to the right of return were taboos in Israel and were positions that even the Communist Party found hard to accept. Although I was still a member of Hadash, I invested my activism in The Emil Touma Institute for Palestinian Studies in Haifa. With the team there, and in cooperation with other NGOs and parties, I organised the first ever Right of Return Conference in Israel. We have also tried to disseminate knowledge about the *Nakba* in Israel and protect its memory. Parallel to this, I continued to research these topics as a professional historian and attempted to teach them as official modules and courses at the University of Haifa. But what was possible to do as an activist in the realm of civil society, proved impossible within the context of narrow-minded and zealot Israeli academia.

My own ideas became clearer, as did those of the Israeli government, society and for that matter mainstream academia, in the aftermath of the Second Intifada, which started in 2000. Society, and academia with it, moved to the right. In the case of academia, it meant abandoning a relatively open decade of self-criticism and discussion that I termed elsewhere post-Zionism.

Now that I look at it in hindsight, the clash between me and the local academic system was inevitable. I have intensified my participation in public activity, condemning Israel's brutal policies in the Occupied Territories. I have also defined my research and teaching more clearly, in a way that in the eyes of the authorities was deemed an act of treason.

Public support for the Palestinian resistance, the teaching of courses such as "The 1948 *Nakba*", and publishing articles on Israel as a rogue state were quite enough for the university of Haifa. In 2002 its management began a process aimed at expelling me from the campus. It took several years, but in the end, I gave in and decided to leave as the persecution was unbearable. The details are in my 2010 book, *Out of the Frame: The Struggle for Academic Freedom in Israel*.

I left Israeli academia in 2007, and in a way also the state of Israel, although not the country that I call Palestine. I moved to Britain and was appointed as a professor in the University of Exeter, where I still am today. In Britain I continue to be active academically and publicly on behalf of Palestine, and peace and reconciliation. Together with Dr. Ghada Karmi I have founded the European Centre for Palestine Studies, and devote my time to writing and public appearances.

Two basic ideas have informed my activities during the past decade. The first is a belief that there is little chance for change from within Israeli society. This is why I supported Palestinian civil society's call for cultural boycott on Israel, as a means of pressuring the Jewish state to stop the Occupation, dispossession and discrimination in Israel and Palestine. The second was a far more focussed and clear commitment to the one-state solution, as the only possible way forward towards a better future.

The first issue, of boycott and sanctions, seemed urgent to me as I still believe that the operation in 1948 which I coined "the ethnic cleansing of Palestine" continues today, and has to be stopped to avert another catastrophe. The second is an issue that demands just as much learning and education, as it does political activity. The venue for finally working on a joint state is there, in Israel and Palestine, but the preparations can begin outside the country. I was fortunate in recent years to be part of a group of Israeli and Palestinian activists, from inside and outside the country, who meet regularly to try and disseminate the importance of building a joint state in Israel and Palestine.

I do feel that more educational work on this should take place on the ground, and I hope one day to return to Israel and push forward this project. In the meantime, I teach wonderful students in England and enjoy a sympathetic and friendly academic environment without forgetting for a moment the people who suffer on the ground and who deserve a much better life.

The Birth of the Israeli State Was my Birthday: Re-living the Past Through a Child's Eye

Ruth Tenne

It was a cold and windy evening. I was only a child, unaware of the date and time. Yet I sensed that it was a special day. The members of our kibbutz, Usha, assembled on the green lawn in front of the ramshackle dining hall, in which the adults had their meals while we children ate in our white stone house. Some heavy and rough wooden benches were placed on the green lawn where we celebrated the summer festivals of the kibbutz. But this was not a summer day, it was a cloudy wintry evening, which came alight by a dangling chain of electric bulbs, tied up to metal poles put up especially for the day.

I was shivering under my worn-out jumper that had been handed down to me by one of the older children of the kibbutz. Looking intently at the glistening raindrops on the rough grass I was wondering why Menasha, the gardener of the kibbutz, did not cut the grass as he always does before a special celebration day. The small light bulbs started flickering in the wind, but no one seemed to worry about it. I was afraid that one of those bulbs would land on my head, which became quite damp without my old woollen hat that I had left behind in the children's house (*beit yeladim*).

I saw the other children in my group standing at different corners of the uncut lawn, quietly staring at an old radio, which had been taken out of the adults' dining hall and was placed on a big chair in the middle of the lawn. It looked as if the old chair was brought in a hurry from one of the wooden shacks (*tzrifim*), in which the young members of the kibbutz were living. I was quite proud that my parents, who were among the founders of the kibbutz, had just moved to a one room mini "flat" in a newly-built white-washed house they shared with three other families.

The new house was built on a steep space, and had a small room at the base, that was used as the general office (*mazkirut*) of our kibbutz. It was stuffed with chunky files piled up on tall rickety shelves, and two big tables with a black telephone in the centre. My father used to go there early in the morning stepping carefully on the stony and uneven stairs that led from my parents' small room to the gloomy office below. I was told by the adult members of the kibbutz that my father holds an important task as the secretary of the kibbutz (*mazkir*), who also looked after the book-keeping records of the whole kibbutz. He was sitting there peering over pages full of figures all day long, taking only a short break for breakfast and lunch. Sometimes when I wanted to see him after school, I went to his *mazkirut* office muttering "Shalom" in a hurry and running back to the children's house without waiting for him to tell me, for the hundredth time, that he was too busy to talk to me.

Tonight, my father gave all his attention to the crackling radio, watching it intently through his silver-rimmed glasses, which made him look like a teacher. He did not take much notice of me, but I was used to that. He was always wrapped up with all the nonsense of the kibbutz and the endless problems of the adult members. I hated going with him anywhere in the kibbutz, because all the time the grownups used to come up to him, bothering him with their silly stories and asking his advice on things I did not much understand. But today no one seemed to bother him with their never-ending problems. They were all watching Aaron, the electrician, bashing the back of the clapped-out radio repeatedly, trying to get some sound out of it, while fiddling with the knobs that move its big red hand from station to station.

Suddenly froze listening to a foreign voice that came out of the coughing radio. Was it English? I could not tell, but I noted that a leading loud voice was announcing some names of places, or countries. I did not know. That was immediately followed by one word that sounded like "ye", or sometimes like "no". In-between, faint voices came out with some other word that I could not understand, but I noticed it was longer than "Yes", or "No". I was quite upset as no one told me what it was all about, but I noticed that there were more "ye"(s) than "no"(s), and that the adults were quite excited when the "ye" was sounded. They were even more thrilled when the "ye" came out of some strange voices, which seemed to be more important than the others for a reason I could not make out.

Suddenly, the whole crowd burst into songs and shouts of excitement. They all linked hands together and started to dance the *Hora* in a circle. The bigger children joined the circle like we used to do on any big celebration day. We all sang the song that we learned at school and knew by heart. It had only one line: "The Nation of Israel is alive" (*Am Israel chai*). It must have been something really special as my mother gripped my hands with great excitement, and then pushed my father into the circle of the *Hora*. My father, who suffered from a very bad heart condition since he was a child, never danced in any of the kibbutz festivals. He used to stand in the corner and watch us dancing in the adults' dining room to the sound of Moshe's accordion. I noticed that my father struggled to get out of the Hora circle but fat Berrel, who worked in the kibbutz cowshed, pulled him right back. It looked as if all the rules were broken tonight, since everyone in the kibbutz knew that the special condition of my father does not allow him to get too excited, and his heart could not stand any special strain.

When I was very small my mother told me that my father suffers from very bad health, and that he was warned by doctors before he left Poland that he would not survive more than a year in the hot weather of Israel. But tonight, fifteen years later, he looked younger and happier than ever, wiping his blurry eye with his big cotton handkerchief, and making an effort not to let his tears drip all over his face. I never saw my father shed tears before and I sensed that something really special happened tonight that made all the adults in the kibbutz forget themselves and behave like children. Even Dov, our strict teacher, seemed to lose his senses, shouting, "We now got our own country", and waving his hands in the air like we children did when we won a game.

I managed to sneak out of the Hora circle, and quite slowly came closer to my father. I had to ask him what it is all about. Why, all of a sudden, at the end of the day, the members of the kibbutz started celebrating and going a bit wild. Were we given a new festival that I had never heard about before? My father looked at me through his misty glasses but could not say anything that made sense. "We got the right to our country. We will have a new state (*medina*) soon, which will be called the State of Israel," he said with excitement. But this did not mean anything to me. "And where do we live now?" I asked him. "Now we live in a kibbutz that is ours but on a land that is not ours," he replied. "So, when are we going to have this State of Israel?" I asked. "It may take a while, Ruthie, there are hard times ahead but we are prepared for it," he said in a faint and shaky voice.

I did not know what my father meant by "hard times". Is he afraid of the English soldiers who came from time to time to our kibbutz, driving their green jeeps and looking for something unknown? We children called the English soldiers anemones (*kalaniot*) because of the red berets they always wore. We were terrified that one day they would start searching the whole kibbutz, looking for weapons hidden deep in the ground. We did not know if there were any guns or other weapons somewhere in the kibbutz, but we saw quite a lot of young people who were not members of our kibbutz walking around with rifles and shooting at targets that were located near the fenced borders of the kibbutz. We were told that they are members of the *Palmach*[72] unit and they are there to protect us, although when the English soldiers came to our kibbutz, they were nowhere to be seen.

Perhaps my father did not mean the English soldiers when he spoke of hard times. Maybe he meant the Arabs. There were two Arab villages near our kibbutz, Husha and Kasayier. Husha was the Arabic name for our kibbutz Usha. We were told at school that our kibbutz was built on the ruins of a Talmudic Jewish town by the same name and therefore we have the right to this land, although the Arabs insist that the land is theirs.

On clear days we could see the Arab villagers (*fallahim*) working in the field with their donkeys and mules, which were pulling behind them some ancient wooden ploughs. They did not have tractors and combine harvesters like ours. Even on a very hot day the women wore long black robes and were covered from head to toe, while the men were wrapped with red and white long headscarf called *keffiyeh*. The hillsides of the Arab villages were dotted with green patches of terraced orchards of almond, olive, and plum trees. Sometimes on Sabbath, or at the end of

---

[72] A Hebrew acronym for *Plugot Machatz* or Strike Forces. The *Palmach* was the fighting force of the *Haganah*, the underground army of the Jewish community in Palestine during the British Mandate. (AA)

the day, just before the sun sank behind the hills, we would sneak out to collect ripe fruit that fell off the trees of those orchards. On other days the children of my class went out to a forest near our neighbouring kibbutz, Ramat Yohanan, from which most of the children in my class came. We loved to go to the forest and collect mushrooms, which were buried underneath the pine trees. On one occasion that I can never forget, two Arab women gushed out of a dense patch of pine trees. The younger one suddenly grabbed me and started kissing my face, mumbling words in Arabic that I did not understand. I stood there shocked and frozen, unable to get a sound out of my mouth. My teacher, who spoke Arabic, rushed to comfort me right away, telling the class that the Arab woman who clutched me to her belly is pregnant and wanted her baby to have my blue-green eyes and curly fair hair. From then on, I was mocked by the other children of my class, especially by the boys, who were telling everyone that I had been kissed by an Arab woman who wished to adopt me.

The hard times seemed to arrive sooner than I expected. Trudging through the muddy ground on my way to school, I noticed that Dan and Meyer, who worked in the field, had started digging trenches around the barbed-wire fence surrounding our kibbutz. The holes in the fence were mended in places where they were broken by the kibbutz's horses and mules, which used to bolt out of their stables, trying to escape into the night. Big sacks of sand arrived from nowhere and were placed next to the stone wall in front of our children's house. The big shelters, to which we were carried out trembling when the German aeroplanes started to bomb the bay of Haifa in the Second World War, were re-opened and cleaned out again.

Some parts of the new trenches were dug deeper and wider. They were filled up with sacks of sand, which were piled up high with some gaps between them for rifles. We were told that those are observation posts from which the adults would guard the kibbutz day and night. I noticed that all the observation posts were facing the hillside, behind which the Arab villages were situated. Some of the adults started to carry guns to the observation posts, and the older children even helped digging the trenches next to our children's house. "Are we going to have a big war with the Arabs now?" I asked my mother, who was also the nurse of our children's house. But she did not take much notice of me and continued to rush around without replying to my questions. The older children, who were reading the newspapers, knew everything. They started whispering about some battles with the Arabs that went on in Haifa, quite near to our kibbutz, and included many soldiers of the *Haganah*. All the adults in the kibbutz seemed very concerned. I noticed that my father's face became more and more worried, and he lost all the happiness he showed on the day we were given our state by the vote of so many foreign countries.

The young men and women of the *Palmach* disappeared sometimes for a few days, returning back at night with rifles and guns dangling off their shoulders. They no longer had time to sit with us around an open fire (*medura*) on Friday evening, singing the songs of the *Palmach*, while drinking hot black coffee from a brass kettle with a long spout (the *finjan*), and playing the accordion or the harmonica. We continued to go to school in the morning, but when we came back from school we had to stay in the children's house and were forbidden from going anywhere. I hated it as I could not go out any more and pick the lovely cyclamen and anemones that sprouted every winter out of the dark cracks in the rocks that surrounded our children's house. I noticed that some of the cyclamen bulbs had been sliced up by the careless trench diggers, and budding flowers were left covered with muddy soil. The deep violet anemones and the scented pink cyclamen were buried deep in the mud, and the rocky hill was left bare, crisscrossed only by ditches and heaps of heavy brown soil that was dug out of the narrow trenches.

The sunny days of the month of *Nisan* (or April, as the adults used to call it) started to chase away the dark clouds of winter, when suddenly we were told to stay at home. A big battle with the Arab legionnaires broke out around Kibbutz Mishmar Ha'Emek, not far from our kibbutz. I became very frightened, worrying that the battle would reach our kibbutz soon, and the adults would not be able to rescue us from the swooping Arab soldiers. And then, a few days later, the fight began. We woke up early to the sound of gunfire. My mother and the other nurse (*metapelt*) urged us to go down to the dining room on the ground floor, which was protected by sand bags that perched on its surrounding stone wall. The noise of the guns was quite faint as if it came from far away, but we saw the adults running to their observation posts with rifles and with a few bigger machine guns. My mother seemed to be a bit confused, hurrying from one room to another and making sure that none of the children stayed in the upper floor of our house, which had no proper protection. Yet we were not very frightened by the gun sound as we were told that the trained soldiers of the *Palmach* have been fighting fiercely against the Arab enemy, and special armed units of the Carmeli Battalion of the *Haganah* are expected to join the battle very soon. The Carmeli Battalion was named after my beloved Carmel mountain, which was the first thing I saw in the morning through the windows of my bedroom.

Then, one day, we had a real fright. My classmate, Amnon, was sitting in the toilet cubicle on the ground floor when a bullet buzzed in and got stuck in the wall just above his head. Amnon run out of the cubicle quivering and holding his head as if it was scratched by the bullet. We all rushed in to see the bullet sticking out of the white wall, which was hardly damaged, leaving only some plaster flakes on the floor. My mother hurried along warning us not to touch the bullet, which looked as if it was still live. Some of the younger children became very frightened, but we were told that the stray bullet was fired by an Arab sniper who escaped the main battle that took place behind the Southern hills. The fight with the Arab legionnaires continued for four days and was not so easy. We heard rumours that some of the members of the neighbouring kibbutz, Ramat Yohanan, were wounded and killed by the continuous barrage of fire and that Eric, the mechanic of our kibbutz, was seriously injured from a single bullet that went through his spine. At night we slept on mattresses that were spread on the ground floor. I listened with great anxiety to the sound of the guns that was interrupted by some heavy blasts.

Then after four days, just before the Sabbath, the gunfire fell silent. It was a heavy silence that made us fear that something dreadful was about to happen. We did not know whether the fight was won by our soldiers, or if they were all lying dead now, slaughtered by the Arab enemy. The menacing silence did not last long. Suddenly it was fiercely broken by heavy bombardments that came one after the other. We all rushed to the floor fearing that we were going to be shelled by the victorious Arab army, but then, once again, a complete silence fell and the gunfire died down for a long while. Soon after, we saw some members of the kibbutz coming out of the observation posts, carrying their guns with relieved smiles all over their faces. They spoke to my mother, muttering some words that I did not catch. When they left, we were told in a solemn and proud voice that the fight was over and that our soldiers crushed the Arab fighters, driving out all the Arabs from the neighbouring villages of Husha and Kasayier. The loud bombardments we had feared so much put an end to these villages that according to the adults, helped the Arab legionnaires who wanted to wipe out our kibbutz and take over our land. We did not know what happened to the people who lived in these villages, and to the Arab fighters who were defeated and chased away. Later we were told that they were not really Arabs but Druze, who had joined the Arab Legion and fought savagely against our brave soldiers.

A few days later we returned to school. We were happy to go outdoors as usual, but we were not allowed to go beyond the hills where the *Haganah* guarded the destroyed villages, making sure that no Arab native would ever dare come back. I did not care about those villages, or about the fate of their Arab inhabitants. I was happy that they were gone and that the fight was over. My classmates from Ramat Yohanan had many stories to tell about the real battle that took place not far from their kibbutz. They boastfully showed us the empty cartridges and shrapnel that they had picked up from the ground. I did not have any of those but was very proud of my father who made a special speech at the funeral of our dead soldiers. The speech brought tears to the eyes of some of the people, but I could not make sense of most of the words, although they were delivered with great force (or pathos as the adults called it). Benny, the kibbutz photographer, took a picture of my father while he was standing straight and tall in front of the big crowd that listened to him with great respect. The picture was kept in our family album and I used to look at it from time to time and show it to my close friends with great pride. The fight of our soldiers was not yet over. In the following days many battles broke out around Haifa, not far from our kibbutz. But then I knew that our soldiers will defeat the Arabs who never wished us to have our new state.

Just few days before my birthday, on the fifth day of the month of *Eyar*[73] the birthday of the state of Israel was announced. All the members of the kibbutz assembled together in the dining room to listen to *Kol Israel*, the Voice of Israel, which was the first Hebrew radio station. The deep and croaky voice of David Ben Gurion, our new

---

[73] *Eyar* is the eighth month in the Jewish calendar. (AA)

Prime Minister, came out of the kibbutz's radio, announcing the birth of the State of Israel. A new blue and white flag was hurriedly raised on the roof of the dining hall and we all gathered around it to sing with great enthusiasm our new national anthem, "We never lost our hope, the hope of 2000 years to be a free nation in our own land of Israel and Jerusalem." I was full of joy. My parents made me a promise that from now on my birthday would be celebrated each year with the birthday of the state. I was ten and the state was just born, but I felt as if I have a new sister who belongs to me and I to her forever and ever.

Confronting the Past

This was my childhood world, dreamy and full of both imagined and real fears that were expressed in simple thoughts and contrasts such as black and white, good and bad, small and big. These contrasting terms helped me to face the unknown world by relating them to the facts, concepts and conventions I was taught to accept unquestioningly throughout my childhood and youth. I no longer speak and think in these terms. I broke out of the confined circles of family, state and faith. They may be convenient frames, but at the same time they foster a strong loyalty that makes their members blind to the fate of others. It took me many years to become aware of the plight of the Palestinians, and the responsibility my own people carry for their fate.

I witnessed the dark realities of dispossession with my own eyes when a few months after the creation of the State of Israel my class visited the razed villages of Husha and Kasayier. We saw the ruins and the desolation of the lively villages that one day disappeared from the face of the earth. No one was there apart from some barking stray dogs and wild cats. The razed houses were stripped of their contents and their dwellers. A few stone walls were still standing, facing bare yards covered with a heavy blanket of prickly grey thistles, shrivelled vegetable beds, and withered cactus shrubs. The almond and fruit trees had all gone. The farming fields of the ruined villages were expropriated by the newly-born Israeli state and leased later to our kibbutz and to the neighbouring municipality that built on them a mass of grey concrete estates for new Jewish immigrants.

The nascent Israeli state seemed to rise proudly out of the remnants of thriving Palestinian villages, whose past existence was obliterated and expunged out of our memories. Words could not remove the guilt but they could break the silence, reach the individual consciousness and etch, drip by drip, on the collective consciousness that has never forgotten the Holocaust but had shut its eyes, heart, and soul to the injustice of the Palestinian *Nakba*. How long could we continue to survive with our false consciousness if it ignores forever that of the Palestinian people?

> *Ruth Tenne was born and brought up in Israel by staunch Zionist parents who were among the founders of the socialist kibbutz movement. She served in the Israeli army during the 1956 Sinai War, and as a reservist in the 1967 Six Day War.*
>
> *Ruth confronted her ingrained Zionist heritage in the aftermath of that war, and became an active supporter of Jews for Justice for Palestinians and the Palestine Solidarity Campaign. She wrote a number of articles and book reviews concerning the Israel-Palestine conflict, that appeared in the press and on websites such as* Middle-East Online, Media Monitors Network *and* Palestine Chronicle.

United States

Shattering the Israel Barrier (A Tikkun Olam Mosaic)

Rae Abileah

Photo by Ben Harris, Jewish Telegraphic Agency

"I have come to rebuild what has been shattered. To rebuild love." — Thich Nhat Hahn

Snapshot One: A Verse for the Homeland

I was raised with an affinity for Israel as my homeland, and a deep love for my Israeli relatives in Jerusalem. Even in the small coastal town in northern California where I grew up, there was some occasional anti-Jewish teasing on the playground. Consequently, the idea of a Jewish state fortified by an army to protect the Jews from future annihilation felt comforting. And the concept, as it was explained to me, of "a land without a people for a people without a land", seemed to make sense.

On the wall of the synagogue classroom was a map of Israel surrounded by Lebanon, Syria, Jordan, and Egypt. To my memory, there was no mention of the West Bank, Palestine or even Palestinians in this classroom. I remember thinking that Arabs were free to go live wherever they wanted in the Middle East. Why did they need this little piece of land? And if they were suffering, why didn't their Arab brothers and sisters in other countries help them?

When I became *Bat Mitzvah* at age twelve, my Reform Jewish community began explicit instruction in Israeli history—a version of history that I have now come to understand as a wild and vivid myth. After being informed and educated by a couple of Holocaust survivors about our horrific genocide in Europe, we were presented with a gleaming portrait of the "land of milk and honey" that provided at last the perfect solution: freedom from persecution. *Eretz Yisrael* (the land of Israel) was a land full of trees planted by our *tzedakah* (charity) money; a land with burgeoning technology, where the *Shechina*, the holy spirit, seemed to whistle by on the wind and flow in through the breath, where bright discotheques blended with deeply mystical spirituality, where *bamba*[74] and hummus were the favourite snacks, all surrounded by some of the world's greatest seas—the Mediterranean to the west, the Red Sea to the south, the *Kinneret* (sea of Galilee) to the north-east, the Dead Sea to the east, and the snaking Jordan River sewing them together. Hearing all this, I deeply believed that Israel and its promised peace flowed through my veins as my own prized birthright.

When I first visited Israel in 1998 on a five-week trip with my Hebrew confirmation class, coordinated by the organisations of Hadassah and Young Judea, I fell in love with the land as soon as I stepped off the plane. I knelt on the tarmac and kissed the ground of what I immediately felt to be my homeland. That same year, the Bureau of Jewish Education hosted a peace poetry contest to commemorate the fiftieth anniversary of Israel. My poem about peace in the holy land was chosen as the winner and I was invited to read it at the *bimah*[75] of San Francisco's prestigious Temple Sherith Israel, where I was presented with the grand prize: a $500 State of Israel bond.

In 2001, I was in my first year of college at Barnard University in New York City when the Second Intifada broke out. Although I was barely aware of the Palestinian uprising, I was painfully aware of the polarisation on campus, where at flag-waving rallies students representing the two sides of the conflict, would shout at one another and get in each other's faces. At some of these demonstrations, I would sit down between the two factions with a group of friends and sing peace songs in English, Hebrew and Arabic, or simply sit in silent meditation, as a way of establishing and forging a middle ground.

That same fall 9/11 hit, and I watched as my country swiftly moved from victim to attacker as the US staged its brutal assault on Afghanistan, despite all our peace marches. When my country invaded Iraq, a country with no connection to the terrorist attacks, I began to dedicate much of my time to peace activism. As soon as I graduated, I

---

[74] A popular peanut-flavoured Israeli snack. (AA)
[75] A raised platform in the middle of a synagogue from which the Torah is read. (AA)

started working, first as a volunteer and then as a staff member, with CODEPINK Women for Peace, a women-initiated peace and justice organisation that was coordinating campaigns to end the US occupations of Iraq and Afghanistan.

Snapshot Two: Seeing What's in Front of You

By December 2008, I was living in San Francisco and still working as local groups coordinator for CODEPINK, when Israel bombed Gaza rendering its landscape a strip of rubble and blood. Many, like myself, who had been more or less silent about Israel's Occupation, could no longer turn away from this gross massacre and violation of human rights. In its twenty-two-day assault, Israel's Operation Cast Lead left in its wake over 1,400 Palestinians, including 300 children and hundreds of unarmed civilians, killed by Israeli forces, who also razed hospitals, schools and thousands of homes. The destruction was so intense, it could not have possibly been an act of "self-defence". The disproportionate brutality of the Israeli Defence Forces was exposed widely, as news channels around the world were flooded with footage of grieving mothers covered in the blood of their children, and grown men sobbing among the ruins of their destroyed homes and families.

Shortly after the assault, my grandmother, my Oma, passed away. The painful images from Gaza kept streaming in as I mourned with my family in Missouri and recalled my Oma's painful childhood growing up in hiding in the cellar of her parents' house in Nazi-occupied Holland. I had always been reluctant to compare the genocide of my people with the oppression in the Holy Land, but the images of death stung just the same.

From our office in San Francisco, I helped CODEPINK organise several delegations to Gaza via Egypt, in an attempt to break the crippling siege, to bear witness to the destruction of people's lives and property, to deliver humanitarian aid, and to bring back first-hand accounts of life in Gaza to the American public and to Members of Congress. The delegates on these trips delivered pink baskets of toiletries to women, built pink playgrounds, and danced and broke bread with women in Gaza. The disarming, creative, life-affirming tactics of CODEPINK once again captured my heart, showing me that taking positive action for peace in the Middle East could be done without the usual name-calling or finger-pointing.

In June 2009, I co-led CODEPINK's delegation to Israel in yet another attempt to break the siege of Gaza, this time at the Erez Crossing. My partner, who grew up Ultra-Orthodox and who had trained as an IDF soldier and ordained as a rabbi, joined me on this trip. During our first days in Israel we rotated between lavish breakfasts on the Tel Aviv beach and walking among the rubble of destroyed Palestinian villages in the Galilee—some of which were purposely hidden by trees planted by the Jewish National Fund, perhaps with my *tzedakah* money—from basking in the warmth of Jerusalem's Old City blushing in the light of sunrise, to standing beside Israel's cold towering separation wall. This juxtaposition ripped our hearts and eyes wide open. For three days our delegation stood at the Gaza border with our valid passports, pleading with the heads of security to let us in. Even one delegate, the famous Dr Patch Adams, and his team of clowns, must have seemed too threatening, and we weren't allowed in. In the end, we tied little notes with messages to the children of Gaza to the barbed wire fence, left peacefully and decided to escalate our actions.

Our hosts, the Israeli Coalition of Women for Peace, encouraged us to join the Palestinian nonviolent call to apply economic pressure on Israel to uphold human rights, known as the Boycott, Divestment and Sanctions (BDS) movement. We found a perfect target to boycott: a brand of women's beauty products called AHAVA, which means "love" in Hebrew. After visiting AHAVA Dead Sea Laboratories and seeing for myself that the factory was located in an illegal Israeli settlement on the coast of the Dead Sea, I joined our delegation in Tel Aviv to launch our international boycott of AHAVA products at the AHAVA flagship store. We walked into the store, stripped down to our bikinis and slathered AHAVA mineral mud on each other, proclaiming "There's no love in Occupation!" and sharing the "dirty secrets" behind the beauty products that are profiting from an illegal occupation! I could never have predicted that I, a feminist and a Jew, would be standing bikini-clad in this chic Tel Aviv store and shutting it down!

Bearing witness to the wanton destruction of Palestinian families and homes and seeing the wall between the West Bank and Israel up close, had changed me. I signed on to boycott illegally-made Israeli products because I had always supported human rights, and these companies were in violation of those rights. Having my muddy boobs all over the news was an unintended consequence of this support.

When we returned home to the US, we didn't stop bearing our bikinis for justice. *Sex and the City* star Kristin Davis dropped her contract with AHAVA, several lawsuits against AHAVA's fraudulent "Made in Israel" labelling were filed in Europe, and the campaign continues to build momentum. It turns out that my action was not such a slight to feminism after all. One of the core principles of feminism is to put your money where your principles are. Following these principles means looking critically at the Israel Bond prize I received as a teen, and giving back this bond, which I have come to see as a symbol of bondage to oppression.

Snapshot Three: Actually Going to Gaza

The morning of New Year's Eve, 31 December 2009. One year after the Israeli assault, I was finally in Gaza participating in the Gaza Freedom March. Nothing about the march had gone as planned. Most of the people in our 1400-person delegation from over forty countries were still in Cairo protesting and battling with the Egyptian police and government, who had denied all but one hundred of us access to Gaza. My best friend and I were among the hundred who were allowed in. As our bus made its way through the busy streets of Gaza City, we witnessed first-hand buildings that one year later were still bombed out. We saw demolished police stations, and marketplaces filled with items still dirty from the tunnels—the only lifeline supplying basic items barred by the Israeli siege of Gaza. We travelled from Gaza City to the Erez Crossing, the main gateway between Gaza and Israel. At the crossing we poured out of the bus and joined throngs of Palestinians already gathered there for a march to the border. Since very few Palestinians are allowed to cross into Israel, this march was to be a symbolic nonviolent act, showing the world what lifting the siege could look like. While we marched to the border from Gaza, activists in Israel were marching toward us from the other side in solidarity.

"Lift the siege of Gaza!" and "Free Palestine!", young men chanted as they slogged along the muddy road toward the border. Noticing me holding out a plastic bag filled with pink peace flags, a group of men crowded around to grab one. The prayer flags quickly dotted the march with soft pink hues and messages of peace collected from children, grandparents, mothers and daughters from all over America. Our pink flags contrasted sharply with the mostly male march, and the loud chants coming from the rear of a pickup truck equipped with mega speakers. I found a group of women towards the back, and told them that as we were marching, women and men in over 150 cities around the world were marching with us, all with the same unified message: "Lift the siege of Gaza!"

That night, after the march, our international delegation gathered with Palestinian youth for New Year's Eve. We lit candles and held a vigil for those who were killed the year before in the Israeli attack. Every Palestinian I spoke to knew someone whose life or home had been crushed. But it was not all mournful—we laughed and took many photos with the boys, promising to "friend" them on Facebook. We listened to Palestinians perform hip-hop and play the *oud*. We sang, danced, and rapped together well into the night.

Upon my return home, my co-workers, friends and parents all wanted to know, "So, how was Gaza?!" My sarcastic mind wanted to respond, "Oh, just a Mediterranean seaside paradise with Biblical beauty surrounded by steel walls and Uzi sub-machine guns." Instead I struggled to find a way to convey how the current circumstances in Gaza relate to people's lives here at home. With a bit of research, I discovered an astounding piece of information: US taxpayers supply Israel with three billion dollars annually in military aid, making it the largest recipient of military aid in the world. This American tax money was used to buy white phosphorus, and other weapons that killed family members of my new friends in Gaza. I began thinking about what we could do to change our own complicity in Israel's siege of Gaza and occupation of the West Bank.

Snapshot Four: Coming Out of the Closet

"*I was raised to love Israel... a dream come true, a miraculous salvation from the grief and terror of the Holocaust... But I was also raised to love justice, not tyranny—no matter who the tyrants profess to be. Without justice for the Palestinians, there can be no security or peace for Israelis. — Starhawk, Jewish-American author and activist*"

My activist work around Israel and Palestine soon started to become more visible. I was giving press interviews about the Gaza trip, and our boycott campaign against AHAVA. I quickly became labelled with names ranging from "self-hating Jew" to "delegitimiser" of Israel—the charge flung at anyone questioning Israeli policy or proposing boycott as a way of pressuring Israel to comply with international law. One reporter went so far as to call his conversation with me the "Most Disheartening Interview" of 2010, adding "We cannot keep losing our kids like this." I scoffed at the idea that Judaism was losing me. I felt I was acting on my faith and the Jewish principle of *tikkun olam*, repairing the world, more than ever before, and was deeply engaged with my local Jewish spiritual community.

When, in the spring of 2010, Israeli soldiers attacked a flotilla attempting to deliver aid to Gaza, killing nine of the boat's aid workers, I was compelled to send out a mass email to friends and family about the reality of the Occupation as I saw it. The blowback I received from this email led me to realise that in speaking out I was "coming out of the closet" in a whole new way. I had broken the "Israel barrier" and was now risking my place in parts of my Jewish community.

But in addition to feeling sad and afraid about what this "outing" would mean in terms of my community, I was also angry. I was fed-up with hearing human rights activists labelled as "anti-Israeli". In all the years I protested against the Iraq War, I never felt I was being "un-American". Yet when I said I wanted to see a new generation of Israeli Jews grow up without a mandatory draft—eighteen-year-olds obliged to defend checkpoints at gunpoint and commanded to kill innocent children with bulldozers—I was called "anti-Israeli". And when I said that I wanted Israel to be held to the same standards of International Law as the rest of the global community, I was also called "a delegitimiser". When I said I wanted freedom of travel for fellow human beings in Palestine, to see integrated schools and shared highways, freedom to eat, pray, and love where they want to, I didn't feel I was against Israel; I felt I was simply for human rights.

Snapshot Five: Young. Jewish. Proud.

"The settlements delegitimise Israel! The settlements betray Jewish values! I'm a twenty-eight-year-old Jewish woman!" I shouted as loud as I could. My words cut through the silence in the grand ballroom of a downtown New Orleans hotel where over 3,000 Jews were listening to Israeli Prime Minister Benjamin Netanyahu address the Jewish Federation's 2010 General Assembly. I was one of five young Jews affiliated with Jewish Voice for Peace, and part of the new youth movement Young Jewish Proud who, one after another over the space of ten minutes, interrupted Netanyahu's speech. We would not sit silent in the face of Israel's flagrant violations of international law, and so one by one we called out what really "delegitimises" Israel: the siege of Gaza, the brutal occupation of the West Bank, the growing settlements usurping more and more Palestinian land, and the silencing of dissent in Israel and Jewish communities around the world.

I was the final disruptor, and as such, subject to the most violent response. While one man in the audience put me in a chokehold and forced me to the ground, another attempted to shove a seat-cover emblazoned with the logo of Israeli airline El-Al down my throat. And while the immediate response in the room was far from friendly, the words we shouted in New Orleans quickly reverberated around the globe, and I received messages of support from rabbis, cantors, Naomi Klein's mum, young Palestinians, and Jewish friends with whom I hadn't yet been "out" on this issue. The overall response to our message was tremendously supportive. The fissure in the narrative about Israel keeps growing, splintering more and more people away from blindly supporting Israel's policies. I found that there were many people like me who considered it pro-Israel to want Israeli Jews and Palestinians to arrive at a just peace rooted in human rights.

Amidst the clamour of emails from both supporters and detractors, a few letters popped up from people who knew a man named Joseph Abileah, wanting to know if I was related to him. And the answer is "yes": Joseph was my great uncle. He was a violinist from Austria whose family moved to Haifa in 1926. He was an ordinary man who in 1948 did something extraordinary: he became one of the first conscientious objectors in the newly founded State of Israel. Joseph had a vision that one day all people—Jews, Muslims, Christians, Druze, and anyone living in the region—would be freed of a dehumanising occupation and granted the right to live with dignity and equality side by side. Yet despite over fifty years of tireless work for reconciliation and peace in the region, Joseph said metaphorically that he would never benefit from the shade of the trees he had planted. Peace in the Middle East still feels as far off now as it probably did then, but the movement towards justice is rapidly building momentum.

In May 2011 I was a co-organiser of "Move Over AIPAC[76]", a national effort involving over one hundred organisations converging in Washington DC to shine a spotlight on the dangerous actions of AIPAC and the Israel Lobby in the US. We organised creative protests and a counter-conference. During the conference Netanyahu met with President Obama, and also addressed Congress and AIPAC. During Bibi's speech to Congress, in which he received twenty-nine standing ovations and outright adulation from our elected officials, I rose from my seat in the Congressional gallery, unfurled a banner and said, "Stop Israeli War Crimes! Equal rights for Palestinians!" I was assaulted by members of the audience, hospitalised, and arrested for disruption of Congress. The outpouring of support from around the world has been tremendous and I feel this was my major "coming out" experience as a Jew on this issue. It doesn't get more public than inside Congress!

A generation after my great uncle Joseph, war and violence were still very prevalent issues in my family. As the offspring of World War II survivors, my parents struggled with their own entanglements in the cycle of fear and abuse. I survived a home in which dishware was routinely hurled across the kitchen and smashed into smithereens amidst episodes of my father's drunkenness. I've seen first-hand how fear can violate our faith and lead to the unconscionable, how families repeat the crimes perpetrated by their governments. And I've also seen how speaking out fearlessly can shatter this vicious cycle. I have come to apply the old adage, "Friends don't let friends drive drunk," to Israel, as I've watched America enabling Israel's Occupation with military aid and unquestioning support in the face of flagrant violations of International Law. As one commentator wrote, "It is time for Israel to sober up and face the reality that their aggressive militarism won't work anymore. Only America has the power to grab Israel's car keys."

My generation will not inherit and repeat the mistakes of our fathers. We are equipped with new tools to rise up non-violently, like our sisters and brothers did during the youth-led uprising in Egypt in January 2011, to create a new future. We've got the keys to the future of American Jewry, and we're not going to hand them over mindlessly to the Israeli government. Joseph's story is about collecting the broken

---

[76] AIPAC, the American Israel Public Affairs Committee is a leader of the Zionist lobby in the United States and a vocal advocate of the state of Israel. (AA)

pieces and forging a unity, through the harmony of a symphony, through living with principles. The challenge for us and my generation, after shattering the Israel barrier, will be to piece the shards together and create something new, sturdy, brave and whole.

As we wrote in our Young Jewish Proud declaration:

> *We commit to re-envisioning 'homeland,' to make room for justice. We will stand in the way of colonisation and displacement. We will teach this in the schools and in our homes. We will grieve the lies we've swallowed. We commit to equality, solidarity, and integrity. We will soothe the deepest tangles of our roots and stretch our strong arms to the sky. We demand daylight for our stories, for all stories. We seek breathing room and dignity for all people. We will become mentors, elders, and radical listeners for the next generation. It is our sacred obligation. We will not stop.*

1996

Jesse Bacon

Through high school, I still barely knew any Jews. I grew up in a town that had only a thousand people in total, and the Jews were my nuclear family, five counting me. I had not considered the number of Jews when I picked a college. In truth I had not considered much of anything beyond the fact that I had a friend who went there, and a kind of process of elimination of other alternatives.

Thus, when I arrived at Carleton College in the fall of 1995, I was utterly unprepared to be blown away by the presence of my coreligionists. But blown away I was. Within a month I had begun to attend their holiday events. *Our* holiday events, but ones I had never heard of. When you grow up as I did, fifty miles from the nearest synagogue, your parents tend to prioritise the big holidays. And the Jewish calendar has a lot of holidays right off the bat in the academic year.

On the third of these holidays, a *Succoth* campout, I met a Jewish woman I could date. I don't remember how we ascertained this, beyond making out. I later realised that Jewish women outnumber men greatly in the "organised" Jewish community, but I did not know then that I was a "catch". I did not know that I was also attracted to men. I did not know anything about Judaism. There was a lot I did not know.

Then came *Simchat Torah*, the raucous conclusion of the fall holiday season that celebrates the yearly completion of the reading of the Jewish Bible. We left our college town of Northfield and ventured up to the

University of Minnesota in Minneapolis for the celebration. The campus was a city unto itself; I got lost there every time in high school visits. To my cornfield-saturated vision, we seemed to be a mighty force of Jewry. This was confirmed for me when during the final *hakafa*[77] with the Torah scrolls, we ran out into the streets of Minneapolis. There we met a Christian evangelist yelling, "Jesus, Jesus is the answer." In my memory, we spun him around, over and over again, cartoon style or maybe body-surfed him along with us. A revolution indeed.

But the Torah ends and begins again, and soon it was time for Carleton's massive six-week winter break. It was apparently the tradition for students to enter a kind of "cryonic torpor", as Utah Phillips—a Leftist Jewish folk singer I was listening to a lot at the time—would say of the complacent. It was becoming clear that I was not interested in actually doing much with my New Jewish Girlfriend (NJG) in bed but we faithfully observed the custom of slumber. My parents were equally horrified at her religious Jewishness and her slumber. My father, at that point a twenty-three-year veteran of marriage, told me that I didn't need a piece of paper from the man to validate my relationships. I had never suggested to him that I was going to marry this lady, but he could tell that I was following a script, and he was anticipating the next scene. He also used his stock phrase, "burning daylight". He may have even invoked his German non-Jewish mother, of his blessed memory, who was apparently a stickler for early rising.

In true egalitarian style the NJG and I alternated our trips, visiting her parents for spring break. These parents, I later learned, scheduled their road trips by the hour and took turns eating the food they packed, while the other one used the bathroom. After our relationship ended, they showed up at my parents' store saying, "Just because our children are idiots, doesn't mean we can't be friends!" I imagine my parents saying to themselves, "Well, actually..."

I attended the family's synagogue, and I appreciated the general sense of Leftish intellectualism. I remember being struck by how much more vital its college town community seemed, compared with the rural Wisconsin congregation of my childhood, where we seemed an ageing,

---

[77] The *hakafot* (plural of *hakafa*) are a series of seven circuits or revolutions around the synagogue with the Torah scrolls. The scrolls, which are removed from the ark for this occasion, are carried around the sanctuary with the entire congregation dancing along and singing. The *hakafot* can sometimes overflow from the synagogue onto the streets around it. (AA)

infirm faith, embodied by one hard of hearing elder chanting at the top of his lungs in his own particular tuneless tune and rhythmless rhythm.

I stood for the Standing Prayer, the *amidah*. To this day, I have not really memorised many of the stands and sits of a Jewish service and am always a split second later than everyone else. Back then I could not read Hebrew at all, so I stood blankly. A rare moment of quiet for a chatty individual, and a still fresh moment of being around other Jews. God, who I must have believed in back then, spoke. S/he piped up with the mission statement of many a group seeking to save the lost American Jews, "Go to Israel." In light of my current oppositional politics, it might seem that I had gotten someone else's divine message, maybe someone who knew the prayers. Or maybe God, or Revelation, or my own subconscious knew exactly what they were doing, that this trip would lay the jagged foundation of my future activism. But at the time, it seemed as orderly as the next instalment of a magazine. My New Jewish Self had simply learned the next thing, the next lesson in who I was to be. Holidays, Girlfriend, Israel Trip, what would the next special issue hold?

Conveniently, my girlfriend was about to embark on her own Israel trip, and I asked if I might tag along. She said yes. Was it grudgingly? Or was it merely the same unenthusiasm we both brought to this entire affair?

My mother's lack of enthusiasm reached such levels that she took the unprecedented step of writing me a letter about her past, something she had never done before (or since). She told me of her own Israel trip in 1968, as a seventeen-year-old. She went there to find a more hopeful world than that of the United States, and instead found, "Jewish racism, Jewish sexism, all of it supposed to be OK because it was Jewish." "Go if you must," she wrote, "but don't be fooled." This was so unprecedented, that I had no schema for it. I tried to say something reassuring, but how do you promise not to be fooled? My father later told me that he reassured my mother, "This is Jesse. He's not going to become some black-hatted fundamentalist." (He probably thought I was too lazy!) But now I am thrilled at his confidence in my ability to resist indoctrination, keep my consistency, even as I have learned that not all fundamentalists wear black hats.

As for me, I had first encountered Palestinians in one of those Public Television specials that aired during the First Intifada, when I was eleven—"Israelis and Palestinians: Fighting for a place they both call home." I do not recall what my parents said when I asked them about it, but I remember the feeling: that I would be always sympathising with the latter group and identified with the first. However, I had not really built on this initial insight, and I was hoping this Israeli-Palestinian conflict would all be wrapped up by the time I got there. This had looked a lot more likely back when I started school in the fall. But two months later, Yitzhak Rabin, who was in charge of ensuring that I would never have to think about this issue again, was assassinated by another Jew. This was the most foreign development yet, but I had nothing to use to alter my outlook; nothing else, despite reading whatever Israel article was in the newspaper every day. Just as in synagogue, I was a blank. The newspaper was no more help than the prayer book, and my hope was an increasingly musty back issue.

The relationship with my girlfriend eventually reached its inevitable end. We couldn't even agree on when the breakup happened, let alone on our views on Israel. Leah (not her real biblical name) claims she ended it in May, just a month before we were supposed to embark on our voyage. But I date it to two earlier events.

In April, Rabin's successor Shimon Peres, a Nobel peace laureate like our current US President, launched a bombing campaign against Lebanon, as part of his larger election campaign. I could recognise my own blankness in response to these actions. But the bombing campaign had much more serious consequences than my own waffling. One of these campaign advertisements landed in a Lebanese refugee camp, exploding and killing hundreds of civilians. In one day, this killed more people than Hamas had managed in its lower-tech horror campaign of suicide bombs up until that point. The bus bombing campaign itself had begun in retaliation for a Jewish civilian mass murderer of Palestinians, whom my rabbi had condemned that *Purim*[78] back home in Wisconsin. The killer was a settler doctor who claimed to be inspired by the story of *Purim*, which I didn't realise until adulthood ends with a Jewish mass murder of the people who had plotted a genocide against them. Like many of us, I suspect, I missed the ending amidst all the rejoicing of survival and wacky costumes. So much to fill you in once you start looking.

---

[78] The Jewish festival of *Purim* is based on the Scroll of Esther in the Jewish Bible. During this festival children dress up in costumes. (AA)

I confronted my girlfriend about the Lebanese camp bombing. I am wordless, beseeching, maybe holding the one Israel article for that day with a picture of bombed rubble. She tells me, "Israel has to defend its borders." In that regurgitated talking point, I hear the echo of what I have become, an empty person who has handed over my religion, my politics, my morals to others, in exchange for belonging. I do not end the relationship on the spot, but it is over. No more.

In early May, my girlfriend is pointedly going to bed and I decline to join her. Her more interesting non-Jewish friends and I stay up and devise an elaborate form of truth or dare that involves group dares and all answering questions together. We introduce ourselves to every stranger we meet, and in the end run naked through the Arboretum. Hello. I am myself, just me.

But "just me" turns out to still be Jewish. I cannot escape it so easily as my own clothing or by fleeing into the Minnesota woods. I go on the trip still, tensely alienated from my now ex-girlfriend and the whole Hebrew language learning camp. I become convinced there is something in the water. I have nothing to say to my roommates, put-off more by their thrice-daily showers and cranking of the air conditioning then their nationalities. I flee for a Hebrew school in Jerusalem. My feminist teacher conducts a daily conversation more lively and political than many a talk show. I hone my arguing more than my Hebrew, though I can read the newspaper and understand the re-broadcast of Yitzhak Rabin's last speech.

At last, I return on Thanksgiving to my rural Wisconsin relatives, and finally feel a sense of belonging. I tell my Jewish professor about my trip; how badly non-Orthodox Jews are treated. He says, "You know I could give a shit about non-Orthodox Jews if Israel would quit oppressing Palestinians." He is right, but I have nothing to say until I meet him again at a Jewish Voice for Peace meeting fourteen years later. All the Hebrew I learned and the peace process fade away and I leave Carleton for a more suitably radical school, the one my parents attended.

Four years later, Israel finds me again. A new Palestinian Intifada has started. I am smoked out of my woods. I met anti and non-Zionist Jews at Antioch College. I never knew there were such creatures. I was so busy recognising them for the first time, that I could not see myself in them. I am living in Seattle. As if hearing a loud explosion, I went out to the street. There was a protest, with signs about Palestinian refugees. I had never heard of them either. It never occurred to me to find out where they came from, or how. I met an actual Palestinian, a great sport who was willing to educate me, and to hear me telling her she shouldn't be so angry without strangling me, which I no doubt richly deserved.

I returned to Israel on a Birthright[79] (or as I dubbed it, "Birthrate") trip and kept right on going, to East Jerusalem, Ramallah, Hebron. I discovered a parallel, mirrored world, one that oddly resembled the mythologised Israel that was all I once knew. This was no coincidence, as the mythos had stolen this world's land, then tried to deny its existence, lest Israel look counterfeit in comparison. Upon return to the United States, I belatedly joined the student divestment movement, and the Palestine Solidarity Movement.

I did not lose any close friends or family members by "coming out" on my views on Israel. With parents like mine, that was probably unlikely. And I gained a community, and eventually I even found my way back to practicing Judaism. The movement was a placeholder, a way for me to stay Jewish when I could not bear to be so any other way. It was also a way to live my values in a direct and connected way, more intimate than a World Bank protest. My own liberation is not more important than anybody else's, but I owe the people who facilitated it, who paid the price, while I slowly, privileged-ly figured out who I was, and what I could do about it.

I have come full circle with Jewish Voice for Peace, a group that honours my past convictions, does not unfairly privilege Jews over others, all the while allowing me to be my full Jewish self in a group of other Jews.

While I am glad I spent years working in non-Jewish specific groups, it is nice to find a real activist home, not a mythologised one. We don't

---

[79] Birthright Israel is an organisation that sponsors young adult Jews aged eighteen to twenty-six from all over the world to travel to Israel. The organisation's website claims that this programme is a "gift" to young Jewish people, and that its purpose is to "diminish the growing division between Israel and Jewish communities around the world; to strengthen the sense of solidarity among world Jewry; and to strengthen participants' personal Jewish identity and connection to the Jewish people." Birthright Israel's funding comes from the Jewish Federation system, the Jewish Agency for Israel (JAFI) and the Government of Israel. (AA)

support one or two states, or any number of state solutions specifically, and while I have my own (singular) views on the question, I have chosen not to emphasise them in my work, focussing instead on human rights, democracy, and equality. The divestment movement has grown into a truly worldwide, Palestinian-led Boycott, Divestment, and Sanctions movement, connected to a beautiful on the ground uprising in Israel-Palestine. I am privileged to have a pretty good seat, and the ability to participate, as me.

Confronting the Sacred Cow

Anna Baltzer

My mother once told me that she was raised on two somewhat contradictory mantras: One, all people are created equal and deserve equal respect, and two, you can't completely trust anyone who isn't Jewish.

An extraordinary woman, my mother grew to shed the bias of the second mantra and fell in love with my father, who isn't Jewish. My parents raised my brother and me to value diversity and cultivate friendships with different kinds of people. At the same time, both my parents still have a kind of affinity for Jews and naturally gravitated towards them. While I was growing up, many of our family friends were Jewish and my babysitter and two closest friends were Israeli Jews.

Although ours was a secular household, I was always keenly aware that I was Jewish. My closest friends' families originated from Sweden, Norway, the Philippines, India, and Israel, so I would occasionally ask my mother about our origins. "We're Jewish," she would reply. "No," I would insist, "What are we? Are we Belgian or Polish or what?" The answer was always the same: "We're Jewish." When pressed, my mother one day explained in a way that made sense to me: "Our family has lived all over. My grandparents lived in Austria and then it was no longer safe there, so they moved to Poland, where your grandparents were born. Then it was no longer safe in Poland, so they moved to Belgium. Then it was no longer safe in Belgium or anywhere else they could reach in Europe, so your grandparents came here to the United

States. It's difficult to say that any of those past countries were really ours because there always came a time when we were no longer welcome."

My grandfather died before I was born, but I was close to my grandmother growing up. She talked often about her story. On my grandparents' wedding night, Hitler invaded. The newlyweds began a harrowing thirteen months of crisscrossing Europe, only narrowly averting arrest and possible deportation at every turn. My grandfather's family went into hiding and eventually joined the Belgian Resistance. His sister was killed and the rest of the family survived. Almost all of my grandmother's family died in Auschwitz, including her parents and beloved fifteen-year-old sister. My grandmother survived but never recovered.

I cannot overestimate the effect that my grandmother's story had on my development. A sense that we could never truly be sure that we were safe pervaded my Jewish identity. I don't remember family discussions about Israel during my childhood. It was a non-issue, because there was nothing to discuss. It was a given that Israel was necessary because there could come a day when the United States would also close its doors. I had no opinion about the Palestinians because I had never heard of them.

Never having experienced religious Jewish life, when I went away to college at Columbia University in New York, I was excited and curious about the large Conservative Jewish student population. I began attending occasional services and celebrations with new Jewish friends, who encouraged me to become more involved in the community. On a campus that was not particularly nurturing or community-oriented, it felt nice to be so warmly welcomed. At the same time, I was troubled that my new friends' openness to me stemmed solely from the fact that I was Jewish.

I remember one student in a philosophy course who was extremely lively and verbose during discussions but kept to herself when class was over. She was by far the best student in the class but had seemingly no interest in her classmates, despite multiple attempts to engage her. One day, she happened to overhear a conversation I was having with another student, in which I mentioned that I was Jewish. She turned around with her eyes lit up and exclaimed, "You're Jewish? I had no idea! We should hang out!"

Israel came up frequently during dinner conversations within the campus Jewish community. I finally had the chance to visit Israel myself on one of the first Birthright Israel trips in January 2000. The all-expenses-paid ten-day tour reinforced my perception of Israel as a peace-seeking democracy—a belief I would carry through the rest of my college career, until my first encounter (knowingly, at least) with Palestinians three years later.

I attended campus events criticising sanctions on Iraq and the new war on Afghanistan. In retrospect, I now remember references to Palestine in discussions and on posters. Yet somehow, without even realising it, I shut out any criticism of Israel, preferring to hear and see no evil, lest I be confronted with something that might be uncomfortable.

My eyes and ears were finally opened the year after college, when I was teaching English in Ankara, Turkey on a Fulbright fellowship. An avid explorer, I travelled during my vacations across Syria, Lebanon, and Iran. As I write in the introduction to my book, *Witness in Palestine*:

I was welcomed everywhere I went, particularly in southern Lebanon, where I was taken in by several families of Palestinian refugees. One family in particular not only showered me with hospitality and warmth but accepted and respected me to an extent that I had rarely experienced, even in my own communities back home. Through my friendship with the eldest son, Mahmoud, and his parents, siblings, and neighbours, I began to hear a different narrative about the state of Israel from the one I had heard growing up as a Jewish American.

My new friends told me stories of past and present military attacks, house demolitions, land confiscation, imprisonment without trial, torture, and government-sponsored assassinations. It seemed that these aggressive actions were not carried out for the protection of the Jewish people... but rather for the creation and expansion of a Jewish state at the expense of the rights, lives, and dignity of the non-Jewish people living in the region. It was hard for me to believe that Israel could act so unjustly. Questioning Israel in any way felt like a betrayal of my grandmother.

At the time, it seemed clear to me that Mahmoud and his family had been brainwashed by anti-Israel propaganda and I set out to prove them wrong. I read books and talked to people who had visited the area outside the context of a Birthright Israel type of tour. To my disappointment, I began to see that I was the one who had been misled.

I resolved to travel to Israel-Palestine to see the situation for myself and was shocked to witness Israel violating the most fundamental values on which I was raised. I found millions of people living under a military occupation characterised by invasions, curfews, humiliation, and the everyday denial of basic human rights like the ability to get to school or earn a living.

I interviewed a mother who was forced to give birth at a checkpoint and lost her two premature children, who couldn't reach proper medical care. I comforted a friend whose six-month-old son died in his arms of a preventable asthma attack, because Israeli soldiers refused them passage to the hospital. I watched Jewish settlers terrorise families trying to harvest their olives, and Israeli soldiers harassing children on their way to school. I visited Palestinians in the Jordan Valley, forced to work on their ancestral farms for the profit of settlements that have taken over their land. Many of the workers have no clean water to drink, while settlers next door enjoy swimming pools filled with water from Palestinian West Bank land.

I watched farmers break down and sob as their trees—their livelihoods, their past, and their future—were ripped from the earth by US-made Caterpillar bulldozers, in preparation for the Apartheid Wall. I held back tears watching mothers cry for their sons wasting their lives in prison, never convicted of a crime.

I learned that there are millions of Muslims and Christians who have waited decades to get a permit to visit their holy sites in Jerusalem—that I can visit freely—and some of them never make it. I enjoyed hospitality from a husband, wife, and child living together in secret, because they have different Israeli-issued ID cards that mandate that they live apart.

I spoke on the phone to a friend in Gaza while bombs rained down, destroying thousands of schools, farms, homes, and lives.

I was devastated by what I saw. The construct of Israel's virtue, which I had always held dear, crumbled before my eyes. I felt confused and scared to have such a deep part of my identity slip away. For every atrocity I witnessed or learned about, I found a corresponding form of Palestinian peaceful resistance. I watched entire villages march to the site of the Wall's construction to protest against the confiscation of their village's olive groves. I watched them return week after week in spite of tear gas, sound bombs, water hoses, and live ammunition used against them. I met a young woman who climbed into the claw of a bulldozer to keep it from uprooting her family's trees. I accompanied families who insist on harvesting their olives in spite of settler attacks.

I met children who have to wake up at 4:30am because they have to cross multiple checkpoints and the Wall to get to school in time. And they still make the journey every day, there and back, because they insist on being educated, refusing to let the Occupation prevent them from carrying on the Palestinian traditional focus on education. I watched children who dodge stones thrown by settlers on the way to school, and who keep walking, steadfast.

I accompanied doctors defying military curfew to deliver food and medical supplies to their neighbours. I worked with families determined to rebuild their demolished homes rather than vacate their properties. I met entire villages who refused to carry their ID cards and be subject to Israel's system of permits, similar to the pass system in Apartheid South Africa. I talked to a mother who sneaks into Jerusalem to pray at Al Aqsa mosque every week, and then sneaks back home.

I saw too many kinds of everyday resistance to list in full. Inspired by Palestinian perseverance and outraged by the crimes being committed in my name as a Jew and with my tax dollars as a US citizen, I was transformed from an English teacher into a political activist against the Occupation. I put together the emails, reports, and photographs I had sent home into a book, *Witness in Palestine: A Jewish American Woman in the Occupied Territories*.

Although I was afraid of the backlash, I pushed myself to give presentations on the Occupation in the United States. I found that I had the ability to move and change people, especially as someone coming from a Jewish background. Soon I was driving around the country in a station wagon full of books, stopping in nearly every city or town, speaking every day at universities, high schools, churches, mosques, policy institutes, and any other venue that had invited me.

My beliefs continued to change with every visit to the Middle East. I came to realise that Israel's abuses went far beyond the Occupation of the West Bank and Gaza Strip. I started visiting Bedouin villages inside Israel, some of which have been bulldozed dozens of times in an attempt to force their inhabitants to relocate. I interviewed exiled refugees in

Syria and Lebanon who still carry the keys and titles to their homes, to which Israel prevents them from returning. I also talked to Palestinians in Israel who are treated as second-class citizens and who cannot return to their lands just a few miles away, simply because they are not Jewish.

What struck me most was the knowledge that I can go to their lands, simply because I am Jewish. In fact, Israel would pay me to leave my life of comfort in the United States to move onto their land. I could lease it, farm it, or build a house on it. And if their houses are still there, I could live in the houses of my exiled Palestinian friends. Yet they are forever excluded because of their ethnic and religious background, as long as Israel remains a state only of the Jewish people.

It is now clear to me that Israel's discriminatory policies are not a perversion of the Jewish state; they are a logical extension of needing to create and maintain an artificial Jewish majority on the ancestral land of millions more Palestinian people.

With the realisation that equal rights for Palestinians are inherently incompatible with the existence of a Jewish state came my second transformation—from anti-Occupation to anti-Zionism. If dispossession, discrimination, and the denial of human rights since the 1967 Occupation began are wrong, how can discrimination, dispossession, and the denial of human rights before 1967 with the mass expulsion of the majority of the non-Jewish population, be acceptable?

Furthermore, I realised that an end to the 1967 Occupation and the creation of a Palestinian state alongside a Jewish one built on exclusivity, do not in fact address the primary grievance and ongoing suffering of the majority of the Palestinian people, either living in exile or as second-class citizens in Israel. I elaborated in an Afterword recently added to my book:

For many, myself included, it is increasingly difficult to imagine a two-state solution that is consistent with the basic human rights of the Palestinian people. The underlying issue remains: how can you have a state representing only the Jewish people that equally advocates and protects the rights and aspirations of non-Jews within it? ...

Those operating from the premise that having a Jewish state trumps all else, find this idea unacceptable because it would mean the end of a Jewish majority. To these people, I would pose the question: is there a limit to what you would accept in order to have such a majority? If the necessity for the perpetual denial of human and equal rights for non-Jews inside and outside Israel is not that limit, I would like to know what is. If creating a safe space for the persecuted Jewish diaspora requires the creation and maintenance of a new persecuted diaspora, is that something we as Jews can accept? And, does Israel really fulfil its stated purpose of being a safe space for Jews? Fundamentally, it is not the choice of Jews whether or not Palestinians should have their rights met, but these are still important questions for us to ask ourselves.

In 2010 I co-led a delegation to Israel-Palestine with the Interfaith Peace-Builders. After a presentation by two representatives of the organisation Combatants for Peace, a Jewish Israeli and a Palestinian who had both lost children due to the conflict, one of the delegates asked Rami Elhanan, the Israeli speaker, how he would feel about living alongside his co-presenter and other Palestinians in a democratic state for both peoples, offering equal rights for all people from Israel-Palestine.

Elhanan's manner abruptly transformed and he barked back at the delegate, "I am not going to commit suicide!"

Elhanan's response encapsulates what I find to be a common perception of the Jewish state and the Jewish people as one and the same. In fact, in some circles I know, Zionism has eclipsed the traditional pillars of Jewish identity, like bloodline and practicing the religion and traditions. It is more acceptable now to question the existence of God than to question the existence of Israel.

As Elhanan's reaction demonstrates, discussion of Israel's right to exist as a Jewish state is heard by many Zionists as a challenge to the right of Jews to live at all. Yet asking Palestinians to recognise the right of Israel to exist as a Jewish state, is to demand that they recognise the right for there to be a state on their historic homeland that explicitly excludes them, their children, and all their people, forever. It takes a simple analogy to demonstrate what an unreasonable demand this is. Would we expect Native Americans to recognise the right of their colonisers to have taken away their lands?

Exposing the nature of Zionism within the context of Jewish identity begins to explain what makes it so hard for so many Jews to free themselves from it. It explains how many Jews and Israelis who oppose the Occupation stop short and refuse to take a stand against the violations of Palestinian rights that are a direct result of the existence of an exclusively Jewish state.

Still, according to an anti-Zionist Israeli friend of mine, the leap from anti-Occupation to anti-Zionism is not even the most significant for Jewish Israeli activists. He explained:

First comes the shift from unconditional support for Israel to criticism of the Occupation. Then, some shift their criticism of the Occupation to criticism of all of Israel's human rights violations, even those required to maintain a Jewish state. But the hardest shift of all is from seeing Palestinians simply as victims to seeing them as the leaders of their own liberation struggle, whom we must follow rather than lead.

It's hard to say what initially made me sensitive to the plight of the Palestinians, while so many remain hardened in unconditional support for Israel. It's clear that talk of Palestine while I was in college was not enough to move me. A strong, personal connection with Mahmoud and his family is what prompted me to begin to seek the truth. In retrospect, it's extraordinary to me how patient my friends were in the face of my insistence on Israel's innocence. Their patience informs my reaction to Zionist opposition I encounter today.

Although I know that in my early years of touring I recruited many to the cause for Palestinian liberation, I have some regrets. One is that I was inadvertently using my Jewish privilege without recognising that by soliciting attention through my Jewish background, I was in fact reinforcing the root of the very injustice that I was trying to help overcome. I was reinforcing the idea that Jewish voices and opinions are more important than the voices and needs of the oppressed themselves, the Palestinian people, the experts and leaders on their plight and struggle.

Second, as a Jew, I was giving permission to non-Jews—especially Christians otherwise hesitant to speak out due to the Church's history of anti-Semitism and complicity during the Nazi Holocaust—to criticise Israeli atrocities, when what needed to be said was that non-Jews do not need permission from Jews to do what they know is right.

I now see my priority as making space for Palestinian voices to be heard. I am happy to see that this transformation is already occurring, with Palestinians increasingly invited to tell their own stories, rather than non-Palestinians telling the stories for them. I believe my role as a speaker is decreasing in importance, and I've consciously transitioned into campaign and movement organising, both locally in my new home of St Louis, and US-wide as national organiser for the US Campaign to End the Israeli Occupation, a coalition of groups committed to justice and equality in Israel-Palestine and beyond.

Another of my regrets from my early talks is that I moved people to sympathy but not to action. I depressed audiences rather than empowered them. But Palestinians don't need any more sympathy—they have plenty of it. Palestinians need freedom, equality, and human rights. These will not manifest simply with a change in public opinion. Change comes from action by a critical mass of people who need not only compassion for the oppressed, but also a willingness to step out of their comfort zones and dedicate time, resources, and energy to support the Palestinian people.

Until several years ago, "supporting the Palestinian people" was easy to say but hard for me to define. Did it mean supporting the Palestinian elected leadership in the West Bank and Gaza? What about all those who didn't feel represented by that leadership? And what about the Palestinian refugees and citizens of Israel who were excluded from those elections? There was no clear, unified voice of Palestinian civil society.

All that changed in 2005, with the historic call for Boycott, Divestment, and Sanctions (BDS) against Israel, until it complies with international law by fulfilling its obligations to end the Occupation, grant equal rights to Palestinian citizens of Israel, and respect the right of return for Palestinian refugees. BDS is a nonviolent method aimed at achieving that which no UN resolution or diplomatic lip-service have: the realisation of full Palestinian rights.

The BDS call includes an invitation to all who believe in justice and equality, including Israeli Jews, to join the BDS movement. Israeli organisations like Boycott from Within and the Coalition of Women for Peace have responded to the call by becoming active BDS advocates. Jews of conscience all over the world are working on BDS. In fact, although I have lost a few relationships over my work, it is within the context of solidarity with Palestinians that I have found a Jewish community to which I feel connected.

Earlier this spring, my grandmother passed away. Packing up her apartment, sorting through the letters from AIPAC and tin cans to collect donations for the JNF—the Jewish National Fund plants trees in Israel, covering up destroyed Palestinian villages—was surreal to say the least. I was and still am overwhelmed with sadness. I wish my work could have been something she understood, since it is an extension of the belief system on which I was raised, not a departure from it. What I do is not in spite of what my grandmother went through, but in light of it. It's not something I choose to do; it's a part of me, as she was and still is.

A Startling Awareness

Rich Forer

Growing up during the 1950s and 1960s, I attended Sunday school at my Reform synagogue from the time I was six until a year after my *bar mitzvah*. Like most people I naturally identified with my religion and culture. Knowing who I was gave me a sense of pride and participation in something deep and mysterious.

The overwhelming majority of Jews I knew were honest and fair in their dealings with others, and taken as a whole, appeared to be more socially and politically aware than other groups of people. Their respect for different cultures impressed me as kind and considerate, especially when contrasted with the racial slurs and ethnic stereotypes I often heard from gentiles.

I appreciated the humour, the food, the warmth, the intelligence and the contributions to humanity spawned by my ancestry; but more than anything else, I willingly embraced my Jewish heritage because of my people's history of wandering and persecution. To question my identity would have felt like a betrayal of an ancient tradition, and an indifference to the suffering of my people.

After graduating from elementary school, I regularly attended Friday night and Saturday morning religious services. Occasionally I would overhear some of the men discussing the possibility of a global nuclear catastrophe. They all agreed that the most likely place for war to be triggered was the Middle East. That region was a powder keg just waiting for a spark and the spark, they argued, was Arab hatred of Israel.

Faced with that prospect, I would often ask myself what we had done to cause the Arabs to hate us. The answer was simple. We had done nothing. We were Jews. That was enough. That was the rule since time immemorial. But, as I would finally figure out many years later, the most honest and accurate answers to my question were not so one-dimensional. The anger the Arab nations felt over Israel's existence had more to do with territory than with inborn hatred for the Jewish people.

As I grew older I rarely dwelled on the enmity between Israel and the Arabs, but I never lost sight of Israel's vulnerability, situated among hostile neighbours, each resenting its very existence and insensitive to the six million unspeakable acts of cruelty that had exterminated a third of world Jewry a generation earlier.

In 1996 I was introduced to Joan Peters' influential work, *From Time Immemorial: the Origins of the Arab-Jewish Conflict over Palestine*. A best-seller, the book claimed that the Palestinian people never existed. They were Arab immigrants who had migrated to Palestine from other areas of the Middle East for the jobs made available by Jewish land development. Any uncertainty I'd had about the circumstances surrounding Israel's birth was completely erased by this remarkable book. *From Time Immemorial* articulated the justification for a Jewish state and provided detailed evidence that enabled me to infer that any and all accusations by Israel's enemies were not only false but antisemitic.

In June 2006, Israeli soldier Gilad Shalit was kidnapped by Hamas militants on the southern Gaza border. Three weeks later Hezbollah, the Lebanese paramilitary organisation, abducted two Israeli soldiers and killed three in a cross-border raid into northern Israel, precipitating the Second Lebanon War. These unwarranted attacks upon my people convinced me that the genocidal intentions of Israel's neighbours were very much alive and unlikely to disappear. Arguments with close friends who were critical of the Jewish state fanned the flames of my distress and I decided to research the history of Israel's existence.

When I began my study, I was determined to read Jewish authors only. I knew that if I chose non-Jewish authors I would suspect bias. First, I went on the internet and scanned reviews of books by Israeli Jews and other Jewish writers. Then I noticed a book by an American professor, Norman Finkelstein. The writer's surname met my chief requirement, and the title drew my attention: *Beyond Chutzpah: On the*

Misuse of Antisemitism and the Abuse of History. After compiling a few other possibilities, I drove to my local library.

Browsing through the bookshelves, I found Finkelstein's book. Perusing the inside jacket, I read that Joan Peters' book *From Time Immemorial* had been "exposed as an academic hoax". Given my enthusiasm for Peters' work, the statement was provocative and threatening. As I was beginning to recover my balance, the jacket held another surprise: it said that Finkelstein was highly critical of the Israel-Palestine analysis that Harvard Law professor Alan Dershowitz communicated in his book, *The Case for Israel*. Although I had not read that book, I had always regarded Dershowitz as an independent and fair-minded thinker. I had admired him, along with Peters, for a long time. I had barely begun my investigation, yet I was already faced with the prospect that long-held, nearly sacred beliefs were about to be deflated.

My inner turmoil had pushed me into a corner. Seeing something I almost wished I hadn't, I was simultaneously repelled and attracted. In the face of this unforeseen impasse, I was left with no choice but to borrow Finkelstein's book from the library as the only possible relief from my dilemma.

Back home, the awareness that I was about to venture into terrain that did not appear to be as clearly demarcated as I had always supposed, became more pronounced. Feeling somewhat anxious, I decided to sleep on my decision and see how I felt after a night's rest.

The following morning, I sat alone in my living room. It was very quiet outside. There was nothing to distract me, nothing I really wanted or needed. At ease, I was finally ready to uncover any evidence that might clarify the issues that had caused such consternation. Resigned to the fact that I was about to discover unsavoury details about Peters and Dershowitz, I picked up *Beyond Chutzpah*.

Over the ensuing days, I read Finkelstein's words with as much tolerance as I could muster. There was no doubt in my mind that I was studying the work of a brilliant scholar who possessed a great deal of confidence in his arguments. Furthermore, Finkelstein was meticulous about documenting the evidence he was presenting. Because of these qualities I restrained myself from abandoning his book, sensing that my endurance would lead to some kind of resolution, though I had no idea what form it might take. Most of the time my reading was marked by an inner struggle: on the one hand, a desire to get to the truth and alleviate my torment; on the other, a curiosity to ascertain whether Finkelstein was in fact a disturbed academic and an antisemite—an ironic possibility, given that the book was purportedly about the misuse of antisemitism. For me the question became: Who was actually misusing antisemitism, he or I?

Part one of *Beyond Chutzpah* was entitled "The Not-So-New 'New Antisemitism'". Here Finkelstein tackled the modern Jewish penchant for ascribing "any challenge inimical to Jewish interests" to antisemitic tendencies. He criticised a wide variety of Jewish sources for their blind and uninformed support of Israel, and their attempts to silence voices that spoke out against its policies, even when those voices were respected human rights organisations like Amnesty International or Human Rights Watch. He especially ridiculed the hypocritical stance of some prominent Jews in defending Christian fundamentalist leaders, like Jerry Falwell of the Moral Majority, and Pat Robertson of the Christian Broadcasting Network, because they backed a "militarised Israel", while ignoring the fact that their theology "reeked of antisemitism". Although I was impressed with the clarity of Finkelstein's reasoning, I was not fully persuaded. He had not overcome my sensitivity to the undercurrent of antisemitism in my society, and the threat it posed to my people.

By the third day, I began to experience a succession of distinct emotions, but was so engrossed in the book that it took a while before I could articulate them. When I eventually shifted my attention onto my mental-emotional state, I remembered the feelings of shock and disbelief that had come over me upon reading that Israel had bulldozed hundreds of homes in the Palestinian areas, sometimes with the inhabitants still inside; that Israel was siphoning off disproportionate amounts of water from those areas for its own use; that collective punishment was a common practice; and that Israel was the only country in the world that legalised torture. As a Jew, I was acutely bothered that human beings were being mistreated in my name and in the name of my people. Considering that I had never treated anyone with such brutality, it seemed unfair that I should have to carry such a burden of culpability.

Pausing briefly, I put the book down and tried to find some respite from this onslaught of disturbing information. After taking a few deep breaths, I forged ahead, only to discover that Israeli security forces had killed or injured dozens of unarmed Palestinians attempting to pass through checkpoints. I also learned that tens of thousands of Palestinians had been tortured or harshly treated, frequently without any evidence that they had committed acts of defiance against Israel.

After reading these and other allegations, my disbelief and shock turned into anger at my Israeli brethren for their unjustified and inhumane deeds. My anger then turned inward as I reflected on my past failure to pay attention to this struggle. My face flushed with heat and a righteous fury seethed within me for the suffering of an entire ethnic group that I had continually ignored. The cries of millions had never even touched me. Waves of remorse passed through my body, and I shuddered at the thought that I had rejected their claims of persecution as propaganda and lies. I was ashamed that I had demonised an entire culture and judged its people as irredeemable. In acknowledging my heartlessness, I was obliged to silently confess to my history of delusion and denial. Many of the positions I had taken on behalf of Israel and against the Palestinian people were factually incorrect.

These positions, so prevalent within my culture, had appeared reasonable, even unassailable. They had taken shape during the impressionable years of childhood and were suffused with the common accounts of my parents, rabbis, Sunday school teachers, relatives and friends. Most significantly, they were founded upon two interconnected, governing beliefs, which were the substratum out of which all other judgments arose.

The first was that Israel unfailingly acted with integrity in its dealings with others. There was never any doubt in my mind that when mistakes were made, Israel's overriding rectitude ensured that the mistakes were redressed. The second and more prominent belief was one that had wielded its authority from the deeper recesses of my mind, indifferent to the fact that I had never been a religious Jew: God had promised the land of Israel to the Jewish people and at last, after thousands of years of persecution, that promise had been fulfilled. And just as the patriarchs Abraham, Isaac and Jacob had acted under God's guidance and protection, so too had Israel. Thus, the judgments I had regarding the Israel-Palestine issue—empowered by holy writ—were so unshakable there was never any thought of deserting them.

Under the influence of these beliefs, I had further rationalised Israel's actions with other, subordinate beliefs that I presumed were equally incontestable. Among these were that Israel, when forced to retaliate against its enemies, did so with great reluctance; that Israeli soldiers did not violate civil rights or kill indiscriminately; that Israel's Supreme Court was a bastion of justice for all citizens, including the Palestinians; and that the reason the Palestinians always subverted Israel's sincere attempts to establish a fair peace was because their true goal was to push Israeli Jews into the sea.

Since I had always believed the United Nations was the primary arena for resolving conflict around the world, I was chronically upset with its myopia to the truth of what was happening in the Middle East, and its insensitivity to the suffering of the Jewish people. Only antisemitism could explain such ignorance. I also couldn't comprehend why some Jews were convinced the Palestinian cause was just. That reasoning was nonsensical to me, so I had attributed their confused logic to misguidance and misinformation.

But now my mind was in the crosshairs, its conception of reality threatened by powerful reasoning and compelling research. My shame and embarrassment receded, and a heavy sadness enveloped me for the oppressive treatment that so many Palestinians had suffered.

Although I had always considered myself capable of clarifying most matters on the basis of my own scrutiny, I saw that when it came to Israel I had brushed aside challenging questions in favour of an irrational but emotionally satisfying appraisal. This realisation quickly passed when I noticed that I could no longer detect an exclusive identity, or "me", differentiated from anyone or anything else. Given my customary outrage at the world's non-acceptance of my people, it was hard to believe at first that I was evaluating my experience accurately. Briefly I speculated that such an evocative ending to a core identity should be accompanied by dramatic emotional, mental and physical overtones. But that was not the case. As hard as I tried to reanimate my Jewish identity—not out of fretfulness, but to confirm the validity of my unanticipated observation—it would not return. So, I surrendered to the inevitability of the moment, and calmly accepted that I was not separate from members of other religious or ethnic groups. I had lost my individual identity as a Jew and discovered my common humanity with all people. I was as much Palestinian as Israeli, as much Muslim as Jew.

My Jewishness had never felt like a burden to me. It was "who I am" or so I'd thought. But now that I was no longer bound to one identity and separate from another, I felt a great relief. This new consciousness of non-separation gave me the freedom to reflect upon the lifelong dominion my former identity had held over me.

Initially, my reflection took the form of a simple exercise. I relaxed and settled into my body. Then, from that calm space I began to compare the new self-sense with the old. At a certain point I noticed an almost imperceptible sensation in my upper abdomen, around my solar plexus. As the sensation captured my attention a memory arose from early childhood. The memory took the form of subtle bodily recoil at the communication that who I was could be defined by others, that I was Jewish and an American. This recoil, which I experienced as doubt, was a natural response to the delimiting of my being—to being informed who I was and, therefore, who I wasn't. It was a warning from my deepest internal perception that by capitulating to a limited identity my most basic understanding of myself would be undermined. But the warning disappeared as fast as it had appeared, and the communication became a part of how I would come to identify myself. I had made a choice, but the choice was not borne of thought; it was borne of innocence, vulnerability and trust. It was a decision from the heart.

As I matured into adulthood, my identity became more entrenched within cultural and social boundaries, beyond which I had no awareness or understanding. These boundaries were analogous to having bridle reins connected to the sides of my head, prescribing how far I could turn in any direction. I could see only that part of the world the restraints permitted. I was so habituated to the restraints, that I didn't even know they existed. As a result, I took for granted that the world I saw was all there was to see. With such a worldview it was not possible to comprehend the motivation for the behaviour of those I perceived as threats to me and my people. What was possible was to label them "terrorists". My irrational fear had reduced them to objects intent on my demise. Only after I was free of irrational fear did I become aware that I had objectified anyone.

Now I could see just how primitive my thinking had been. A reasonable need for safety had been transformed into an irrational fear that could be satisfied only by incapacitating or destroying the objects of my fear. Only then would no harm befall me. Fear persuaded me to deny the humanity of others and more easily condone their destruction. By interpreting the world through the prism of fear, my mind had created enemy images and then superimposed those images onto other people, unconsciously presuming that they actually existed as reality. I had played God by determining the substance of a man or a woman without even knowing that man or woman. Those whom I defined as enemies, as threats to my being or way of life, were transmuted by my fear into monsters whose potential for violence could never be discounted.

Deceived by a belief system consisting of antagonists and protagonists and aligning myself with the presumption that one part of the world represented sanity and the other insanity, I was supporting indiscriminate and massive destruction; in a word: insanity. This careless choice emanated from a single error in consciousness: my unquestioned devotion to a limited identity. Until I acknowledged the profound influence of this primal error, my participation in the generational re-enactment of hatred and retribution, of chronic hostility and mistrust, was destined to continue.

I noticed that I didn't seem to suffer a fear of terrorists. Where once there was fear, now there was emptiness, and this emptiness manifested as the absence of any impulse or desire to judge or define the other. My curiosity was stirred, so I designed an experiment to check the accuracy of my observation.

Like someone who pinches himself to see if he is really awake, I visualised a series of horrifying scenarios that were similar to news reports that once stimulated great agitation within me. My objective was to see if I could rekindle my former feelings. I imagined bloody atrocities against innocent children and meditated on nightmare visions of my brutal death at the hands of Islamist extremists. Surprisingly, the physical and mental stress that normally sprang from such images did not appear. What materialised instead was a feeling of equanimity. There was an immeasurable relief in knowing that the rage extremists felt was not based solely upon irrational hatred. With this understanding they became human, and the irrational fear and anger I once felt for them were translated into compassion, equal to the compassion I felt for Jews. Compassion became the doorway to understanding the suffering of my former enemy.

In classical psychology, projection is defined as "the attribution of one's own ideas, feelings, or attitudes to other people or to objects; especially the externalisation of blame, guilt, or responsibility as a defence against anxiety." Although I was familiar with this defence mechanism, I had really only understood it with my intellect. Now I understood it with the natural intelligence of my heart, and I found myself able to inquire directly into the grievances that catalyse the anger of others.

I realised that my past appraisal of the motivations of the extremists had more to do with me than it had to do with them. Believing that my fear and hatred were justified, I had been certain that my intentions arose out of fairness, while theirs arose out of hatred. That was pure projection. Their anger simmered and then exploded, because my culture withheld the fairness they longed for. Now I had to consider the possibility that they didn't become our enemies because of *who we were*; they became our enemies because of *what we did*.

Before, I had scoffed at their torment and ridiculed as pure fiction the reasons they gave for their anger. Now I could feel how callous that attitude had been, and I understood why the level of violence in parts of the Muslim world had grown over the years, and why my fellow man could act with such murderous intent. After years of frustration, of not having his hopes and needs considered, he was enraged. Demoralised by the deaths of family and friends and anguished over the persistent inequality between his people and their occupier, he was intent on ridding his homeland of an unwelcome and foreign presence. Once I understood how these feelings ignited his passions, I knew that what the Palestinian people truly wanted was not the gratuitous deaths of Israeli Jews but the implementation of the same God-given rights on which the state of Israel was built—self-determination and equality.

Notwithstanding my continued abhorrence for premeditated acts of violence, I had to admit that no matter how cold-hearted I judged their behaviour, the extremists had adopted the only means they knew to pursue the quest for justice that was hidden within the heart of their struggle. They had as much right to self-determination and equality as anyone else. I also understood why so many Jews and Americans were emotional, even hysterical, in their condemnation of Islamist extremists and how — as I had once done — they generalised that reaction to include all of Islamic society.

Our beliefs convince us how the world should appear. When we look out at the world, if it does not conform to our beliefs—especially when we see conflict and violence—we suffer fear, anger and despair. We struggle with these emotions. Usually, we deny them: either we suppress them and disavow our humanity; or we find suitable individuals or groups to project them onto and disavow their humanity. Neither choice satisfies. But there is another choice that gets to the root of the problem: we can examine our beliefs, lay bare their emptiness and let true compassion awaken. It is my experience that this choice leads to peace.

An Accidental Activist

Hazel Kahan

I am uncomfortable with calling myself an activist because I'm not sure where activism begins: Writing a letter to the editor? An argument around the family dinner table? Waving a flag? I know where activism can lead a person—to death, or jail, or exile, and so I am uncomfortable with defining myself as an activist: the label is grander than my actions justify. Being a witness requires being present in the killing fields.

Writing this piece has encouraged me to look for coherence in these actions of mine, to see whether I've always planted myself in defiance on the other side, or whether I've taken up whatever cause matched my outlook of the moment.

Ever since I was seven or eight I have been outspoken, protesting not just at injustices or foul play but at rules, constraints and authorities. Speaking out implies opposition: one is speaking out against something or other, and I have always found much to be against. Perhaps it's a matter of temperament as much as conviction!

I look back at how much over the years I have talked and talked and talked, and written too, until the moment when I understood that if I wanted not just to talk but also to be heard, I would have to start walking that talk. That's where I left the safety of opining and philosophising and took on risk. My risk threshold will be different from those of other writers in this book and our risk thresholds will not be static. We often become bolder with each action we take.

I am a Jew, born in what is now Pakistan. My parents were German refugees, medical students, who had left Germany when Jews were barred from studying medicine and continued their studies in Italy until Mussolini and Hitler became allies and being Jewish was once again an undesirable thing to be. On the advice of a Catholic monsignore who told them India would welcome young German physicians, they set sail for India in 1937 and settled in Lahore, then part of the British Empire. When war broke out, our family was interned by the British from 1940 to 1946. On our release, we returned to Lahore, where we were the only Jewish family in what a year later became Pakistan, a Muslim country. I went to several schools, ranging from convents in Lahore, an American missionary boarding school in India, and a progressive secular boarding school in England.

Being classified by others as "Jewish" is not sufficient — nor necessary — for Jewish consciousness. There was no Jewish community or synagogue in Lahore and I had only the wispiest knowledge of Jewish prayers, rituals and holidays. I knew I was Jewish because I knew I wasn't Christian or Muslim. Israel was referred to in whispers as *eretz* (Hebrew for land) so that the servants wouldn't know what we were talking about. My grandparents, uncles and aunts had all left Europe in the early 1930s for Palestine, becoming part of the foundation of Israel, where those still alive today continue to live. There were several occasions when my parents could have chosen to live in Israel. They eventually moved there only after Pakistan became hostile to Israel following the Six Day War in 1967 and living in Pakistan was no longer what it had been for the past twenty-five years.

I was almost fourteen and my mother was taking my brother and me to our new boarding school in England. Until then I had never been outside India or Pakistan. On the way, we stopped in Israel to meet our relatives, including my grandparents, for the first time. A Jewish country, everybody Jewish—it was a daunting and confusing experience but one that I didn't dwell on for long, facing instead the challenges of a new school in a new country.

Four years later I spent the summer in Israel. I arrived with visions of the Israel Miracle dancing in my head—Golda, *Exodus*, Moshe Dayan, kibbutzim, humming the tune if not the words to *Hatikvah* as I marvelled at the Jewishness of everything, the olives, grapes, oranges, bread and yoghurt, all Jewish, and the policemen and the leaders, the soldiers and the street signs—all Jewish. And me, I was Jewish too. I cried when I had to go back to London to start university and swore I would return—forever.

Twenty years and two children, two husbands and two academic degrees later, I did—without giving much thought in the intervening years to being Jewish. I had married first a non-Jew and then a Jew, and although we didn't belong to a Jewish community, I knew I was a Jew just because I was born one. What else could I be under such circumstances? Once a Jew, always a Jew. I also knew I was against war and had marched in CND (Committee for Nuclear Disarmament) demonstrations [80] with Bertrand Russell in London, but the word "activist" was not part of my vocabulary.

In-between, we lived in Australia and protested against the Vietnam war and Australia's Aborigine policies. I wrote a letter to *The Canberra Times* protesting against the Australian preferential voting system because it forced me to assign the Nazi candidate a preference, or have my vote nullified. We were academics and found our friends among the most radical of our fellow students, with Marxists at the helm. My T-shirt with a red clenched fist asserted my credibility as a radical feminist. It was the late sixties and we agreed with our comrades on everything important, until the day we discovered we had been excluded from a meeting. Hurt and confused, we asked why. "You're okay on almost everything," we were told, "but you're unreliable on Israel and Palestine." We were not accused of any specific ideological transgression but the implicit message was: You're Jews and you don't think like us on this issue.

Nursing our wounds, we decided on flight rather than fight. Exodus *redux*. We would go to Israel where we would find solidarity among our fellow Jews. We handed in our doctoral theses, took the *aliyah* path, accepting without cynicism the benefits this conferred on us. Learning Hebrew is part of Israel's immigrant absorption process and we were assigned to a six-month programme in kibbutz Giva'at Brenner. We had language instruction for half the day and worked in the fields or dining rooms or laundry the other half. I was in love again—this time

---

[80] There is a photograph of me pushing my two-year old son in a stroller under the CND banners and another one of the same son, forty years later, at a demonstration protesting against the Iraq invasion in 2003. I conclude that demonstrations don't do much for the cause!

with Socialist Israel (and a little bit with the leader of the vineyards who taught us about grapevine care). Imagine being in a place where property is theft, child rearing is communal, the workers own the means of production and each receives according to his needs! No income, free cigarettes and soap, kibbutz-owned shorts, and the iconic blue *kovah tembel*[81]. And that is not all! These socialists are Jewish! I was giddy with the wonder of it all.

As our stay came to an end, we could see the kibbutz was in flux: the kibbutzniks were tired of carrying the socialist banner for everyone else. Communal practices were creating dissent and Palestinians ("Arabs") were being hired to work in the orange juice factory. I wrote articles debunking early pioneer (*chalutzim*) myths that women had equal rights, when they came to "redeem" the land in the 1920s. My research revealed that these women chafed under their assigned roles, rejecting their place in the kitchen and with the children and demanding equal time on the tractors and in the fields with the men. My Socialist Dream was crumbling as my Miracle Dream had before.

Fully planted in reality now, we began life in an apartment generously handed to us by the Jewish Agency and the Israeli government. We lived in Kfar Saba, then a new development town just within the original 1967 boundaries. On Saturdays we went to Qalqilya to shop for groceries, barely aware that we were in occupied land. Today, Qalqilya is entirely surrounded by the Wall with only one exit/entrance for the entire town.

In our new life, we felt happy to be Jews among Jews, and had not yet understood that we were actually foreigners among *sabras*, outsiders among Israelis. *Siakh* was one of the peace groups we gathered with on Saturday evenings, trying to keep up with the conversations that took place mostly in Hebrew, about the future of the Palestinians.

But the *Siakhniks* did not take our opinions seriously: we weren't born in Israel, they reminded us, and therefore couldn't comprehend "the situation". We had similar experiences with cousins, aunts and uncles who were hostile to our political observations and resentful that my

---

[81] A tembel hat is an iconic Jewish Israeli national symbol, worn until the 1970s. It has no brim for shadowing the face or the neck, and it is small enough to fit into a pocket. Tembel in Hebrew means fool, but it's not known whether the word tembel came from the name of the hat, or the other way around. (AA)

parents had not come to Palestine to "build the land and be built by it" (*livnot u' le'hibanot*), that while "we were busy having a good time in Pakistan, they had had to carry the load for all of us". "What can you know?" they asked, "You don't know what it was like here."

Slowly it dawned on us that we had not found our brethren after all, that we were no more accepted in Israel than we had been in Australia. Here in Israel we were being marginalised by left-wing Israeli Jews and blood relatives! (Since then, I have come to understand the imperative in Israeli culture to separate and differentiate, (*le'hafrid ve le'havdil*), so clearly manifested in the "separation" or "apartheid" Wall, its 700 kilometres re-shaping the land.)

With that sobering realisation we reviewed our *aliyah* commitment. Staying in Israel would mean that our children would one day be inducted into the Army. Worse, they would become Israelis, harsh, intolerant, arrogant Israelis. We wondered if we could relate to such children? Would our own values stand up to the overpowering and homogenising effect of Israeli culture? The answers were not reassuring. It was time to leave again, to acknowledge our failure to participate in the Zionist story, and to wander again among the nations, rather than "be a light unto them". We moved to Brooklyn and our children went to a Friends school.

Although I felt Israel had deprived me of my dreams, I didn't turn against the country. Rather, memories of the dreams lay fallow on my frequent visits to Jerusalem, where my parents had bought an apartment in North Talpiot, just within the 1967 borders, with a panoramic view of the Old City and Arab villages nestling in the Kidron Valley and the Old City. I went for daily walks on the Sherover Promenade, greeting the Palestinian families who were doing the same thing. "Be careful," my parents would say, relating stories of crime and "ugliness". "They live here too," I answered. I loved going to the Old City, referred to by my parents as "the bazaar" because somehow it reminded us of Lahore. I befriended a Palestinian shopkeeper who, over a cup of mint tea, would answer my political questions with a sigh, preferring to tell me wonderful family stories. One day Rashid Khalidi[82] was leaving the shop as I entered. The shopkeeper introduced me to

---

[82] Rashid Ismail Khalidi is a Palestinian-American born in 1948. He is a Professor of Modern Arab Studies at Columbia University. (AA)

him, extolling Khalidi's great kindnesses to his and other Palestinian families.

In those days, running my own business, my family, and now my ageing parents occupied most of my consciousness, and I paid little attention to what was going on in Israel or in the rest of the world. I was a founding member of North Fork People of Conscience, a group protesting against the war through a large, ever growing display of the names and faces of Americans who had died in Iraq and, later, in Afghanistan.

One day everything changed. It was 2006. I was back in Jerusalem, walking on the Promenade and I saw the Wall for the first time, stalking its pernicious way across the hills, encircling Abu Dis. I was on the phone with Jeff Halper, setting up a time to meet and I said to him, "Oh my god, what is that? How could they do such a thing? They are destroying the hills." "They don't even care that it's Jerusalem they are doing this to", he said, his voice unexpectedly emotional.

From that day on, the Wall became the lens through which I looked at Israel. Although its construction had begun in 2002, it did not reach my radar until that day. I had just been given a half-hour time slot on a Connecticut-based radio station and the first person I interviewed was Yusuf, a fifty-two-year-old man who lived in the West Bank town of Batir. The wall had not yet reached their land, but the entire village was waiting in suspended animation for the construction that would alter— and destroy—their lives forever. Yusuf invited me to his house but I had to return to Jerusalem. When I interviewed him a year later, the Wall had surrounded Batir, and Yusuf did not repeat his invitation.

I became obsessed by the Wall. My Israel dream, no longer fallow, had turned into a nightmare. I hired a taxi to take me to Hares in the Salfit region, where the International Women's Peace Group are located. They introduced me to several Palestinians in the area, including Issa, an activist whose spinal cord was shattered by an Israeli bullet. I took a bus to Bethlehem and Aida camp to photograph the art on the wall as the beginning of "Resistance as Art", a presentation of the images along the wall, to show Americans how the Wall was destroying Palestinian community and livelihood.

My radio programme became a platform for informing Americans and Israeli Jews about the Occupation, the checkpoints, the olive farmers and their imperilled trees, the shifting face of American Jewish opinion, Palestinian women singers, Palestinian Israelis, authors—anything that would be informative, interesting and powerful. That is how I met Avigail, the editor of this book. I interviewed her in her professional capacity as a psychotherapist, asking how she would analyse Israel, if Israel were a person rather than a country.

No longer quiescent, my inner Jew became a provocateur. Speaking in measured tones was no longer an option. Galvanised, I released my outspoken and confrontational voice. When I visited my father, then in his nineties, he took issue with my side trips to East Jerusalem and the West Bank, and to my contact with Palestinians—dinner in a Palestinian home, inviting a Palestinian artist to the Talpiot house. My mother had died some years earlier, so she was spared the passionate arguments that raised the decibel volume in the house—he defending Israel's right to do anything in the name of security, and I despairing about what the Occupation was doing to the Jewish ethos. I invoked our long harmonious life among the Muslims of Pakistan as a reason that he must respect the Palestinians since most of them were Muslims too. He died without our resolving our differences, although I did persuade him to replace his subscription to the conservative *Jerusalem Post* with the more enlightened *Ha'aretz* newspaper. My views on Zionism and the Occupation have lost me some friends and chilled my relationships with others, but they have also gained me many new and vibrant friendships.

Am I an activist? I refer the question to whoever asks it. I know that my activities in the past seven years have clarified what being a Jew means to me, but it's personal and idiosyncratic and I would not offer it as a metric for anybody else. Would I take the same actions against Israel if I were not a Jew? I can't answer that, but I do know that I absolutely reject Israel's claim that "delegitimising" Israel means I am not a "real" Jew. I do not know how otherwise enlightened American Jews can be so blind to Israel's treatment of Palestinians within Israel, in Gaza or the occupied West Bank, nor how they justify the brutality by invoking ancient history or the Holocaust. Jews do not have special dispensation, divine or otherwise. "A crime is a crime", I say to them, "irrespective of who commits it." But such discussions, all too familiar to the authors in this book, lead nowhere, and I have grown weary of engaging in them. Quite honestly, I am not up to the task of persuading those for whom Israel-Palestine is a single story, a solely Jewish narrative, and who refuse to see the second story.

So, reflecting on how to best use my time and assets, I have decided to no longer try to persuade these tellers of the single story. They live behind a construction that protects them from seeing the other side, and I am unable to scale an eight-meter wall!

For now, I believe that what I do best is to preach to the converted and the wavering, because I know that to be a Jew has always been difficult and that internal conflicts and contradictions are never completely resolved. When I communicate with birds of my feather, less time is spent in disagreement. I will continue to drive two hours to gatherings in New York City and I will continue to forward emails to refresh my network (but not forget how we are all prone to email fatigue!). With the Occupation in full force, there is always so much to hear and tell and know—and never enough time.

I am grateful that the radio waves carry my message, and that technology helps me to convert the sound into podcasts and blog entries, giving me a valuable platform, from which I can remain in an outspoken opposition.

Hybrid States

Yaniv Reich

When I was very young, at the time of my earliest memories, my father and I would build model aeroplanes together. This joint activity was his way of sharing his intellectual interests with me, and it became a grounding force in my childhood. After careful assembly, we would gather our minute brushes and fine modelling paint to decorate the F-15s and F-16s, especially the F-16s, those perennial favourites, with small Stars of David to match those flown by the Israeli Air Force. My bedroom walls were plastered with action shots of Apache helicopters and the latest high-technology permutations of fighter planes. As a consequence of this passion, I could by the age of eight, inform curious listeners about the entire fleet of the IDF, including detailed information about aeronautical capabilities and weapon payloads.

Early Israeli Nationalism

As part of Israel's compulsory conscription, my father joined an IDF infantry unit in late 1966. It would have been a terrifying time to become an Israeli soldier. Just a few months later, in spring 1967, Egypt's President Nasser was busily amassing 100,000 troops in Sinai, near Israel's south-western border. He had just expelled the UN peacekeeping mission that had been in the Sinai Peninsula since the Suez War in 1956, when Israel, the United Kingdom and France jointly attacked Egypt in response to Egypt's attempted nationalisation of the canal. Then, on 22 May 1967, Nasser closed the Straits of Tiran to Israeli shipping, despite explicit warnings that Israel would consider this *casus belli*, a justification for war.

My father's unit, under the overall command of a thirty-nine-year-old Major General named Ariel Sharon, prepared for war. When Israel struck first and destroyed the entire Egyptian air force in about two hours, the tone for this outbreak of war was set. As the mythology goes, Israel was attacked by all its neighbours, and still managed to defeat the combined armies of Egypt, Syria, and Jordan in just six days.

The story of the Six Day War stirred in me a distinct nationalistic pride. My family, after being massacred in the death camps of Poland, was now on the winning side—and not just any victorious side, but one famed for its technical expertise, discipline, and morality. This was something my youthful, and later adolescent male mind, could really appreciate. I saw my father as a sort of military hero.

Holocaust: Death and Survival

After occupying an Egyptian town on the Sinai Peninsula for a year, my father's military service was complete. He then left Israel to go to an American university, where he pursued his longstanding interest in aerospace engineering. A couple of years later, my grandparents followed him to the US, after growing concern about the future of Israel. My grandparents were ever-present when I was small and became two of the primary recipients of my attention, love, and respect. Their biographies, their lives, more than any influence of which I am conscious, give shape to my current perspective on Israel-Palestine.

My grandmother was one of five siblings, and her family lived in a medium-sized town in south-eastern Poland, where they were prominent and relatively wealthy members of their community. Among other local activities, they were principal benefactors of the town's only synagogue. My grandmother was fourteen years old when the Second World War began, and the family fled their home upon hearing rumours of advancing German troops. The family was quickly fragmented. Some family members went into hiding, and others were captured and sent to labour camps. By the time the war ended, two brothers, one sister, and my grandmother had survived, largely because they were young, strong and were able to work as slave labour instead of being murdered outright. The rest, including the extended family, were dead.

My grandfather and his family fared much worse. He was one of eight brothers and sisters and a proportionally large extended family.

By the time the Holocaust ended, he was alone—completely alone. He spent a few weeks wandering around the ruins of concentration camps, searching for the only sibling that he did not know for certain had been killed. This missing brother was never found.

After several months, my grandparents met each other in a refugee camp in Germany. They were among the group of early Jewish marriages in post-Holocaust Europe—people desperate to re-build their lives and regain some modicum of the humanity that had been stripped away. Every time I pass by the final series of images of newly wedded Jewish refugees in the main hall of Yad Vashem, Israel's stunning Holocaust museum, I am overcome with the notion, and emotion, of those tormented souls, who were resilient enough to start new lives, to gamble with love, when they had nothing. I imagine I am looking at my grandparents as young twenty-somethings. My father was born there, in that same refugee camp, in 1948. One month later, with my grandmother extremely ill from a breast infection, my grandparents and baby father boarded a boat for the new, three-month-old country called Israel.

Growing up, Israel always carried for me the aura of redemption that one can easily imagine existing in the minds of these Jewish boat-people, refugees from ovens and mass graves. Every time I heard *Hatikvah*, I thought about this redemption. Israel's almost metaphysical quality was never tarnished by what I thought was the irrational hatred and violence of the Arabs in the Middle East, which was to my mind, just a continuation of the prejudice and hostility through which my grandparents had already gone. It wasn't until much later, as an adult, that the first couple of blemishes emerged in my almost uniformly glowing thoughts about Israel.

Overdue Recognition

I distinctly remember the first cracks in my Zionist nationalism. One fissure-inducing moment arrived when I came across Edward Said's *Orientalism* in a university class on global change and world order. Enraptured not only by his argument, but also his writing, I sought other things he had written. Of course, I very quickly arrived at commentary on Israel and Palestine.

I cannot remember the name of the text that so troubled me, but I can still recall my feeling, as a young Zionist proud of my Jewish and

Israeli heritage, when I grappled with Said's potent arguments and their unyielding emphasis on Palestinian rights. I was already sympathetic to and interested in human rights, although I must admit that Israel and Palestine were not a particular focus then. Still, I had been so deeply and continuously immersed in Jewish victimhood, that it had never occurred to me to focus on any aspect of the Arab-Israeli conflict other than what I perceived as the ongoing threat to Jewish security. Said dragged me through my tribal narcissism and taught me how to ask what has now become just as obvious and important a question as the one about how to make Jews more secure. That question is simply: What about Palestinian security?

Another moment that year that became a personal, intellectual watershed, was learning more about the Six Day War. I was always taught that Israel was attacked by all its neighbours in that war, which was of course largely why the victory was so impressive. But then I learned that it was Israel that had attacked first, in what had become a classic case of pre-emptive self-defence. Yes, Egypt had moved soldiers to the border and closed the Straits, but it was Israel that struck the first military blow. The Egyptian air force was destroyed on the tarmac.

This was worrying mostly because of how startlingly at odds it was with the traditional story of Israel being attacked by all its neighbours. Pre-emptive self-defence, as was emphasised later by the US military misadventures in Iraq and many other incidents, is an ambiguous and politically charged endeavour. It suddenly seemed to me that Israel was possibly guilty of the same failings. Would war have broken out if Israel had not attacked? We will of course never know, but I was certain that being an aggressor was not something to be taken lightly.

The third instance that fundamentally altered the way I thought about Israel was learning about the *Nakba* in Benny Morris' *The Birth of the Palestinian Refugee Problem*. Reading about the more than one million Palestinians who lived in Palestine before Israel was established, and of the destruction and depopulation of the network of many hundreds of Palestinian villages and towns that comprised Palestinian society, tormented me then, and still does now. Given the fact of Palestinian life and society, where did the idea of, "A land without a people for a people without a land" come from? The catchy idiom adopted a very sinister character, amply reinforced by the knowledge of how much Zionist thought, effort, and, ultimately, action went into the removal of

Palestinians from Palestine. This openly stated and discussed project of ethnic cleansing remains, for me, the most unsettling, sickening part of the Israeli history that I was not taught. Because of this, I began to question all my received wisdom on Israel.

What I discovered made for an unpleasant, deeply disconcerting period of my life. I learned about Jewish paramilitary activity against the British, much more about Jewish massacres and expulsions of Palestinians in 1948, about the burial of these now empty Arab towns under Jewish National Fund forests and Hebrew names, about Israel's relentless bombing of urban Beirut in 1982, about Israel's responsibility in the massacres of Palestinian civilians in Sabra and Shatila, about settlements. I had not even heard about the settlements in all my years as a member of the Jewish community! I was ashamed not only of this behaviour, but of my ignorance until then. My worldview was shifted by this new knowledge. I would never be the same again.

Comfortable and Uncomfortable Knowledge

Today, as a thirty-two-year-old, I have lived over one-third of my life with a conscientious and critical eye over Israeli policies. During this time, I have seen little reason for celebration or optimism beyond the huge impact of communication technology on information about the conflict. This technological revolution has brought images and stories from Israel-Palestine to a much wider audience than was possible when a small set of media sources framed nearly all news. Notable examples of this shift include the explosion of Palestinian bloggers and Twitter users, whose highly personal and often tragic updates challenge their routine dehumanisation at the hands of Israeli and Western media. Millions of people around the world are able to see shocking images through video documentation by Palestinians, of Jewish colonists and Israeli army violence. Of course, my own small contribution in the form of my blog on Israel-Palestine affairs, *Hybrid States*, can also be considered part of this new technology of information.

This medium has allowed me to reach a large number of geographically and ideologically diverse readers, something for which I am grateful. But *Hybrid States* is also a more personal project, that takes the form of a continuous, interminable conversation with my family, in which we engage with and dissect our disagreements. It is therefore a forum not only for sharing news and analysis, but for negotiating the most difficult questions raised as a result of being a Jew whose history is constructed, and must be understood, in the context of both victimhood and victimisation.

When I debate Israeli history and Zionist ideology with my family and friends, I am struck by a recurring pattern in their arguments. First, the historical events that challenge Zionist mythology are denied flatly. After I provide a mountain of references to support a particular point, that first phase typically evolves into excuse-making for any bad Israeli behaviour (even before any given atrocity has been accepted, as if at the core even Israel's greatest defenders know something is amiss). In the third stage there comes highly qualified acceptance of the incident, usually with citations of extenuating circumstances. The conversation nearly always gets stuck here, or if it continues, stumbles backward to basic affirmations of belief in the inherent rightness of the Zionist project and/or Israeli intentions. It is not easy to overcome these rigid psychological barriers.

It is unclear to me why my initial reaction to unsavoury Israeli history managed to escape this pattern. I can offer, however, a couple of reasons that help explain the attitudinal differences. The first is my academic and personal background in human rights. I arrived at critical arguments and facts on Israel in the middle of an undergraduate education in peace and conflict studies that emphasised human rights and structural violence. In the course of that programme I developed a worldview and ethics that were universal rather than tribal or relativistic. This knowledge was complemented by an understanding of both the limitations of universal conceptions of justice, and the problem of implementation that exists in a flawed international system for protecting human rights. This background, which at the time included human rights work in Indonesia, Timor Leste (East Timor), and Mexico, as well as with refugees from all over the world seeking political asylum in the US, caused me to be more sensitive to war crimes, and to the stories and rights of those dispossessed by violence.

My ethical perspective as a young adult is related to another factor that, I would argue, makes me more willing to engage with the darker sides of Israeli history. This second factor is a consequence of growing up in the post-civil rights era in the US. Although the US remains cursed with discrimination and social injustice, the state of the civil rights debate in the US is extremely advanced compared to many other countries, including Israel. The words that give shape to civil rights discourse in the US are, in a real sense, more powerful than the still widespread socioeconomic realities that try to constrain them. Americans, in the main, love freedom and equality as much as they tend to express that on their bumper stickers and T-shirts, even if they haven't the foggiest idea about their individual and national roles in suppressing freedoms and perpetuating inequality.

This emphasis on equality and civil rights, accompanied with indignation when these objectives are violated, is something into which I was socialised and which shapes how I view systems of ethnic and racial privilege. Martin Luther King's "Letter from a Birmingham Jail"[83] is, for me, just as much about the Palestinian liberation struggle as it is about the US civil rights movement. It holds universal lessons about militarism, equality, and the characteristics of principled support for justice, even when uncomfortable or unpopular. In this way, a tinge of the most beautiful parts of Americana informs my engagement with Israel, including and especially when I see it violating the principles of justice into which I was socialised, at least in theory if insufficiently in practice.

Once I began to question my received wisdom on Israel, I resolved to take a more proactive role in pushing for positive change in the Arab-Israeli conflict. I began writing much more, as well as giving lectures and seminars at the university. I engaged in debates, big and small, with all the Jews around me but most of all with my family. It's natural of course to want to persuade those who are closest to you.

At the first reasonable opportunity, I moved to Israel and volunteered with the Israeli Committee Against Housing Demolitions (ICAHD), an organisation that aims to prevent and resist the all-too-common demolitions of Palestinian homes. In this period, I supplemented a growing academic understanding of Israeli history and occupation with infuriating personal observation of Israel's mundane brutality against Palestinians. I also lived the insecurity of the Second Intifada's waves of suicide attacks against restaurants, buses and markets all around me and my family. After some time, despite my intention to continue working in Israel, I accepted an offer from a graduate school at an overseas university, where I studied international

---

[83] Available at: http://web.cn.edu/kwheeler/documents/letter_birmingham_jail.pdf (AA)

development. My academic career has thus taken me a bit far from Israel geographically, although I remain active in terms of writing and lecturing.

A Chance to Heal

My family and friends, indeed my people, escaped from Europe's ghettos and death camps not to an empty and inviting land, as was commonly argued. The essential fact is that the Jews sought a new life, a new state of a particular, ethnically defined form, that could only arise at the expense of the Palestinians. In my view, the fundamental contradiction of this spiritual and physical project is the primary source of Jewish-Arab conflict since the early twentieth century.

My grandparents are no longer alive. Yet because of their suffering, shared with me during a million Polish meals, conveyed as another million words left unsaid because of unhealed wounds, I learned how to identify suffering and its social consequences. Because of hearing my grandparents discuss the sheer joy of speaking Yiddish and Hebrew in Israel, of being surrounded by Yiddish and Hebrew speakers without fear of being pelted with rocks thrown by racist Poles, or being rounded-up by German executioners, I can grasp perfectly the intoxicating pull of community and power. In other words, my grandparents' history has taught me to empathise with *all* those who have been dehumanised by violence, both as victim and victimiser. This lesson is in many ways the essence of a hybrid state, a concept I often use to break down static, superficial, and ultimately unhelpful categories like "pro" or "anti" Israel or Palestinian.

As Jews, Israelis, Americans, and the entire global Jewish community, we must recognise not only that the maintenance of an ethnically exclusive state for Jews is anachronistic in its nineteenth-century demographic nationalism. We must also accept that Israel was and continues to be possible only through massive violence. We need to embrace the fact that Israel's establishment in the first instance required the wholesale denial of Palestinian rights, the same rights we were simultaneously claiming for ourselves. Jews built a state that granted them privilege over land, economy, and political power by excluding, through violence and law, the large majority of Palestinians who lived in that place. This contradiction is the profound burden that Zionism carries, and that cannot be avoided except by coming to terms with the historical and contemporary injustice for which Jews are responsible.

There is a way for Israel-Palestine to heal. Jews do not need to live under paranoia-causing insecurity. Palestinians do not need to live under the twin boots of dispossession and occupation. The security of Jews and Palestinians is intertwined with the inherent human rights of both peoples. Our fates are inextricably linked, our national identities are forever interwoven, and so our collective healing is jointly determined. Peace and justice for each nation will come only with peace and justice for both nations. This is the fact of Israel-Palestine.

The Cult of Atheist Zionism Posing as Judaism

Rich Siegel

Photo by Thomas Anomalous

I consider myself a cult survivor. I was raised in the cult of Atheist-Zionism-Posing-as-Judaism. I stated this to a few select friends several years ago, and they thought it was funny. The statement brought with it a pregnant pause, as though a punch line was going to follow, as though I were telling a joke. No punch line. I'm serious. More recently, subsequent to Israel's 2006 Lebanon war and the massacre in Gaza of 2008-2009, I find that I can say this and it is taken seriously. People know that something is very seriously wrong with Israel, and with the culture that supports Israel. They may not understand it, but they're more open than they were.

My family's involvement with Zionism goes back to its beginnings. It includes a grandfather who fought with the Jewish Legion to "liberate" Palestine from the Turks in WWI, great-great-grandparents who went to Jerusalem for their retirement in the 1920's, the best buddy of an uncle who smuggled arms from Czechoslovakia to Jewish terrorist groups in Palestine in the lead-up to the 1948 war, grandparents who were officers in their local B'nai Brith[84] chapter, and a cousin who was involved in "Operation Mural" [85]. He currently represents

---

[84] *B'nai Brith*, Hebrew for "Sons of the Covenant", is a Jewish service organisation. It was founded in 1843 in New York City. B'nai Brith is engaged in a wide variety of activities such as the promotion of Jewish rights and the state of Israel, assisting hospitals and victims of natural disasters, awarding scholarships to Jewish college students, sponsoring low-income senior housing, and opposing antisemitism. (AA)

[85] "Operation Mural" was an undercover operation led by Mossad, Israel's intelligence agency, to smuggle Jewish Moroccan children to Israel. The operation took place in the late 1950s and early 1960s, when the newly independent Morocco restricted Jewish emigration out of the country. (AA)

Jewish/Zionist NGOs at the United Nations office in Geneva. His wife writes Muslim-bashing books under a pseudonym.

During my childhood, Zionism and Israel were held up on a pedestal. They were central to our existence, our identity, our *raison d'être*. They were our sub-cultural equivalent of "Mom and apple pie". I grew up convinced that they were perfect and beyond reproach. There was simply nothing in my environment to indicate otherwise. Finding out that I had been lied to all my life, and that I had been supporting something that I would never have supported had I been told anything resembling the truth, has been absolutely shattering.

My Atheist-Jewish parents got together with a group of their Jewish friends in 1963 to start up a new Reform synagogue in the suburb of Pearl River, New York, which previously had not had a synagogue. Some in this group were atheists, some had religious beliefs. I grew up in Beth Am Temple, where the belief system echoed that of my parents: "We're proud to be Jews, members of this ancient group that everybody hates for no reason. We love Israel, our Jewish country that we need as our refuge in case another Hitler comes to power. Everybody hates Israel for no reason, just like everybody hates Jews for no reason."

We knew about relatives who had perished in the holocaust. Although they were distant cousins, the Holocaust loomed large for us. Our awareness of the massive loss of Jewish life during that dark time formed a significant part of our sense of who we were. This combined with the liberal political agenda of the 1960s and 1970s. We opposed the war in Vietnam. We supported African Americans in their struggle for equal rights. We opposed American overseas military activity while supporting Israeli military activity and saw no contradiction in this. Israel was different. There were antisemitic Arab hordes trying to drive the Jews into the sea. It was about survival.

I took Hebrew School and Judaism seriously. When I was old enough, I began fasting on *Yom Kippur*[86] even though my parents did not fast. Lessons on the Holocaust were presented to me both in Hebrew School and in my parents' discussions of their personal philosophy. One aspect of the history made a big impression on me: There were Germans and other Europeans who protected Jews from the Nazis,

---

[86] *Yom Kippur* is the Jewish Day of Atonement. It's a day of fasting and atonement, observed exactly ten days after *Rosh Hashana*, the Jewish New Year. (AA)

often at great personal risk. I thought about what I might do if I were in their situation. What would it be like to know that your people were committing monstrous crimes against humanity, and to have to make a choice between loyalty to them and doing the right thing? Opposing America's crimes in Vietnam was a clear choice but considering the possibility of having to oppose my people, the Jews, seemed impossible. I was glad that there was no reason to do this.

There was a paradoxical element to our worldview. We considered that it was through our "Jewish values", our superior Jewish intellect and morality, that we were able to embrace progressive agendas. As contradictory as this was—I consider chauvinism antithetical to anything progressive—there was evidence to support it in my environment. Jews tended to be liberal Democrats, anti-war and pro-civil rights. The majority of the population in my town, Irish and Italian Catholics, tended to be conservative Republicans, pro-war, and racist. This was back when there were real differences between Democrats and Republicans.

My sub-culture didn't mix well with the local majority culture. In the second grade a girl told me that her father said I killed Jesus. I told her I'd never killed anybody. I was a skinny smart kid who wore glasses, got very good grades, and sucked at sports. In my family, sport was not stressed and academic achievement was. I was a target for the tough non-Jewish kids I grew up with. And I was bullied quite a lot. Taunts of "Jew-boy" and "faggot" were frequent—lack of prowess in sport being ample evidence of homosexuality in the tribe of the playground, and there was occasional violence. I was also a bully, although it took me many years to see this. I took my humiliation out on kids who were more vulnerable than me: the fat kid at school, and my younger brother at home.

I found refuge in music, discovering early on that music was power. It earned the respect of my peers. I didn't get bullied on school concert days. Music also provided something else, which I did not have language to describe at the time. It filled a void produced by the spiritual desert I was raised in. The rejection of God, the belief in the privilege of belonging to a universally despised and superior people, and the pressure to achieve academically to prove that we were indeed superior, were not working for me, although consciously I accepted all of it. Music was spirituality—a term I would have rejected at the time. It provided a sense of wholeness, which my anti-religious religion was not providing.

There was one childhood incident that gave me pause. On a visit to see an elderly aunt who lived at an Orthodox Jewish nursing home, my brother and I encountered Orthodox Jewish kids. Their parents did not allow them to play with us. My parents explained that because they were Orthodox they viewed us as *goyim*. It occurred to me that even the kids at school who bullied me were still allowed to play with me.

By the time I reached high school the bullying had become overt Jew-hatred. Kids would throw pennies at me. "Pick it up, Jew boy." They were just as cruel to the very few African American kids at Pearl River High School, delivering taunts of "nigger" and making jungle noises. My parents decided to leave this racist town and move to a place with a larger Jewish population.

Spring Valley was only a few miles away but worlds apart. The daily humiliations ended and I thrived. My experience of what we called antisemitism had served to make me more committed to Judaism, and by extension to Zionism, as the two were inseparable in our belief system. I believed Jews were persecuted, and that I had been personally persecuted, for being moral, intelligent, progressive.

I was an active teenage Zionist. In 1974 I went with a group of kids from my Jewish summer camp to protest against Arafat's appearance at the UN, on the grounds that he was a terrorist. I had never seen so many people in one place before. The sea of humanity stretching several city blocks reassured me that I was on the right side.

There was a disturbing incident at a Zionist youth group I attended. Our adult sponsors wrote Zionist lyrics to songs from *West Side Story* and passed around lyric sheets for a sing-along: "When you're a Jew you're a Jew all the way." One repeated line stated, "We'll kill those Syrians." I remember feeling uncomfortable. Did I really want to sing about killing people? I rationalised that it must be OK. Arabs are our enemies. The adults in charge wouldn't do something wrong. I sang along. (Apologies to Leonard Bernstein, and to Syria.)

After I graduated from college I took a trip with my family to Israel, to celebrate my youngest brother's *Bar Mitzvah*. The previous *Bar Mitzvahs* in my family, mine and my other brother's, were held at Beth Am, but now my mother was fulfilling a life-long dream with her youngest, celebrating a *Bar Mitzvah* at the Wailing Wall in Jerusalem.

Afterwards I was approached by an Orthodox Rabbi and it was the first and only time in my life that I've ever laid *tefillin*.

While we toured Israel, I managed to secure employment playing piano at a luxury hotel. My family left, and I began my adventure in my Jewish country. My experience there was confusing. I was often taken for being a *goy*. I am light-complexioned, with light hair and green eyes, but so are many Ashkenazi Jews. Perhaps I don't carry myself Jewish. I often heard disparaging comments like *sheygetz*[87], that people assumed I didn't understand. Then when it was revealed that I was indeed Jewish, there was warmth and welcome. Acceptance was clearly conditional. I didn't like the way it felt. It was not lost on me that I'd had my ass kicked as a kid for being a Jew, that Orthodox Jewish kids were not permitted to associate with me, and now as an adult in my Jewish country, I was rejected as a presumed *goy*.

I didn't like the feel of the place and was glad to leave when an offer came to play shows on a Caribbean cruise ship. The job was fun at first but it soon became a challenge. I was getting burned out from many months at sea, but I was afraid of getting off ship, being unemployed and forced into medical school—something my father wanted me to do. It wasn't just that I didn't want to be a Jewish stereotype ("my son the doctor"), but that I had my own direction as a musician. I would take a week or two off here and there, and run up to New York to look for work, without success. On one road trip back to the Port of Miami I checked into a road-side motel in Southern Georgia.

I realise that in discussing my "revelation on the road to Miami" I leave myself open to various interpretations. Some might not be so kind. However, simply stated, I checked into a motel an atheist who was going through some emotional turmoil and checked out a believer in One God. I have remained one ever since. Not a god who had an only son who died for my sins, and not a god who deals in real estate, but One God, One Love that connects us all to Him/Her/It, to each other, and to Eternity, to the fabric of the Universe, which is One Love.

I immediately had to re-think my childhood, my atheist parents who were founders of a synagogue, the tribal paranoia and martyrdom and the disdain for any notion of spirituality. I saw clearly the worship of the

---

[87] A Yiddish word for a non-Jewish boy or young man. It can have different degrees of pejorative connotations depending on context. A Jewish boy who has been naughty could be called a *sheygetz*. (AA)

twin idols of Jewish identity and Israel. I identified the spiritual desert for what it was and brought my new awareness home to a family that included two troubled younger brothers. My parents assumed that I had been converted by a Catholic girlfriend. I offered that if they would care to look into the Jewish religion, they would find that God is actually a big part of it.

I quit working the ships, settled in New York and soon became an in-demand freelance musician. I began to look for a Jewish place of worship where I would be comfortable. Orthodox Judaism was out of the question because of its multitudes of laws and the endless debate and analysis about them. Why would the Master of the Universe give a hoot if I push a baby carriage on the Sabbath, inside or outside a wire perimeter hung between telephone poles[88]? I wasn't going near any of that. I investigated Reconstructionist Judaism but found that they were worshipping Jewish tribal identity and Israel much the same as in my Reform synagogue.

Finally, and reluctantly I began looking outside Judaism. The "New Thought" movement, consisting of various types of churches and centres, has worked nicely for me for many years. I'm a member of the Congregation of Universal Wisdom, which does not offer religious services, and I attend services regularly at Unity churches and Religious Science centres. I enjoy the focus on One God without tribalism, and often provide music for religious services.

Remarkably, for many years, having identified contemporary Jewish culture as a cult, and having gone outside Judaism to worship, I was still so totally indoctrinated into Zionism, that I continued to believe all the mythology. I still believed that Israel had never done anything to harm anyone, that we went to Palestine wanting good neighbourly relations, but the Arabs just hated us for no reason. Distanced from Judaism and Jewish culture, I still held a "liberal Zionist" stand politically.

I got married in 1998 to my lovely wife Xuan who is Chinese. I married for love disregarding the Jewish directive against intermarriage. The following year we left the city for suburban New Jersey. In 2004 my wife, pregnant with our daughter Emily, came to visit me at an out-of-town job. While waiting for her outside the train

---

[88] This is a reference to the ritual enclosure of *eruv* that is constructed in some Jewish neighbourhoods. The *eruv* permits religious Jews to carry objects from a private to a public domain on the *Shabbat*. (AA)

station in Providence, Rhode Island, I discovered a table that activists had put out displaying literature about the Israel-Palestine conflict. (Outreach works!). Curious, I picked up some material, including *Understanding the Palestinian-Israeli Conflict: A Primer*, by Phyllis Bennis. I got to the section about the Deir Yassin massacre. Jews massacring Arabs. My jaw dropped. This had somehow been concealed from me all my life.

I've been reading continuously since then. I've come to understand that Zionism has been a political agenda that sought to take a land with a 95% non-Jewish population and turn it into a Jewish-exclusivist state. It achieved this in 1948 through massacres, campaigns of fear, and military forced mass expulsions—taking over most of Palestine and making over three quarters of a million people homeless, establishing the state of Israel on mostly stolen land. In 1967 it conquered the balance of Palestine, beginning an era of brutal occupation and settlement in occupied areas. It's not rocket science to come to the conclusion that this is criminal, and just as easy to dismiss the various excuses commonly given for it.

Becoming active in the cause was automatic. I remembered having learned as a child about individual Europeans who protected Jews against Nazis and having admired their commitment to doing right while insanity prevailed in the world around them. I had pondered what I would do in their position, later to discover that I had been in their position all my life without knowing it. I also credit my parents, because even in their atheism, and even though they taught me the lies they had been taught about Israel, they always valued justice and human rights more than anything else. I learned that from them. Today they are disillusioned with Israel.

It hasn't been easy. I've lost long-term friends and some family members. But I really don't feel a sense of loss about it. I see those relationships as having been Jewish relationships, based on a requisite tribal agenda, rather than genuine friendships. The friends and family that matter are still with me.

Perhaps the most difficult part was coming to appreciate the reality of the criminality of Zionism at the same time as becoming a father. It's excruciating to know that Palestinian fathers cannot keep their children safe because of the insanity of this programme that unknowingly I supported all my life. This adds to my passion as an activist.

I find it painful to witness the spectacular hypocrisy of a people who are still whining, "Where was the world during the holocaust?" while committing another holocaust in Palestine. It's a depravity that paradoxically I find both familiar and unfathomable. The willingness among Jews to obsess with Jewish suffering while being completely immune to Palestinian suffering, scares me. I don't want to believe that I come from a place that sick.

Remembering myself as a child, both a victim of bullying and an unconscious bully, I've sometimes been tempted to excuse Israel. But Israel's leaders know. Zionism's leaders through history have always known. And the public has always had the responsibility to know.

Having made a U-turn on Zionism, I still had to resolve my relationship with my Jewish tribal identity. Two incidents served to cement a decision about this issue. The first was in 2006. It was the story of Tove Johannson, a young Swedish peace worker. While escorting Palestinian children home from school in Hebron, the group was attacked by settlers chanting, "We killed Jesus. We'll kill you, too." A settler broke a bottle over the young woman's face and caused her severe injuries. I remembered having been accused of killing Jesus at the tender age of seven and was shocked that members of my tribe were admitting it, and proud of it, while acting in a depraved and violent manner. It seemed to me that they were almost begging for the next holocaust and were making it unsafe to be a Jew.

Soon after, in 2007, I found out that a local Orthodox synagogue was planning to host a West Bank settlement real estate event. An Israeli company was touring American synagogues selling settlement homes directly to American Jews. I organised a demonstration against it (with no help from the local "peace and justice coalition", a largely Jewish organisation that refused to get involved) and thought it a good idea to contact the rabbi and ask him to cancel the event. This led to a lively email correspondence, as the rabbi saw an opportunity to try to bring a wayward son back into the fold.

When it came up that I have a Chinese wife and a mixed-race daughter, he became disgusted and ordered me to not raise my daughter Jewish, because by Jewish law she is not[89]. When I told him

---

[89] Jewishness is determined by the maternal line. According to Jewish law a Jewish father and a non-Jewish mother will produce a non-Jewish child. (AA)

about having come to believe in God and that my belief directs me to reject tribal chauvinism, he insisted that I had invented my own god. It became clear to me that his god only exists in a book that can be misinterpreted and manipulated so perversely that it can lead to the justification of murder and theft. I saw clearly that he, and those like him, are atheists just as much as the atheist Jews of my childhood synagogue. (The real estate event went on as planned.)

I made the decision to stop calling myself a Jew, to simply leave the cult. I respect the Jewish activists who speak about the crimes of Zionism as antithetical to "Jewish values", but I've had quite enough of "Jewish values", and embrace only universal values. Judaism, like all ancient religions, is a mixed bag. You have to take what you like and leave the rest, or else be subject to its contradictions. Orthodox Zionists, who would be aghast at this notion, are the foremost practitioners of this, rejecting the "golden rule" found in Leviticus[90] in favour of the tribalism and nationalism also found in various other writings.

The honourable agenda of Reform Jewish anti-Zionists like Elmer Berger and Alfred Lilienthal failed miserably. They promoted a Judaism based on the universalism of the prophets, rejecting Jewish nationalism. Not only were they unsuccessful, but they've been all but forgotten. I take this as evidence that, despite other possibilities in the religion, the ethos of Jewish life is more about tribalism and nationalism than anything else. I do not wish to be part of it.

In considering whether I can be of better service to Palestine as an Anti-Zionist Jew or as an Anti-Zionist ex-Jew, I finally decided that representing myself honestly was the best path— the path more likely to bring better results.

I find I have little patience for those who advocate for a "two state solution" or for any solution that calls for continued Jewish exclusivity in any part of historic Palestine. Clearly, peace will come with justice, and justice calls for the return of the refugees and their descendants, and the re-making of this land into a pluralistic society.

---

[90] Leviticus 19:18 states, "...Love your neighbour as yourself", and 19:34 states, "The stranger who resides with you shall be to you as one of your citizens; you shall love him as yourself". These are considered the Jewish version of the "Golden Rule": One should treat others as one would like others to treat oneself. (AA)

For me it's simple: One God, one human race, equality, justice. We live in a world that tries to make those things very complicated. They are not.

How I Became a Self-Loving Anti-Occupation Jew

Wendy Elisheva Somerson

"And among all the sins we hurled into the ocean, the sin of self-hate and the sin of failing to feel compassion for others mingled, as indeed they should, for they are the same sin." —Melanie Kaye-Kantrowitz

At a protest against Israel's horrendous attacks on Gaza, "Operation Cast Lead," in 2008, a friend asks if I've seen the sign with swastikas and Jewish stars in a circle with arrows connecting them like a recycling symbol on a grocery bag. I claim that I have not, though I did catch a glimpse of it out of the corner of my eye. I just didn't look too hard; I was trying not to see it, not to notice that anti-Jewish feelings arise when people are angry at the Israeli government for its violent actions against Palestinians. I'm at the rally to protest against the current trauma being imposed on Palestinians, not to deal with my own historical trauma. Unfortunately, when it comes to Israel-Palestine, these two traumas have become inextricably linked.

Jewish historical trauma, from centuries of persecution and genocide, has left many Jews so fearful that we see ourselves always and forever as victims. This blinds us to our role in the current oppression of Palestinians. Our families often pass on Jewish trauma to us through the notion that any criticism of the Israeli government is an attack that will lead to our imminent destruction, and through the related feeling that we are always in danger. Even as I overtly contest this thinking through my politics, the fearful feelings lie inside me, ready to seep out when I am least prepared to feel them. To really see this swastika sign means to open myself up to old and new fears: fear of being visible as a Jew, shame about Israel, and even more shame that I am focussed on my own trauma, when I am there to speak out against Israel's aggressions.

A Jewish friend and I walk up to the guy with the swastika sign, and we start talking about the attacks on Gaza. We are clearly Jewish because we are holding signs that say, "As a Jew, I believe in liberation for all people" and the name of our group, Jewish Voice for Peace (JVP). We discuss Israel's blatant disregard for Palestinian life, and we agree on how important it is to differentiate between Jewish people and the state of Israel. I keep staring at the circle of swastikas and Jewish stars going around and around, attempting to conflate Jews with Nazis. It both evokes and oversimplifies the cycle of trauma.

I eventually get to my point, telling him that I like his other sign (a map of the land Israel controls in former Palestine) better than the one with the swastikas. He explains that he is simply trying to demonstrate how the Nazis persecuted Jews, and now Jews are persecuting Palestinians. Yes, we tell him, but not all Jews are Israeli; Israeli Jews are not Nazis; and not all Israeli Jews support their government. We also explain how signs like this make it difficult for other Jews to join in these demonstrations. He says that he will take our points into consideration.

Unfortunately, at the next large protest against the attacks on Gaza a few days later, I see him again holding the same sign. And I see a few more disturbing signs, including a swastika embedded inside of a Jewish star. I give up. I don't have the energy to talk to all of these protesters. People are angry at the Israeli government. I get it. I am also angry, and I don't want to expend all my energy on this, but my stomach hurts every time I glimpse one of the swastikas.

When the protest turns into a march, a bunch of us start singing peace songs in Hebrew. One of our signs says, "Israel distorts Jewish values." A man behind us yells that we shouldn't be there, and that "Jewish values are dead." We stop singing. We find it difficult to stay together during the march. Our group of Jews disperses among the crowd.

I wonder: How do we create a space to hold the contradiction between loving ourselves as Jews, and protesting against what is being done in our name by the Israeli and US governments? How do I, in particular, balance my hard-won pride in being Jewish, with my shame about Israel's militarism and its ardent supporters, many of them Jews?

Between a Swastika and a Jewish Star

A few days later, I meet a few other JVP members at a "Stand with Israel" rally at a local synagogue. Stand with Us, an Israeli advocacy organisation, and the Jewish Federation are sponsoring the rally. When I get there, I see four of my friends on the footpath across the street from the synagogue holding our banner that says, "Jewish Voice for Peace" and "Not in our names". About twenty people who presumably came to attend the rally have decided to stand in front of the synagogue (instead of going inside), simply to yell things at us. As I approach, they start yelling that I should try living in an Arab country where I would be killed for being homosexual. I sigh and pick up one side of the banner.

Again, I see a swastika sign, but this time it is being held by a Jew, and his sign shows the swastika, an equal, and a picture of Palestinians. While extreme, this sign is simply the most blatant representation of projecting a historical threat to Jews onto a current victim of Israeli policy. From the steps of the synagogue, these pro-Occupation people yell at us that we aren't really Jews, threaten to cut off our heads, and tell us that we should be ashamed of ourselves. The police stand in the street between our two factions and say that they are worried that the folks "on the other side" might try to hurt us. When people stream out of the synagogue, they wave their mini-Israeli flags, and a few of them flip us off.

These people, my fellow Jews, are actually scarier to me than the people holding the swastika signs at the Gaza protests; their intense anger that we dare show "disloyalty" to our people is palpable. So many American Jews unthinkingly support Israeli militarism out of fear for the Jewish people—a fear that is sadly reinforced by most mainstream Jewish institutions. I wonder what it would take as a Jewish people to heal from our historical trauma and find the strength to recognise that true safety cannot be found by oppressing other people.

During the time of "Cast Lead", I attend only one *Shabbat* (Sabbath) service at my synagogue. We are asked to pray for the state of Israel. This unquestioning support for Israel intrudes into my spiritual space and disrupts my connection to Jewish prayers. I feel sad that I do not have a ritual space to grieve what is happening in Gaza, or to feel connected to a wider spiritual community of Jews.

Assimilation, Midwestern Style

Growing up in a suburb of Columbus, Ohio as one of a handful of Jewish families scattered among the thousands of WASPs[91], I didn't have any Jewish community or culture. In fact, I didn't even know any other Jews outside my family. Both my parents were from working class Jewish families in Pennsylvania. They got married in 1955 and were part of a movement of American Jews after World War II who were encouraged and enabled to move up in class status by assimilating into a white Christian-dominated culture. My parents conveyed the message that while we were Jewish, it was not central to who we were.

I spent my childhood feeling mostly invisible as a Jew. When our Jewish identity was acknowledged, it was rarely a positive experience. One time driving back from a hiking trip, we stopped at a farmer's stand to get corn. My Dad and the farmer joked around, and as the farmer bundled up his corn, he threw in a few extra ears, saying, "Don't worry, I won't be a Jew about it." There was a pause, and then my dad threw back his head and laughed, a little too loudly. We filed back into the station wagon in an uncomfortable silence. I knew we were Jews, but I didn't understand what the farmer said about us, or why my dad laughed when it didn't seem funny.

At every sport banquet and extracurricular event at my school, we prayed to Jesus, and in third grade, I co-starred in my class' Christmas play. When my teacher picked me out to be one of the stars, she knew that I was Jewish, but said that my parents were really cool about things like that—things like assimilation? My teacher later wanted another girl to play my part, but I refused to be demoted to an elf or a reindeer. They all wore the same costumes and faded into the background! So, proudly wearing my nightgown, after fighting with my play "brother" on Christmas morning, I gave a little speech in front of the whole school about how the real meaning of Christmas was not about presents, but about Jesus. I had no idea who Jesus was, but I liked the attention.

My family celebrated Chanukah[92], but we began celebrating it right around Christmas time, and it mostly involved exchanging presents

---

[91] White Anglo-Saxon Protestants. (AA)
[92] The Jewish festival of lights. (AA)

with one another. I don't remember celebrating any other Jewish holidays: No Passover *seders*, no High Holy days. I didn't have access to any Jewish culture to counter the implicit and explicit negative messages that surrounded me.

Towards Judaism (and Justice)

As an adult, I felt sadness and confusion about my identity. I had some sense of my family history, but no feeling of belonging or community. When I first moved to Seattle, I kept trying to connect with other Jews, but they seemed reluctant to discuss their Jewishness: I often heard from them that they had moved out here to get away from the Judaism that they grew up with.

Eventually I was invited to join political conversations about Israel-Palestine with other, mostly queer Lefty Jews. I was excited yet nervous about connecting with other Jews over such a difficult topic. While I had written my dissertation in graduate school on transnational feminism, I had always shied away from the topic of Israel-Palestine because it seemed too unwieldy and overwhelming to be my only connection to Jewish culture. However, my desire to connect with other Jews outweighed my fear, and I kept showing up at meetings.

We had *Shabbat* dinners where we discussed different topics surrounding Israel-Palestine. When people said prayers and lit candles, I felt like an imposter—unschooled and unsure of my identity or politics. As I started meeting more folks like myself, I began recognising that my experience of growing up in an assimilated family was not an anomaly, but an integral part of Jewish experience in the United States. I also gradually became more politicised as our group morphed into a study group on the history of Zionism, and eventually became the Seattle chapter of JVP.

I feel blessed that, unlike so many Jews, I have found connection to a Jewish community that is critical of Zionism and the Israeli government. Through studying the history of Zionism, I came to understand how Jewish historical trauma was central to the founding of Israel. I developed a growing conviction that we needed to break the hold of this trauma to see the situation clearly and to work as allies of Palestinians. On the journey to deepening my connection to Judaism, I found myself becoming more and more committed to speaking up for

Palestinian human rights.
I eventually joined a "progressive" (i.e. queer friendly) Reform Jewish synagogue, where I discovered a love for Jewish rituals and prayers. But I learned that being critical of Israel was a potential point of disconnection from the synagogue community. Soon after joining the synagogue, my friend and I were asked to write about our work with JVP for the synagogue's newsletter. One day after the newsletter appeared in print, we received an extremely long and angry email from a congregant who had written to us, the board, the rabbi, and the president of our synagogue. After claiming that we were promoting antisemitism and the destruction of the state of Israel, she then asked us a series of questions, some of which included, "Do you think there is a difference in the value Jews place on life and the value Muslims place on life? Do you understand the concept of martyrdom among Muslims? Are you aware that Muslim families rejoice in the death of their young people in suicide attacks?"

Having recently joined the congregation, I was jolted and upset by her letter's blatantly racist anti-Muslim sentiment, as well as her attack on us. When we asked the rabbi for support, he told us to "buck up" because we should have expected that this topic would engender strong feelings. When I told him that we felt attacked, he responded that he didn't think the letter was attacking, just powerful.

The board went on to discuss the issue without including us. With no input from us, the next newsletter apologised for not clarifying that our "controversial" piece was not synonymous with the views of the synagogue, even though there had been a disclaimer stating just that above our article. While individual synagogue members were supportive of us, we got no institutional support during this "controversy", and we were quickly cut out of the process to contain it.

This was my introduction to the way even a "progressive" synagogue leaves very little space for critical views of Israel. I continued to participate in this congregation, while simultaneously developing relationships with Jews in JVP who shared my political values. In my quest to feel more at home with Judaism, I spent two years preparing for an adult *Bat Mitzvah* at the synagogue. When the day arrived, I was proud to help lead prayers and chant from the Torah. But I was even more proud that I used my *Dvar Torah*[93] to connect my Torah portion's theme that "we are all alike before G-d" to equal rights for Palestinians. The people who most supported and cheered me on that day were my radical Jewish friends in JVP.

Reclaiming Jewish Resistance

While a few of us struggled for years in the synagogue community to begin a serious conversation about Israel-Palestine, the war on Gaza proved to be a tipping point for me. I stopped attending services regularly because I could not find a holy space where unthinking support for Israeli militarism was promoted. I value the time I spent learning prayers, rituals, and Hebrew, but what I discovered was that I no longer needed institutional validation as a Jew. I helped create a place in JVP to be my whole self by participating in rituals that combined spirituality with politics. These rituals help me feel grounded in a positive Jewish identity that is not based on a false image of an unchanging, monolithic Judaism. It is based, instead, on the holiest of values—*tzedek* or just action—which means responding to current oppression in the world as we see it, not as we have been told to see it.

These spaces also help me reconcile the contradiction between loving myself as a Jew and continuing to protest against the status quo; in fact, sometimes they make living inside this contradiction feel like home. At a protest in downtown Seattle following the cease fire in Gaza in early 2009, a group of us radical Jews contributed what felt like our most powerful protest statement. Dressed in our *kippot* (yarmulkahs) and *tallitot* (prayer shawls), we recited the Mourner's *Kaddish* for all the victims of the attacks on Gaza, for the more than 1400 Palestinians and eleven Israelis who died. Saying the Mourner's *Kaddish* in prayer shawls at a protest was powerful; our visibility as Jews undermined the notion that Jews mourn only for the loss of other Jewish lives. At a time when so many synagogues were lining up to support Israel, we reclaimed the power of our spiritual heritage by demonstrating how the Israeli government's actions distort our Jewish values. Standing on our makeshift *bimah* on that cold winter's day, I felt rooted in my community, grateful, and unafraid.

As anti-Occupation Jews, we honour the legacy of Jewish resistance when we consciously choose solidarity, even when we feel fear. By

---

[93] *Dvar Torah* is a talk on topics relating to a section of the Torah being read.

focusing on a present that is informed but not dictated by the past, we are creating a vibrant, sustainable Jewish culture that refuses to be complicit in another people's oppression.

I look forward to the day when Palestinians gain self-determination, Israel is forced to change its ways, and we are all released from the cycle of re-enacting historical trauma.

My Journey Home

Ariel Vegosen

I am thirty, cleaning out my grandmother's apartment in Sheepshead Bay, Brooklyn: her mother's plates, my grandfather's army papers, scripts from every play she's ever performed, old writings, a list of college classes she took when she was seventy, a story about her mother standing in the living room with other suffragettes debating the best strategy for women to get the right to vote, my strawberry shortcake cup. I search for my beloved pink stuffed rabbit and instead come up with my grandmother's work papers stating her family origin as England.

England? I remember in the second grade being charged with the task of creating a family tree. I stood in the kitchen in Valley Stream, Long Island and asked my mum and Dad, "Where are we from?" "Brooklyn." "No, I mean where is my great grandfather who I am named after from?" "Brooklyn." "What about before that?" "Brooklyn."

We are a Brooklyn family on both sides. We are bagels, lox, cream cheese eating, fast-talking, Left-leaning Jews. We value education, public radio, family dinners, giving back to others, and a good *knish*[94]. We believe it is important to take a day off from school or work on *Yom Kippur*, and to attend synagogue. We also have no problem enjoying crab and lobster. We do not sing songs about Jesus, even when the rest of our public school does. We have Hebrew names and although no one will tell me for sure, I know we are not just from Brooklyn. As a second

---

[94] A baked or fried filled dumpling originating in Eastern Europe. (AA)

grader the best answer I could get was "We are Jewish—this is our nation, our culture, and our religion."

As I grew up I started to discover more of my ancestral past. It turns out that on both sides of my family the story involves fleeing, pogroms, name changes and hidden identity. We come from Eastern Europe. My grandmother's father came over to America speaking twelve languages. I can only speak one. Like many other groups of people my family's priority was assimilation for survival. One of the languages my great-grandfather spoke was Yiddish. I only know words like *kvetch*[95] and *schvitz*[96], which I always thought were part of New York language, since even my non-Jewish friends use them.

I grew up going to Hebrew school, giving *tzedakah* in a blue box, hearing my grandmother's stories of not being able to get a job or an apartment due to antisemitism, and learning about great intellectuals and revolutionaries like Emma Goldman. Most of my friends in the neighbourhood were Italian American and I always thought of myself as Jewish American, since we were very clearly not Russian, Polish, Lithuanian or any number of other countries my family ran from in an effort to find freedom and acceptance.

I have always felt proud of my religion and culture and its contributions to society as a whole. In high school we had a tolerance awareness day and part of the curriculum was watching the film *Schindler's List*. I came to school the next day wearing my Jewish star. Both in public school and in Hebrew school I was drawn to understanding oppression, and I always wanted to make a difference.

I did not grow up in a super Zionist or Arab-bashing community. I grew up in a Hebrew school that talked about Israel, but never mentioned Palestine or Palestinians. I grew up in a public elementary school and high school with a tolerance awareness day, but no real plan to deal with the mocking on the playground or in the halls, of anyone who was not Christian and white.

It wasn't until I became an adult that any of this seemed weird. The way oppression works is sneaky, confusing, and mind bending. It isn't always obvious. Oppression feeds on lack of words and lack of knowledge. It relies on an unknowing population of people to continue the cycle. It relies on isolation and silence.

---

[95] Yiddish for a person who always complains. (AA)
[96] To sweat, perspire. (AA)

My parents have never been to Israel, so when I asked at seventeen to go on the United Synagogue Youth Poland-Israel pilgrimage, they were a bit surprised. They must have thought it was because of my deep interest in the Holocaust or because my best friend was going. Maybe they thought that it was my way of staying connected to the Jewish community, since my days in Hebrew school ended at age thirteen.

Looking back, I am not sure why I wanted to go so badly. It could be that I had heard that we Jews did have a place to call home—the land of Milk and Honey—*Eretz Yisrael*. Or maybe after years of saying "next year in Jerusalem" at every Passover *Seder*, it seemed like I should go and see such an important city. Or it could be the same feeling I have today of not fully belonging anywhere. My ancestors left their place of origin to find a home because of oppression. They landed here in America, on a shore that was not theirs, on land taken generations ago.

I thought that maybe Israel would be a place where we could go and not feel like we were living on someone else's sacred earth. I had heard the story of "a land without a people for a people without a land", and I longed to go there. I wanted and still do want a homeland.

At seventeen Israel looked beautiful. I climbed Masada, swam in the Dead Sea, cried at the *Kotel* (Wailing Wall), celebrated *Shabbat*, rappelled down Mitzpe Ramon, met cute Israeli soldiers (or at least my friend said they were cute), and I felt connected to the place as if it really was mine. Never mind the fact that I knew nothing about the government, couldn't speak Hebrew, and had only seen a small fraction of reality. I felt like I could move to Israel and finally have a homeland.

I had come from visiting Poland—devastation, a whole community wiped out, the gas chambers of Treblinka, the train tracks of Auschwitz, the stains on the walls. I had stared at Nazi photographs trying to imagine them as children and looked at piles and piles of hair and ashes and shoes. I knew my ancestors had burned in those camps and that my identity was wrapped up in that fire. I needed to be safe. I needed a place to call my own, and Israel was designed for that reason, right?

Part of being Jewish has always been *Tikkun Olam*, which means repairing the world and practicing *tzedakah*, which means righteousness or charity. In college I learned about these words in Torah study sessions, and as part of *Tzedek Hillel*. My understanding of *tzedakah* is that it is not enough to just give charity; you have to go to the root of the problem and work from a place of solidarity. You cannot just hand a homeless person a dollar and feel like you have done a *mitzvah*, a good deed. You have to understand homelessness, and work to end the causes of homelessness.

Thus, I became a radical activist, someone who is interested in going to the root of the situation and repairing it so the world can be a better, more whole place.

In college I launched full on into activism and direct radical actions resulting in being arrested. I led workshops on ending racism and sexism to community service projects, and about living and working in a collective. I learned about nonviolent communication, consensus processing, and creating coalitions. I joined a movement to end the war in Iraq and Afghanistan. I protested against the IMF and World Bank. It was only natural for me to find out about Palestine.

The equation was heart-breaking, but obvious. I was raised and educated to struggle and work for justice. If it's wrong to occupy Iraq, wrong to colonise women's bodies, wrong to segregate people based on race, then it's obviously wrong to take Palestinian land, put Palestinians behind walls, suppress them economically, and bomb their cities and villages.

Once you know the truth you can't ever go back. The only time Israel was ever pure and dripping with milk and honey, a place of working together like they do on the kibbutzim, a place of glory, love, joy, and equality, a place of true democracy, a place of freedom, the Jewish homeland, my homeland, was when I was seventeen and didn't know any better. That journey to Israel was so innocent, sweet, fun, and simple.

Now when I go to Israel I see walls, brutality, bombed-out villages, silence, a mask hiding the truth, racism. The tears I shed at the *Kotel* are tears of heartbreak, sorrow, and a longing that might never be healed. I cried at the *Kotel* when I was seventeen because I thought I was home and that I had made it, finally, after generations of struggle. Now I cry at the *Kotel* because I know this is not my home and I am still wandering.

As a white Jewish genderqueer person, I am not sure where my home is. I can't claim American soil, although I was raised here and it is the only culture and language I fully know. I realise this land was stolen from people and that my identity as genderqueer raised female, as Jewish, and as radical is not accepted. I do not belong in Israel because it also is not my land and because the way it is being governed goes against my Jewish values.

I am trying desperately to navigate two conflicting messages coming from Judaism. One message tells me that historically this land is connected to my people, that currently it is the state of Israel and therefore violence in the name of security is acceptable. The other message that my religion teaches is one of peace—that I am to love my neighbour as myself and to work for justice. The Jewish religion I grew up on teaches nonviolence, love, and standing up against oppression. The Torah says, "Justice, justice you shall pursue." Therefore, the logical conclusion is that I, as a Jew, must stand up against the Occupation of Palestinian people and the land.

It wasn't hard for me to find other Jews who were concerned about the Occupation. While attending the University of Maryland, a small group of us banded together and formed our own version of Women in Black, holding weekly silent vigils to mourn the loss of lives on both sides, and calling for an end to the Occupation.

At this time, I was on the board of Hillel, the co-founder of the Muslim-Jewish dialogue group and a member of the Maryland Activist Collective. I took part in "boycott Caterpillar" actions, I set up mock checkpoints on campus to educate the public on the situation in the West Bank, I brought in speakers, I mourned the loss of life, and I held space with flowers in the middle of the on-campus war between the Jewish Student Union and the Arab Student Union.

I quickly realised that it also wasn't hard for me to find Jews who disagreed with our stance against the Occupation. Once on the way to my Hillel board meeting, I was faced with a poster calling me a traitor. Rabbis called me to ask if I would reconsider my weekly Women in Black vigils. When I returned to Long Island, numerous people in my Jewish community told me they agreed that the Occupation was wrong, but they said now was not the time to speak out.

As Jews they hold so much fear of antisemitism that they have become silent in the face of another group's oppression. I do not heed their warning to stop standing up against the Occupation. Instead, I think about the great scholar Rabbi Hillel who said, "If I am not for myself, who will be for me? But if I am only for myself, who am I? If not now, when?" For me that has become a lifetime commitment to justice.

Two days after graduation I boarded a flight to Tel Aviv. I spent two months on the front lines in the West Bank. It was the first time I experienced war directly. One rainy Saturday, along with other members of *Kvisa Shchora*[97], I was shot at by Israeli settlers from Ma'on while doing a direct action in solidarity with the Palestinian farmers of At'tuwani. I was shocked. What were Jews dressed in Orthodox attire doing shooting guns, especially on *Shabbat*!?

It went against everything I had learned about my religion and culture. In this moment I realised the Occupation is deep and complex. Here we were, a group of Israelis, Palestinians and Internationals, holding a circle around a small farm as farmers tried to till their land, and settlers were shooting at us. Then the Israeli military came, arrested some of the Palestinians and forced us to leave the area. The war was right here. Added to checkpoints, bombs in Gaza, Qassam rockets in Sderot, suicide bombers in Sbarro's Pizza in Jerusalem, a giant occupation wall separating families, and US tax dollars backing Israel's army—the war was right here, people versus people. A small Palestinian village teamed up with nonviolent "end the Occupation" activists versus Israeli settlers. Rocks were thrown, guns were shot, I ran and ran and ran, looked back and saw one of my comrades bleeding from the face. The battlefield here is not an army versus an army. War, as I have learned, rarely is.

War, it turns out, takes place in people's homes, villages, and olive groves. War takes place on people's bodies and in people's minds. War is the moment at a checkpoint— one human in military uniform, the other longing to see the rest of their family. War is decisions made quickly, a thousand messages of fear versus a person's smile and eye contact. War is loss of humanity. War has ironic moments too, like my Palestinian friends in Tulkarem selling meat to Israelis because they need the money, all the queer Palestinian and Israeli couples I know, the Palestinians working in settlements to build houses, or even on the Occupation Wall because they need the money. It's these intricate ironic moments when people talk to each other, learn about each other, and discover that ultimately, we are all just people. It's these moments that I see as potential for war to end, for occupation to end. It is sunlight slipping through the cracks of a thick wall of concrete.

---

[97] Black Laundry, a direct-action group of lesbians, gays, bisexuals, transgenders and others.

I see a new day on the horizon. I, as a Jewish American, have sat in Nablus in a small shop drinking coffee with Rami, a Palestinian man who spent ten years in an Israeli prison. I have danced on the occupation wall in Bethlehem as part of the Borders Project. I have done workshops with Palestinian and Israeli poets. I have picked olives with farmers in Jenin. As part of the Gaza Freedom March, I spent two days in Gaza. There I shared a bed with my former Seeds of Peace camper's sister. We cried tears for the Occupation, the loss of her father who was a peacemaker, and the fact that she spent her childhood living in a house with Israeli soldiers who had taken it over and were using it as a base. I have picked up seashells on the shores of Gaza and returned with them to Brooklyn, placing them in the hand of my ninety-eight-year-old grandmother who falsified work papers claiming she was English in order to get a job in America.

I believe relationships and people coming together are stronger than military and government agendas. The Occupation is killing Palestinians. It is also hurting the humanity of Israeli Jews and the fabric of what it means to be Jewish. I am standing up with many others to rise above this violence. We are creating space for mainstream Judaism to change their message from, "Wherever we stand we stand with Israel" to, "Wherever we stand we stand with justice."

The media often refer to the occupation of the Palestinian people as a conflict between Israelis and Palestinians. I do not see it that way. There are nonviolent Palestinian and Israeli resisters working every day together along with internationals to end the Occupation. I refuse to see the divide of sides being Israel versus Palestine. I see it more as the military industrial complex and corporate interests versus people. My personal liberation is deeply bound with all those who seek liberation.

I have found beautiful communities to work with, including The Community of Living Traditions, Shomer Shalom, Jewish Voice for Peace, and the cast and crew of *An olive on the seder plate*. I have found a space to be queer, Jewish, and against the Occupation. I have found a community, a family, a dedicated group of creative, loving people who are consistently taking risks and standing up to end the occupation of Palestine. I have found rabbis like Rabbi Lynn Gottlieb and Rabbi Brant Rosen who are willing to take a stand against the Occupation, and who do it from a Jewish perspective. I have found mentors like Jen Marlowe and Starhawk who are fierce and courageous. I have friends like Rae Abileah, Jacob Rosenblum, and many others who are willing to put their heart, bodies, and minds into creating justice. I know that my religion encourages me to stand up for the end of occupation everywhere, from Palestine, to Iraq, to Sudan, to New Orleans, to Trenton, NJ. I believe that through nonviolent resistance, creating community, and working in solidarity we will overcome oppression. I believe that one day the wall will come down, Gaza will be free, and young Israeli Jews will do community service instead of joining the army.

There is still so much work to do, and I am proud to be part of a movement to end the Occupation. I am also incredibly proud of my roots and my Jewish identity. I see my Jewish identity as an intricate part of my work in ending the Occupation. I see my grandmother's struggle as part of a greater struggle. What makes me human, Jewish, American is my desire to see a just, free, loving world, a world in which we are all safe to be whatever it is that we are.

My religion has always taught me to speak out, to disagree when needed, to dissent, to be peaceful, and to love big. I am proud to continue the traditions and heritage I was given. I am proud to be my grandmother's granddaughter. I am proud to be a Jew for liberation.

Since my first trip to Israel when I was seventeen, I have returned to Israel and Palestine numerous times. I can no longer go there in naïve innocence. My tear stains and broken heart are splattered on the *Kotel*. The journey to the Holy Land is no longer fun and exciting, it is filled with hurt, fear and desire to see a change. I am still questing for a better future, an end to the Occupation in Palestine, as well as an end to the occupation I see worldwide. I am working for a world free from racism, sexism, homophobia, ableism, classism, militarism, antisemitism, Islamophobia, and other interlocking oppressions. Perhaps when that world is reached, I will finally feel at home. Until then I continue to wander.

A Lighthouse in Gaza
by
Ariel Vegosen

There is a lighthouse in Gaza,
this small shimmering of hope
and from the smallest spark comes the largest fire.

There are fishermen who can't go more than three miles out
because Israeli guards are in border boats waiting with guns
and there are young Israelis in boats waiting and shaking
confused and afraid,
told their neighbours are the enemy
because rockets have hit Sderot
and there are men in high places with fish on their table
making policies that don't benefit the soldier or the fisherman

and the cycle continues
those on the ground battling each other
while others get richer and profit from this hell

I am ready to meet in the field out beyond right and wrong
I am ready to heal our wounds
share our bread
and figure out how to stop this machine.

Afterword

Avigail Abarbanel

The purpose of this book was to try to understand what makes it possible for the contributors, and others like them, to question their loyalty to Israel and Zionism. As I explained in my introduction and as so many of the stories describe and explain, Zionism is not easy to resist. Criticism or resistance to Zionist ideology elicits internal conflict as well as external opposition, some of which can be vicious.

I looked for common themes in the stories. I thought that if I could find something that all the writers have in common, I would have my answer. Some of the themes I looked at were: growing up with Jewish values and morality, education, the opportunity to meet Palestinians as equals at a young age, growing up without a clear sense of place or belonging, and a particularly rebellious or questioning nature in childhood.

For example, if like Sivan Barak, every single one of the writers had an opportunity at a young age to meet Palestinians as equals, this could perhaps explain why they were able to be more sympathetic to the Palestinians at a later age. But this isn't the case. A number of the writers, myself included, met Palestinians as equals only after we became activists.

As for the experience of growing up with the understanding of Judaism and the Jewish people as moral and ethical—that wasn't the answer either. But this is an interesting theme because the writers who did grow up this way are saying that when they object to the Occupation and support the Palestinian people, they are merely following the ethics they grew up with. They refuse to be PEPs, and they do not distinguish between the Palestinians and other victims of injustice and persecution. It is precisely the values and ethics they grew up with that make it possible for them to do what they are doing.

But alas, not everyone grew up this way. I certainly didn't. Growing up in Israel in the harsh reality that I did, surrounded only by Jewish people, made it obvious to me from a young age that we were not a particularly nice, just or moral people. My teachers certainly tried to tell us that we were a special people because we were more moral and ethical than other people. But they also knew that we were growing up in Bat Yam, and that most of us had experienced in our families and neighbourhoods the exact opposite of justice, morality or ethics. When children are sexually abused, when they are beaten or neglected, when mothers and their children are demeaned, oppressed or suffer domestic abuse, when the general atmosphere in society is rude, nasty or inconsiderate and when kindness or compassion are rare, it really makes no difference whether the perpetrators are Jewish or non-Jewish. The harm is the same, and we couldn't blame nasty antisemites for any of it.

More than anything, my upbringing in Israel taught me that Jews are no different from other people. The evils that exist in every human society exist also in Israel—in a society run by Jews, mainly for Jews, and with a majority of Jews—and I experienced many of them first hand. For me there was no noble Jewish tradition, or special Jewish values that I could see or believe in. Unlike other writers, my own transformation required me to change my values, not follow them. I did not become an activist *because* my values were noble. It's my activism that has made me a better person. I was a product of mainstream Jewish Israeli society, and Israel is a very different place, with a profoundly different culture and values, to many of the Jewish communities outside of it.

None of themes I looked at were present in every story. So, they could not provide a reasonable explanation for what makes it possible for us to be critical of Israel and Zionism when the majority of Jews are not. There are too many differences between us. We come from different backgrounds and were educated differently. We are also from different generations and were born and raised in different countries and circumstances. Some of us were rebels as children or young people, but not all of us. Some grew up in stable, loving families, and others were not so fortunate. Some of us were successful academically, and some of us weren't. Some were brought up in an environment that already questioned Israel and Zionism and didn't need to have a "conversion" experience as adults, but many of us were brought up within a Zionist mindset, and our doubts and questions came later in life.

I thought I would simply have to concede that I couldn't find an answer to my question and that it must for now remain a mystery to me. But then as I was reflecting on the stories something suddenly stood out for me. I realised that there is in fact something that all the activists in this book have in common: they all have the capacity to tolerate difficult emotions. They don't just shrink or panic when they feel uncomfortable. They are not afraid of their emotions. I call this *emotional resilience*.

Emotional resilience is the ability to tolerate uncomfortable feelings without avoiding them or trying to make them go away. Emotional resilience enables people to act according to their values and do the right thing *even* when they experience fear, guilt, insecurity, turmoil, confusion or pain, and even when some of these feelings are reinforced by outside opposition or even persecution. Even in the face of internal and external turmoil they do not lose their clarity and identity, or their capacity to act according to their values.

Emotional resilience also includes the ability to tolerate the experience of being disapproved of, disliked and rejected by others, sometimes even by relatives and close friends.

I believe that this answers not only the question about the activists in this book. The same applies to anyone who is prepared to stand up for what they believe against a hostile mainstream and the difficult and conflicting emotions it can trigger.

I don't know if any of the writers in this book have ever considered themselves in such terms. I also don't know how they have evolved to have the capacity for emotional resilience but somehow, they did and that's what makes them special.

In his piece Jeff Halper says:

> *What I learned that day proved crucial to my ability to deal with such a charged, emotionally-laden issue like Israel-Palestine. One of the hardest parts of critical thinking is the ability to detect in yourself elements of irrationality, prejudice, fear, peer pressure and social conditioning—and to confront them.*

In this paragraph Jeff describes the realisation that he felt prejudice and fear, and that he would have to confront them. He doesn't say how he did it, but it is clear that he didn't avoid what he was feeling, and that in the end he was able to use reason. The easier way out would have been to remain defensive and to hold on to prejudice, fear and unsupportable views, just to avoid discomfort.

In her moving piece Maya Wind describes her feelings at the military induction base. She says:

> Amidst the chaos I look around at all the young men and women my age, all staring at me either in anger or bewilderment. And suddenly I feel guilty. I know how long they have all waited for this important rite of passage, and I am ruining it for them with my protest. I stand there and for a moment I feel deeply proud and terribly ashamed at the same time. 'You are doing the right thing', I whisper to myself as I walk forward, and show the guard my ID card and draft papers.

The feelings she felt were clearly disturbing. While she felt proud of what she was doing, she also felt deeply guilty. She had to face the accusations of the people around her that she was a traitor who was putting everyone at risk. But she was able to reassure herself in the midst of all this turmoil and did not back down from her decision to refuse to serve in the military.

At a rally in Melbourne in 2008 Sivan Barak also struggled with difficult feelings. She too kept going:

> Now as I march I keep looking around to see if anyone recognises me. I'm genuinely concerned that I would be labelled an "Israel-hater" or "an enemy from within". Despite my fears I march, as my heart tells me to do the right thing. Let my friends gaze in horror. "Palestine will be free, from the river to the sea!" The chanting made me cringe, but I marched on.

Anna Baltzer describes how she unconsciously tried to avoid feeling uncomfortable about her relationship with Israel:

> I attended campus events criticising sanctions on Iraq and the new war on Afghanistan. In retrospect, I now remember references to Palestine in discussions and on posters. Yet somehow, without even realising it, I shut out any criticism of Israel, preferring to hear and see no evil, lest I be confronted with something that might be uncomfortable.

However, this did not last and she later says:

> I was devastated by what I saw. The construct of Israel's virtue, which I had always held dear, crumbled before my eyes. I felt confused and scared to have such a deep part of my identity slip away.

Despite these feelings, she continued her journey to become an outspoken activist for Palestinian rights.

In his story, Rich Forer describes his emotional journey in detail. Recalling his conflicting feelings when he started to read Norman Finkelstein's book *Beyond Chutzpah*, he says:

> *Most of the time my reading was marked by an inner struggle: on the one hand, a desire to get to the truth and alleviate my torment; on the other, a curiosity to ascertain whether Finkelstein was in fact a disturbed academic and an antisemite...*

A little later he says, "But now my mind was in the crosshairs, its conception of reality threatened by powerful reasoning and compelling research." In the end he came to the realisation that:

> *Although I had always considered myself capable of clarifying most matters on the basis of my own scrutiny, I saw that when it came to Israel I had brushed aside challenging questions in favour of an irrational but emotionally satisfying appraisal.*

Forer went through a deep and complex emotional process. He was initially tempted to vilify Finkelstein as a way of protecting himself from the uncomfortable feelings triggered by the book, and the inevitable collapse of his reality, but he did not.

He says that it is the reasoning and the evidence behind what he read that helped him resist the urge to protect himself from the new information. This is similar to what Halper says about the importance of intellectual honesty. However, people who do not have the ability to tolerate uncomfortable emotions will not listen to or accept evidence or reason, no matter how compelling. Although it's crucial, it's not the evidence itself that did the trick here. Emotional resilience is a prerequisite to the ability to assimilate a new truth and to be intellectually honest. Without enough emotional resilience, Forer would never have been convinced. Like many staunch supporters of Israel, he would have abandoned the book, told himself that it was nonsense or that the writer was crazy, and would have carried on with his belief system unchanged. The many labels and accusations that Zionists throw at people like us are an example of this process.

My own reaction to reading *The Iron Wall*, was similar to Forer's experience. I too wanted to discredit the author, in this case Avi Shlaim, so that I could ignore what he was saying, and by so doing keep my sense of reality intact. Forer wondered if Finkelstein was insane or an antisemite. I wanted to convince myself that Shlaim had an "agenda", and that "there was something wrong with him". As I described in my story, my feelings were intense and deeply disturbing. But I kept on going because I couldn't deny the truth, and because I was apparently able to tolerate the emotional discomfort that this truth had caused me, and gradually develop as an activist. Every story in this book is the story of emotional resilience.

෮෴

There is no doubt that all the people in this book, and others like them, are courageous. But courage is a manifestation of, or a quality that comes out of, emotional resilience. Courage is not the absence of fear or emotional turmoil. It is the ability to do something that has to be done, *despite* fear or other inner resistance. By contrast, people who avoid difficult or uncomfortable emotions do not tend to act courageously. This is because they give in to what they feel and use a lot of their energy to try to suppress their "bad" feelings, avoid them or make them go away.

In the context of Israel-Palestine, that can take the form of avoiding exposure to any information that contradicts the Zionist narrative, choosing to believe in the accepted mythology even in the face of clear evidence that it is untrue or inaccurate, excluding, vilifying, discrediting, demonising or attacking writers, researchers, speakers and activists, justifying the unjustifiable, or simply avoiding the whole thing. "Shooting the messenger" is a well-known defence mechanism that people can use to protect themselves from something that they don't want to hear, because it might make them question their beliefs or behaviour.

Such psychological defences are designed to push away the feelings that are triggered by a challenge to people's existing worldview. When that worldview is also tied up so strongly with people's identity, as in the case of Zionism, it becomes doubly difficult to challenge it. Because then it's truly personal, and the feelings that are triggered can be devastating. We know from the intensity of the responses we often receive from supporters of Israel that some people can be pushed to deep distress, fanaticism and violence by our opposition to Israel's actions. Rae Abileah was assaulted on two occasions by Zionists when she expressed her protest in public peacefully, and Ilan Pappé had to leave Israel because of the growing hostility against him. Disagreement doesn't have to translate to violence or hostility. But it often does when the challenge to people's point of view is perceived as a challenge to their identity and survival.

The opposite of courage is cowardice. But to say that someone is a coward is not satisfying to me. Cowardice is not something that we can do anything about and saying the word "coward" doesn't explain much about what is really going on for the person in question. It is much more informative, I believe, to say that a person is unable to tolerate his or her fear or discomfort, and as a result acts in a cowardly way.

Israel and its *hasbara* machinery count on the fact that most people don't want to feel uncomfortable and they know that the majority of people are not emotionally resilient. *Hasbara* agents know perfectly well that fear of antisemitism runs deep in Jewish communities around the world and in Israel, and that it can be used and manipulated to ensure that the majority of Jews won't question Israel and will support it "right or wrong".

Poor emotional resilience is a human, not a Jewish, trait. The non-Jewish world that does not stand up to Israel, and that has been colluding in the destruction of the Palestinian people, also lacks the ability to tolerate uncomfortable feelings. I am told that the reason there is so much support for Israel in the Western world is because of guilt over the Holocaust. If this is true, then it means that collusion with Israel is designed to soothe this guilt, manage it, or make it go away.

I presume the reasoning—albeit unconscious—goes something like this: "We were not fair to the Jews in the past and we did nothing to stop the Holocaust. We feel terribly guilty about it and we don't like feeling guilty. This is very, very uncomfortable. So, in order to not feel it, we should now support the Jewish state. When this state does bad things, we have to overlook them or pretend that we are doing something about it, but not *really* do anything because we don't want to upset Jewish people. When we try to do or say something, we are immediately accused of being antisemitic and that reawakens the guilt we already feel. To justify doing nothing, we can pretend that the

Palestinians are the 'bad guys'. That way we don't have to feel guilty about what Israel does to them", and so on[98].

People who are emotionally resilient are more likely to act rationally and less likely to be emotionally reactive. People with poor emotional resilience spend a lot of energy in an attempt to "medicate", avoid, or push away emotions that they don't like. All addictions have to do with this, but not just addictions. I know many people who try to intellectualise their feelings away, meditate as a way of escaping feelings, exercise their feelings away, or marry and have children or renovate their house for exactly the same purpose. Almost every human activity can be used to try to banish, control, suppress or manage uncomfortable feelings. The amount of mental and physical energy required to do that is huge, and it is taken away from more important and valuable things we can do.

No matter what theories or rationalisations we come up with, it is clear to me that in the last analysis most humans would sacrifice themselves and others, just to avoid feeling uncomfortable. This is a staggering point. Because of nothing more than feelings, so much wrong is done in the world, and so much unnecessary suffering is experienced and inflicted!

※

I am glad I have found my answer. I now understand that if we want to teach people to stand up and speak out against injustices, we must first make sure that they are capable of tolerating their emotions. There is a skill to this and it can be taught. I do it all the time in my work as a psychotherapist. If we teach this to young people, we can raise generations of resilient human beings who will have the necessary strength to question the things around them that are wrong, and to take action to remedy them.

However, as I am writing this I am also wondering if the world would want to do this. Would our societies be prepared to nurture and educate "trouble-makers", whistle-blowers, activists who can think for themselves and who do not just accept things as they are? I am not so

---

[98] I don't have the scope in this book to discuss it, but Leon Festinger's theory of 'cognitive dissonance' comes to mind in relation to some of the topics I raise in this book.

sure they would. Peter Slezak quoted Bertrand Russell who said that "[a] certain percentage of children have the habit of thinking; one of the aims of education is to cure them of this habit." If this is as true today as it was in Russell's time, then we are still far away from having a mature and healthy society.

Societies populated with a majority of rational and independent thinkers who know their feelings and embrace them, are likely to be more just than the ones we have now. They would also be harder to manipulate by any power structure and their tolerance for wrongdoing and human-made injustice would be low. We, the "little people", would no longer be so little or insignificant. We would have more power simply because power would be distributed more evenly through society.

When we learn how to tolerate our feelings we become more whole, and we know so much more about ourselves. It's very hard to push around someone with a strong sense of self.

As a humanistic psychotherapist, this vision of the world sounds wonderful to me. This is the world I would like to live in; a world where all human beings can develop to their full potential, where human beings will not allow themselves to be easily manipulated, victimised or disenfranchised. To get there we all have to learn how to be more fully human, by learning to accept and tolerate everything that we feel. The stories in this book demonstrate what is possible when we do that.

Printed in Poland
by Amazon Fulfillment
Poland Sp. z o.o., Wrocław